PARALEGALS AND LEGAL ASSISTANTS

PARALEGALS AND LEGAL ASSISTANTS

by
M. Vanidevi
Soumya Asokan

Wordpen Academics
Publishing Science That Matter

ISBN: 978-93-6084-566-7

Published by : **WORDPEN ACADEMICS**
4736/23, Ansari Road, Darya Ganj,
New Delhi – 110 002
Phone: +91-011-35004336
E-mail: info@wordpenacademics.com

Exclusive Distributor: ***Bio-Green Books, New Delhi***

Preface

The legal profession is vast and multifaceted, and at its core lies a dedicated group of professionals who ensure the smooth functioning of legal systems—paralegals and legal assistants. These individuals play a crucial role in supporting attorneys, conducting legal research, managing case documentation, and maintaining client communication. As the demand for efficient and cost-effective legal services grows, the importance of trained and knowledgeable paralegals and legal assistants has never been greater.

This book, titled *Paralegals and Legal Assistants*, is crafted to serve as a foundational guide for individuals aspiring to enter or advance within this dynamic field. It is intended for students of legal studies, early-career professionals, and anyone interested in understanding the structure and scope of paralegal and legal assistant responsibilities within modern legal practice.

The book begins by exploring the history and evolution of the paralegal profession, providing context on how these roles have become integral to law firms, corporations, government agencies, and non-profit organizations. It outlines the ethical responsibilities, essential skills, and legal knowledge expected from paralegals and legal assistants across various areas of law, including criminal, corporate, family, and civil law.

Chapters provide detailed guidance on legal research techniques, drafting legal documents, case preparation, interviewing clients and witnesses, and navigating legal databases and technologies. The book also includes insights into certification pathways, career development strategies, and the regulatory framework governing paralegal practice in different jurisdictions.

With an emphasis on practical application, *Paralegals and Legal Assistants* incorporates real-world scenarios, sample documents, and checklists to bridge the gap between academic learning and professional duties. It also addresses the impact of technology, such as legal management software and digital communication tools, which are reshaping the daily work of legal support professionals.

We hope this book will empower readers with the knowledge and confidence to pursue a meaningful and impactful career in the legal field, contributing to justice and access to legal services through their specialized support.

M. Vanidevi

Soumya Asokan

Contents

1

Introduction to Paralegal

1.1. Definition of Paralegal

Paralegal is a person who is qualified by education, training or work experience and is employed or retained by a lawyer, law office, corporation, governmental agency, to perform specifically delegated substantive legal work for which a lawyer is responsible.

Paralegals play an important role in the provision of legal services as they carry out broad variety of tasks in all areas of law and are an important resource to an organisation. Normally, paralegals are not permitted to practice law, however as paralegals normally gain a high level of experience in a particular practice area, they offer high level of services. Under supervision of a senior lawyer, paralegals run their own files and conduct work which may have otherwise been undertaken by a junior lawyer.

Paralegals are important members of the legal team, playing key roles in the legal process. The work that Paralegals undertake is quite often virtually indistinguishable from that undertaken by the Solicitors who employ them. Apart from engaging in file specific work, paralegals can also help in training new employees and ensure consistency in a firm. They also provide information to new lawyers and staff, related to research tools, case preparation and protocol in a particular firm.

Paralegal is not formalized in any way in many states as some states have programs for certification of paralegals. Some paralegals obtain college degrees in paralegal studies or criminal justice, but this is often not required. In many cases, to become a paralegal, one must merely be hired by an attorney and given the title. The paralegal is able to research and draft most legal documents and often assists with the day-to-day operations of a law firm, like scheduling hearings, interacting with clients, and keeping case files and evidence in order. Paralegals cannot give legal advice or represent clients in legal proceedings, and cannot independently prepare legal documents that have not been approved by an attorney.

Paralegals typically work for lawyers. Just as lawyers are employed by different types of organisations, paralegals also are employed by organisations for providing legal advice related to:

- law firms
- governments
- courts
- corporations

Paralegals also perform administrative and clerical functions in common along with typical duties of legal assistants, legal secretaries and file clerks in different organisations.

Paralegals can work in the areas of:

- Financial Services
- Insurance
- Banking
- Building Societies
- Retail Sector
- Credit Control
- Export
- Entertainment
- Media

In Public Sector, Paralegals work with:

- Government Departments
- Local Authorities
- Court and Tribunal Staff
- Welfare
- Probation Services
- Social Services
- Police

Paralegals are not lawyers, but their responsibilities are similar in all matters related to working on implications, consequences, issues, liability, important gaps in knowledge and strategy. The work of a paralegal is to carry out a course of action as directed by the lawyer which involves:

- interviewing the witness
- research on questions
- incorporating that company
- completing and filing legal documents

Paralegal display a mix of the following skills:

- ❖ Analytical skills
- ❖ Administrative skills
- ❖ Managerial skills
- ❖ Research skills
- ❖ Communication skills

Such skills include the ability to:

- ❖ organize complex tasks
- ❖ independently solve problems
- ❖ pay attention to detail
- ❖ manage time effectively
- ❖ research factual data
- ❖ possess knowledge of legal issues
- ❖ communicate effectively

Apart from having knowledge of legal environment, paralegals require proficiency in computer and Internet skills. They typically use word processors, spread sheet programs, data bases, and on-line resources, and also learn and adapt to new and specialized software programs unique to their specialty and place of employment. Many paralegals function as coordinators to manage other paralegals. They also have the ability to constantly learn about new developments in law and new technologies since they are integrated in the legal profession. They also further train attorneys and other paralegals on new technologies.

In the areas of practice where many cases are similar in nature involving conveyancing or probate or following simplified process driven route, paralegals are increasingly handling cases from start to finish.

However lawyers continue to deal with more complex matters or matters where large sums of money are at stake involving mergers and acquisitions work, murder trials, aircraft financing deals, celebrity divorces etc., The involvement of Paralegals in such instances tends to be on a peripheral basis.

The growing number of paralegal law firms (commercial entities offering legal services to the public and business without any lawyer involvement) shows that paralegals would be doing the more complex work eventually although it probably won't be any time soon.

Some of popular areas of paralegal specialization are:

- Bankruptcy
- Corporate law
- Family law
- Immigration
- Litigation
- Nurse paralegal
- Military paralegal specialist
- Real Estate
- Estate planning, probate and trust paralegal
- Intellectual property
- Criminal defense law
- Banking and finance law
- Public defense
- Judicial paralegals

1.2. Functions of Paralegals

1.2.1 Introduction

Paralegals form an important part of the legal industry and are responsible for handling a plethora of tasks and for providing support for the lawyers they work for. Under directions issued by an attorney, most paralegals look after minor legal issues. They help lawyers in different tasks such as research of laws, judicial decisions, articles, treaties, and other legal documents that are pivotal to the current legal cases. They may even have to coordinate in the filing of financial records and case documents.

Paralegals work closely with lawyers to assist them with legal research, preparing documents, and maintaining files. In both civil and criminal cases, paralegals may conduct interviews with victims, suspects, witnesses, clients, or client families. Paralegals take notes or record these interviews to prepare a written transcript for review.

Legal assistants to an attorney who specializes in health law may help locate federal regulations, statutes (federal and state), and pertinent periodical articles regarding healthcare issues. They have to prepare asset reports and locate information on a daily basis. Employment opportunities for paralegals are in many different practice areas of law including real estate, probate, litigation, corporate, and employment law.

If one wants to learn the nuts and bolts of the legal profession and understand the vitality of legal research, then the profession of a paralegal will suit them just fine. The paralegal profession is the first step to a successful legal career and includes many professionals who have not ventured to law school. There are various tasks which both paralegals and lawyers do, but paralegals do not practice law and are prohibited from dispensing legal advice, accepting legal fees, or conducting trials.

Paralegals help lawyers prepare cases for trial and try to uncover all facts of the case. They conduct relevant research to aid the lawyers for whom they work, in order to get the decision in their favor. Much of the paralegal's work involves writing reports and drafting legal documents for litigation. Paralegals who work in other areas, such as patent and copyright, real estate, and corporate law, assist in drafting contracts, mortgages, estate planning, and separation agreements.

Paralegals working in government agencies have the responsibility of maintaining reference files and analyzing research material for internal use. Those who work in community legal services help people who live in obscurity and are in search of legal aid. In short, paralegals spend much of their time in preparing and filing documents and researching legal stuff like affidavits, previous court cases, and helping in depositions.

The pay rates of paralegals vary to a great extent depending on the type of employer, practice area, billing rates, location, level of education, and experience. The US Department of Labor has projected a bright employment outlook for paralegals, because employers are increasingly trying to hire paralegals and legal assistants to cut on costs for tasks which are usually carried out by lawyers. There are very interesting prospects for paralegals in the near future, as well as good advancement opportunities.

Paralegals are involved in the delivery of legal services in a variety of ways. Traditionally a large number of paralegals worked on conveyancing matters. However, there is a role for paralegals in just about every area of the law, including commercial, , criminal, debt collection, environmental, family, HR, immigration, insurance, litigation, personal injury, procedural skills, research, wills and estates, and WorkCover.

Paralegals generally provide practical, hands-on assistance in relation to all aspects of legal work. The type of work performed by a paralegal will depend both upon the nature of the organisation and the practice area.

Under the supervision of lawyers, paralegals may perform duties such as:

- acting as an initial contact point for legal inquiries
- taking instructions for and drafting wills
- engaging in legal research

- drafting correspondence
- preparing agreements
- compiling court documentation
- providing general assistance in relation to commercial transactions
- managing a debt recovery practice
- conveyancing
- designing and operating databases
- liaising with clients

Each area of the law offers different opportunities for paralegal work. For example, paralegals can function as the point person for large projects, ensuring that the project is properly managed. They can also act as a liaison between lawyers and their clients or witnesses, return phone calls, conduct research or help with case preparation.

Another responsibility is to prepare what is known as the trial notebook. Each attorney has a certain way to organize the notebook. These are indexed and organized so that attorneys can just follow along in the notebook as they present their case to the judge and jury.

Paralegals prepare rough drafts of wills, contracts, bankruptcy filings, motions, and pleas. Attorneys will review these and note any changes to be made.

1.2.2 Duties:

Below is an outline of the major duties and responsibilities of the litigation paralegal from investigation through appeal.

Investigation

Litigation paralegals often take the lead in the pre-claim investigation. The paralegal's role may involve locating and interviewing witnesses, taking witness statements, gathering documents and evidence, creating case investigation notebooks, organizing documents and creating a chronology of facts. Litigation paralegals on the plaintiff side may conduct initial client interviews and perform initial case assessments.

Pleadings

Litigation paralegals on the plaintiff side may assist in drafting pleadings including the summons, complaint, and supporting affidavits. Paralegals on the defense side may collaborate with the client to investigate the allegations and formulate responses.

Litigation paralegals are often charged with the task of creating and maintaining pleadings, indexes and filing pleadings with the court. Paralegals also calendar hearing dates and filing deadlines.

Discovery

The majority of the litigation paralegal's time is spent in discovery. Litigation paralegals aid attorneys in drafting interrogatories, requests for production and requests for admissions and other discovery.

Paralegals on the defense side may track down knowledgeable persons within the client organization to help develop responses to interrogatories and other discovery requests.

Paralegals also create and maintain discovery indexes; organize voluminous case files; calendar discovery deadlines; organize, review and analyze documents for production; prepare deposition summaries; organize, summarize and analyze medical records and assist with e-discovery.

Litigation paralegals often conduct legal research, analyze issues and craft legal research memos. Litigation paralegals also conduct factual research, gathering relevant information from a variety of resources, such as newspapers, libraries, police and fire departments, trade associations and the media.

Pre-Trial

The litigation paralegal's communication and organization skills are invaluable in the pre-trial stage of litigation. Litigation paralegals organize and index exhibits; prepare trial binders, and manage document-intensive files.

Litigation paralegals also serve as a liaison between the trial team and third parties such as witnesses, clients, vendors, experts and courtroom personnel. If the trial takes place out of town, litigation paralegals often coordinate the logistics such as setting up the war room, reserving hotel and office space and acquiring equipment.

Trial

At trial, litigation paralegals are the attorney's right hand. Paralegals organize exhibits, documents, and evidence; arrange for transporting and setting up files and exhibits in the courtroom; prepare and issue subpoenas; assist in preparing witnesses; research and evaluate prospective jurors; and serve as a liaison between clients, witnesses, experts, vendors and the trial team.

In the courtroom, litigation paralegals assist with voir dire and jury selection; handle exhibits; pull together necessary documents; prep witnesses; prepare witness files; observe the jury; take notes on the attorney's behalf; order and review trial transcripts; and interact with clients, vendors, experts, and courtroom personnel. Paralegals may also help prepare jury instructions and conduct post-trial interviews of the jurors.

Settlement

Litigation paralegals often assist attorneys with case settlement. Their role may include gathering and organizing data and information needed for settlement; creating settlement brochures, distribution statements or negotiations checklists; drafting settlement agreements and releases, and assisting at pretrial conferences.

Appeal

Litigation paralegals assist with identifying issues for appeal; gather and organize documents for a record on appeal and/or a joint appendix; indexes cases for a table of authorities; assists in research and drafting of appellate documents, and filing documents with the court.

1.2.3 Examples

- Working on/handling probate and family law (divorce etc.) cases in a solicitors' firm
- Involvement in purchasing land and selling finished properties for a property development company
- Registering and defending trademarks for a food company
- Prosecuting people who have been cruel to animals as part of the RSPCA prosecutions team
- Giving immigration law advice to clients when working for a paralegal law firm
- Advising on consumer law protection as part of a local authority trading standards department
- Helping members of the public on a wide variety of issues (e.g. employment/ housing) as a Citizens Advice volunteer adviser
- Working for the Crown Prosecution Service
- Incorporating companies and doing other company secretarial work for a solicitors' firm, accountancy firm or company formation practice.

1.2.4 Legal Research

Paralegals are an integral part of our legal system, as they provide many valuable services to lawyers, including editing and drafting of legal documentation, preparing correspondence, performing legal research, preparing case summaries, among other things. Without paralegals, our legal system wouldn't work as well and there would be too much work for lawyers to do.

Successful paralegals combine a basic understanding of law with curiosity and fact-finding skills. Much of a typical day is spent digging through old case files and trying to find information useful to lawyers in court cases. Efficiency is critical since one would normally work on multiple cases for multiple lawyers each day. A lawyer would ask for cases that help establish precedent or offer insights on how to handle a trial or court proceeding. A paralegal's job is to find relevant cases and take notes on how they apply to the current case.

All paralegals are required to have a vast knowledge of the legal system, no matter where they choose to work or what area of law they work in. Most lawyers will expect paralegals to have a solid understanding of how to prepare affidavits or other documents, such as legal correspondence, and organize and maintain documents in paper or electronic filing system, as well as prepare for trial by performing tasks such as organizing exhibits. These skills, among others, are taught in a paralegal training program, designed to help students navigate today's legal landscape.

The ability to do effective legal research is like any other learned skill; it takes effort and hands-on practice to get good at it. Whether you do your research in the local law library, at an on-campus law school library, or inside your own firm, you need to have a plan before you begin. Without a clear idea of where to start, what to look for, where to look for it, and how to document what you've found, you may end up spinning your wheels and wasting valuable time.

These valuable tomes might be known under different names in your particular state, but they include:

- ❖ The state Penal Code-Explains the elements, violations, sentences, and statutes regulating crime and punishment.
- ❖ The state Vehicle Code-Explains the administrative, enabling, enforcement, and punishment statutes pertaining to motor vehicles.
- ❖ The city Municipal Code-Covers various laws and infractions specific to the community.
- ❖ The state Civil Code-Covers civil procedures.
- ❖ The state Business and Professions Code-Gives rules and regulations governing fair business practices and procedures.
- ❖ The state Welfare and Institutions-Covers state welfare issues, mental health concerns, juvenile protection, etc.
- ❖ The state Health and Safety Code-Covers occupational safety rules, narcotics violations, and state safety issues.
- ❖ The state Probate Code-Used to help determine will and probate cases.
- ❖ The state Real Estate Code-Governs real estate transactions with rules, regulations, and guidelines.

- The state Tax Code-Covers the state tax system for collection and enforcement of tax revenues and the associated laws.
- The U.S. Tax Code-The federal code that governs the collection of taxes by the IRS.
- The U.S. Title Code-A wide-sweeping document that governs many legislative actions for the entire U.S. government, including civil rights, law enforcement, and employment rights.

1.2.5 Legal Writing

Earlier the task of legal writing has been assumed by the attorney. However, paralegals are now being asked by their supervising attorneys to prepare many legal documents where certain documents are created for internal purposes relied upon by the attorney in preparation for litigation or appeal. The written documents are reviewed and revised by the attorney and ultimately filed in court. It is seen that in law offices, it is not uncommon for experienced paralegals to write brief case histories, research memoranda, motions, memoranda of points and authorities and even appellate briefs.

Legal writing is scary for many seasoned legal professionals, however many paralegals are involved in and follow correct writing. Paralegals use their writing skills throughout their careers whether for their independent work on provincial matters, landlord and tenant disputes, immigration and small claims, or in legal office under the direction of a lawyer, writing becomes an essential part of their job as paralegals are responsible for preparing and reviewing documents related to:

- Affidavits
- Legal documents
- Estate transactions
- Wills
- Court reports
- Trial briefs

Points to be considered for Good Legal Document Writing

There are certain tips which every paralegal needs to follow which would help them in proper legal writing skills such as:

Establishing G.O.A.L. for writing project

Before starting your pen on paper, paralegal must first gather some essential information, regarding the GOAL of the project which covers:

- G = ground rules for your project: Familiarizing with document format that follows type font and font size with proper margins. If writing a document, be certain to follow the format preferred by the attorney. Take samples of earlier submitted work while completing the assignment. If preparing an appellate court brief, take an idea about the procedure for incorporating references to record and transcript.

- O = objective of your project: After knowing the ground rules, you should have an idea about the purpose of your assignment; whether you want to write to inform or persuade, writing research memorandum to inform the attorney about the client's viable defenses under state law, or writing to persuade the court to deny the opposing party's motion for judgment. Keeping the objective in mind will help to focus and structure your writing by safeguarding it against the likelihood that key information will be overlooked or omitted.
- A = audience: If writing to your attorney or other paralegal, opposing counsel, client or to the court, it is important to tailor the writing style, tone and formality in a way which is correct for the intended audience.
- L = limitations for the project: When the attorney gives an assignment, you should confirm the due date. If you are preparing a document that would ultimately be filed with the court, in such case, you should know the filing deadline. As per the type of document you are preparing, it would be important to know the applicable statute of limitations for causes of action being asserted.

Organizing research material

Hours of research are meaningless when the seminal case you need is inside somewhere under piles of paper and stacks of folders. For easy organization and worry-free retrieval, hole-punch the research materials and file them by category. Apply color-code tabs and mark dividers to separate the material into primary and secondary authority, mandatory and persuasive authority, and federal and state authority.

Also, in upper right-hand part of the first page of each case, note the client-matter number, date you retrieved the case, and legal principles for which the case is important. On filing the case and retrieving it later, you will not have to re-read it to recollect why you printed it out in the first place. Do make an index or table of contents of the research materials and update it as and when required. After doing all these tasks, save the document on the computer and place a hard copy in the binder.

Preparing an outline

Once the research is done, before you start writing, prepare an outline of information you want to include in your document. Apply proper formatting for your document as a tool to create an outline. If you are writing an appellate brief, your outline should mirror each section of the brief covering the statement of issues, statement of facts, and argument components.

When writing a legal memorandum or appellate brief, it is better to list out the main points that you would address in the argument section and corresponding subheadings under each point, such that strong arguments will appear before weaker ones. Once the preparation of the preliminary outline is completed, break it down further into paragraph levels and identify the topic of each paragraph. Now list the information which will be included in a paragraph with applicable references to authority you cite. Such processes are cumbersome, boring and hard, but investing significant time to prepare your outline would really save time in the long run.

Keep writing simple and short

Legal writing will not involve use of flowery phrases or melodic prose, but is about reducing the complex to simple. Inspite of addressing attorneys and judges, your document should be written in such a way that the average person can understand it.

Good legal writing should be short or concise without multisyllabic words. Write in short sentences to heighten your reader's understanding.. Also, don't overwhelm the reader with paragraphs that extend three-quarters of the page; long paragraphs should be divided into more palatable two or three short paragraphs.

Keep reader's interest

Good writing helps in capturing the reader's interest at the beginning and -and helps to sustain his/her interest till the end. At the beginning of your document, give your reader a roadmap of where you are going and explain how you intend to get there. Throughout your document, insert mile markers to orient your reader as to how the section he or she is reading fits within the bigger picture.

Prevent reading induced hypnosis by varying the length of the sentences and paragraphs. Apply headings and subheadings for breaking bigger text on the page and apply sufficient white space to give your readers a visual resting place. Stress on key points or phrases with special formatting like italics and bold with bulleted lists. Strategically placed graphs, charts, and tables add substantive value to your writing and also help further engage your reader.

Use of topic sentences and transition bridges

As discussed, readers should have a complete road map of your document with proper guidelines. A good way of doing this is to start each paragraph with a topic sentence to introduce the subject matter you intend to discuss. You should end each paragraph with a transition bridge to the next paragraph. Use transition language to move from one point to the other, which would contribute to overall cohesiveness of writing.

Using active voice

For writing a legal document, it is always better to use active voice. For this, arrange the sentence so that the subject performs the action expressed by the verb. In many cases, a sentence written using active voice is more clear and direct as compared to a sentence written in passive voice, although , there are times when the facts in your case dictate the use of passive voice. In criminal cases where your attorney represents the accused, you certainly would not want to write, "The defendant assaulted the victim." Instead, you would write, "The victim was assaulted."

Write in positive voice

Use a glass half-full approach to write your legal documents using a positive voice. Change negative statements into affirmative statements. For ex.compare "The defendant should not be prohibited from asserting a contributory negligence." with "The defendant must be permitted to assert a contributory negligence defense." Notice how the second sentence reads better and is more direct.

Avoid legalese and legal jargon

Professional legal practitioners avoid the use of old legal jargon and legalese in their legal documents, as legalese and jargon only increase the complexity of the message, leading to confusion, hence it is better to include them only if really required.

Edit writing for 7 Cs

Once the draft is completed, review your work and edit for the following:

❖ Clarity – Add information if required to clarify your point and remove information that makes your point ambiguous or unclear. Rephrase or re-work passages to ensure your point are conveyed clearly and meaningfully.

❖ Completeness – Use the outline you prepared from above as a checklist to ensure that your document is complete. Thoroughly review your document to ensure that you have included the required elements and necessary information.

❖ Conciseness – Remove unnecessary words, fillers and redundancies. Remember to keep your sentences and paragraphs simple, short, and to the point.

❖ Concreteness – Remove lengthy legal phrases and replace it with shorter concrete words and phrases.

❖ Consistency – Read through the writing to make sure that your use of tenses and pronouns is consistent from beginning to end. Check to see that you have used the same word or phrase each time when referring to a particular concept.

- Continuity – Review your work for organizational continuity. Sentences and paragraphs should flow logically from one to the next. Read the first and last sentences of each paragraph. If you are able to glean the major points by reading these sentences alone, your writing has excellent continuity.
- Correctness – Verify that the legal authority you cited is still valid by double checking the citation format. Review your work to see that you have accurately stated the facts. Finally, carefully proofread your work for spelling, grammar, typographical and other kinds of errors that would detract from the message you want to convey.

1.2.6 Investigation

Introduction

Paralegals and legal assistants are typically part of the support staff for a law firm. Their main tasks include performing legal research, typing up drafts of documents and organizing files. Although paralegals can be found in all types of organizations including government agencies, most work for law firms.

In their primary role, paralegals and legal assistants help lawyers to prepare for hearings, trials and corporate meetings. Depending on the size of the law firm they work for and the focus of that firm's primary workload, paralegals' day-to-day duties may vary.

However, most paralegals will at some time or the other do some of the following duties:

- conduct research on relevant laws and regulations
- look up legal articles to help substantiate the reasoning behind a lawyer's legal position
- gather and arrange evidence for attorneys to review
- draft correspondence and legal documents
- file exhibits, briefs and appeals and other legal documents with the courts or opposing counsel
- call clients
- call witnesses
- call lawyers and outside experts to schedule meetings and depositions
- get affidavits
- organize and maintain both paper and electronic files

In big firms, paralegals may specialize in a certain aspect of case preparation such as legal research or collecting evidence. In smaller firms, paralegals may be tasked with a broader list of jobs, perhaps helping out in nearly all phases of trial preparation. Regardless of the size of the firm, paralegals must be comfortable using technology to manage the amount of documents and data a case can generate. Many of today's law firms utilize databases to catalog documents so that they may be searched and found utilizing just a few key words.

Investigation

Similar to attorneys, paralegals assist in various specialized areas of law such as personal injury, corporate law, criminal law, litigation, intellectual property, family law, real estate, immigration law or bankruptcy filings.

In case of personal injury litigation, when representing the injured party, paralegals mainly do many types of investigative work. An early, thorough investigation can lay the ground work for a solid case. While hiring a professional investigator may often be necessary, paralegals can perform a significant portion of the essential investigative work, sometimes without leaving the office.

During the investigation process, a paralegal will interview an assortment of witnesses, as every witness interviewed during the extensive investigation, would help to enlighten a paralegal about the intricacies and details of the case. While each witness is being interviewed a proper statement must be constructed to document the findings or opinions of the particular witness.

Following the conclusion of the interview a paralegal must create a memo or statement to provide an overview or summary of the information exchanged. Lawyers are often too busy to conduct interviews with witnesses, hence they rely on the paralegal to assist in this role.

The paralegal must provide the supervising attorney with a witness statement to bridge the absence and streamline the investigation process. In case of the supervising attorney's absence in the interview process, the witness statement would provide a summary of all the necessary information, statements, and findings from the questioning process.

A witness statement is a formally written legal document which paraphrases what the witness said during the interview. The witness statement must include a thorough evaluation of all facts relevant to the case.

In addition, the witness's credibility or lack thereof must be documented. In order to satisfy the competency requirements a paralegal will subdivide the witnesses into different categories.

There are many classifications of witnesses, each group contains necessary obligations in regards to the individual's presence in the legal matter or his or her expertise. For instance, an expert witness will prove competent if he/she reveals a certain knowledge for the matter in question.

Choosing an expert witness is a painstakingly detailed process. The appropriate expert witness must not only possess a general knowledge of the background information involved in the case, but a specific understanding of the varying complexities present.

Choosing and evaluating an expert witness based on investigation is an arduous task, therefore the paralegal must have a thorough understanding of the background and general matters involved in the case.

In contrast, the competency test for a lay witness is more exact. A lay witness will be marked as "competent and usable" in a witness statement if the individual actually saw, heard, or perceived the events of the issue in some way.

During the investigation the paralegal must undoubtedly conclude that the lay witness was in fact present during the incident. After the witness is proved competent the paralegal must also denote whether or not the individual is credible. Credibility will arise simply from the questions during the investigation.

The credibility of a witness will be up to the paralegal to decide, based on his/her findings. Along with the credibility and competency of the witness, the paralegal must also document any substantial non-verbal communication during the interview. Non-verbal communication includes any emotion, nervous ticks, "tells", smiles, or seemingly anything that will make the paralegal believe that the witness is biased, prejudiced, or supplying misinformation.

The witness statement exemplifies the importance of the paralegal. Although it is a simple reporting of facts from an interview, the witness statement will provide the lawyer with invaluable information relevant to the case.

Investigation proceedings

The investigation process starts as soon as the law firm is contacted by a potential client or even before it is retained. If the call involves a motor vehicle accident, check the local papers or television stations for reports concerning the accident; this is where the internet is an invaluable tool. This early information may be useful to the attorney when deciding whether to take the case or when speaking to the client for the first time. Or if the potential case involves a product defect or surgical complication, a quick internet search can help determine if there was a product recall or if the surgical complication is a recognized risk.

Once the client has retained the firm, the investigation begins in earnest. The paralegal / investigator must gather as much data/information as possible about the people and events associated with the accident. It is important to locate and take statements from potential witnesses; photograph and document the accident scene; locate, collect and preserve physical evidence; and photograph the client's injuries. In addition to obtaining all medical records concerning the instant injury, it may also be necessary to obtain prior medical records in order to fully understand the client's injuries and disabilities.

Gathering and reviewing records is an integral part of the investigation where all related records are considered as soon as the file is opened which includes:

- police records
- paramedic reports
- fire rescue reports
- weather records etc.

In this phase of investigation, the internet becomes an invaluable tool for gathering information about locations, people, products, drugs, medical procedures, etc. Maps and aerial photographs can shed light on accident locations. A large number of public records, like property (ownership) records, are available on the internet. Photographs of required products or instrumentalities that are used in an accident are useful in understanding the mechanics of the accident/incident which also can be retrieved from the internet. Social media sites also offer other sources for locating witnesses, hence to the delight of many employers, all such investigative research can be carried out without the paralegal leaving the office.

However, a thorough investigation does require work away from the office. The paralegal may be required to visit the accident site and take photographs and measurements. Try to go there at the same time of day as the accident and observe the traffic conditions. Never assume that the accident site is the same as the accident scene; accident sites change. There may be changes to the lights, contour of the road, street signs, timing sequence of traffic lights, etc. If possible, it may be helpful to visit the accident scene with the client.

1.2.7 Relationship with Attorneys

While lawyers are responsible for the creative thinking behind court cases, their legal assistants are responsible for preparation, logistics, obtaining affidavits and other forms required for court cases, as well as general duties in a law office. The best way that you can build and maintain a great working relationship with lawyers is to perform these duties as faithfully as possible and to make sure that all of your supervising lawyers understand what your paralegal training has taught you. If you come across as being persistently thorough in your communication, the lawyers in your office will acknowledge you as a professional and dependable assistant.

Lawyers and paralegals have different ways of thinking, and because the paralegal profession is relatively new, lawyers often have trouble understanding how best to utilize the skills of a paralegal. The most important way for a paralegal to establish a good working relationship with lawyers is to communicate every thought as clearly as possible. Communication is even more important for paralegals than for lawyers because lawyers can assume, without being reprimanded, that all their personnel are on the same page. It's the responsibility of the legal assistant to completely understand the information passed along from lawyers.

Another important point is a bit of general advice for any workplace. A professional relationship isn't the same as a personal relationship. Establishing good relations with superiors in the workplace requires a different approach than befriending them. In fact, managers of law offices cite this mistake as being the cause of the complete unraveling of a work environment. When lawyers and paralegals have trouble separating personal interests from professional matters, the working relationship suffers.

For managing attorney, paralegals should never:

- ❖ assume that you can catch him/her in the hallway for anything unless he/she has a publicly understood open-door policy.
- ❖ take his/her company policies personally unless he/she sits you down in the office and tells you of implementing something or unless he/she publicly recognizes the ideas and its implementation.
- ❖ expect him/her to take your side in any disagreement you may have with any attorney or manager; he/she won't.
- ❖ expect him/her to defend you to a client; again, he/she won't.
- ❖ expect him/her to make excuses or speak in your defense to another firm's attorneys; again, he/she won't. He/she expects you to be professional at all times with attorneys from other firms regardless of what is said within your firm about those same attorneys or their firm.

1.3 Functions in Law Office

1.3.1 Structure of Law Office

Law office normally comprise of the following staff:

Partners

People commonly refer to the owners of a law firm as being the "partners." Partners are usually the most experienced lawyers in a firm and, consequently, they charge the highest fee and receive a share of the overall profits. Depending on the legal structure of the firm, they might be called "Members" or "Shareholders." While law firms often have a "Managing Partner" who runs the operations of the firm, most firms do not typically use the more corporate-style language of "CEO" or "President."

Associates

Lawyers who are employed by a firm, but who aren't owners, are usually called "associates." Associates can be excellent lawyers, but typically have less experience than the partners of the firm. Much of their work will be reviewed by partners, and they may have very little personal contact with clients for their first few years at the firm. Although practices vary from firm to firm, associates may have to work for perhaps three to ten years before they are considered for partnership. Given their experience, associates tend to bill clients at lower rates than partners. Therefore, as a client, you might prefer that certain work is handled by a smart associate for a lower hourly rate.

Contract lawyers

A firm will sometimes hire outside lawyers as independent contractors to do part-time work. The firm will usually pay a contract lawyer on an hourly basis and then bill out his or her time at a higher rate in order to cover overhead costs and hopefully make a profit. It is common for a firm to do this when they are particularly busy, or when the Contract Lawyer has specific expertise on a matter.

Of counsel lawyers

Many firms will also develop an affiliation with one or more lawyers under an "of counsel" arrangement. These types of arrangements that can be called "of counsel" are sometimes hard to neatly define, but it usually is something more than a part-time contracting relationship.

Law clerks

Law clerks are ordinarily current law students working at a firm for academic credit, or for a small amount of money. Clerks will do legal research and otherwise assist lawyers in preparing cases and working on other law-related matters. Like associates, firms will bill out clerks at a much lower rate than partners. Thus, clients would find it beneficial in law clerks doing certain types of time-intensive work, where significant expertise is not required. Hiring a law clerk is also a good way for a firm to recruit new associates; clerks are often given job offers following their law school graduation.

Paralegals

A paralegal is someone who performs quasi-legal functions and assists attorneys, but is not an attorney. Paralegals can serve a very important role in a law firm by providing critical support to lawyers when they are working on cases. In many instances, paralegals have a practical working knowledge of the law and of court or administrative procedures that makes them valuable to a law firm. They are able to work under the supervision of a lawyer and carry out detailed work that is required on every case, but that cannot justify the high billing rates of a lawyer.

Legal assistants

This is a catchall term that is sometimes used by law firms to describe anyone in a law office who assists attorneys in working on legal matters. It may include paralegals, legal secretaries, and other support staff. These individuals generally do not have law licenses, but do have experience with legal practice, or are recent college graduates who have sufficient education to handle tedious tasks like summarizing deposition transcripts.

Legal secretaries

Every lawyer is burdened with an endless barrage of administrative details and procedural requirements that are a part of practicing law. These duties and requirements can be a huge disruption for a lawyer who doesn't have a competent legal secretary to organize and assist with the day-to-day affairs of his or her practice. Depending on the law firm, "legal assistant" and "legal secretary" are sometimes interchangeable titles.

Receptionists

Almost all law firms employ a legal receptionist. He or she is the firm's initial contact with the outside world, and generally answers phones and greets clients at the door. Some receptionists double as paralegals or legal assistants, depending on the nature of the law firm.

Investigators: Depending on the type of law they practice;some law firms will hire their own investigators who investigate background facts on a case. This is particularly common in criminal or personal injury practices.

Administrative personnel

Big law firms will have their own administrative personnel to run internal operations. While administrative staff generally dont charge clients directly for their services, they do constitute an overhead cost that is ultimately reflected in billing rates. Administrative staff may include accountants, bookkeepers, librarians, billing and accounts receivable personnel, and human resources personnel.

Other personnel

Many law firms will have runners, part-time clerical help, technology experts, and other staff members to perform certain functions of the law office. The larger the law office, the more likely you will find such personnel as staff. Clients are unlikely to interact with many of these behind-the-scenes employees.

1.3.2 Attorneys in Law House

An attorney is like a lawyer who also passed the bar examination and has been admitted to practice law in a particular jurisdiction. They also go beyond the realm of lawyer and provide legal representation to an individual. The relationship is more than merely providing the factual state of the law and delves into providing strategy for the client's needs in reference to the law. An attorney can also appear in court and other settings on behalf of a client.

Attorneys are bound by a code of professional responsibility. There may be limits on what an attorney can do for talent such as soliciting material for roles. Also, an attorney would only be able to represent multiple parties in a single project with signed waivers and by advising the parties to obtain independent counsel. In any event, attorneys can make a talent aware of industry standards, provide additional knowledge, negotiate deals and help with development of a career.

Roles and Duties

The following are the role and duties of an Attorney:

Being accountable

An attorney is accountable to the adult. Attorneys may also encounter questions from the Public Guardian and Trustee, Health Authorities or Community Living BC, who have a role to investigate complaints of abuse of adults who are incapable.

Knowing the scope of authority

As per Power of Attorney Act, EPA covers an adult's financial affairs which cover adult's business and property, and conduct adult's legal affairs. In such case, property includes: money, assets like vehicle or real estate, and personal belongings such as jewelry and clothes.

Exercising general duties of an attorney

An attorney has to act honestly, in good faith and within the law. An attorney can do anything on behalf of adult with respect to legal and financial affairs, except for making or changing the adult's Will, and as long as it is something that the adult could do while considered capable.

Acting in adult's interests

An attorney's first legal responsibility is to act in adult's best interests by making decisions on behalf of the adult as per opinion of what is best for them. While making decisions about what is in the adult's best interests, an Attorney needs to take into account the adult's current wishes, their known beliefs and values, and any directions they set out in EPA document. When it is reasonable, an Attorney must foster the adult's independence and encourage their involvement in decision making, keeping their personal effects at disposal and giving priority to meeting health and personal care requirements.

Keeping records

An attorney while acting on behalf of the adult should make a reasonable effort to determine the extent of the adult's property and liabilities as of the date your first start acting, which is similar to taking an inventory. While acting as an attorney, the following records are to be considered:

- A current list of the adult's property and liabilities including estimating value if reasonable
- Accounts and records related to actions taken as an attorney
- Invoices, bank statements and records necessary to create full accounts about receiving or spending capital or income on behalf of the adult

Non-delegation of authority

Delegating authority is giving someone else the power to make a decision about the adult's financial affairs. Unless specific instructions is provided in EPA, an Attorney cannot delegate any of the decision making authority, except for decisions about investments.

Keeping information confidential

An attorney must keep the adult's personal information private, except when necessary to:

- Carry out your duties
- Providing information to or comply with requirement of Public Guardian and Trustee
- Making an application to court, or comply with court order

Changing beneficiary designations

- An attorney can manage the adult's beneficiary designations on their behalf
- Attorneys have such power for all types of instruments that covers life insurance policies, RRSPs, and RRIFs but not the adult's Will.
- An attorney can renew, convert or replace an instrument that the adult sets up while capable, as long as it is similar and you name the same beneficiary the adult named in the original.
- He/she may also set up a new instrument as long as the beneficiary designation of adult's estate remains the same. Attorney must apply to court for permission to change who is named as a beneficiary on an instrument the adult made.

Dealing with real estate matters

Unless the EPA document restricts it, an attorney may manage the adult's real estate affairs provided that certain requirements of the Land Title Act are met. The adult and the attorney must each sign the EPA in front of a lawyer or notary public who will also sign the EPA to certify the adult's and attorney's signatures. The adult and attorney do not have to sign at the same time or with the same lawyer or notary public.

Keeping your property and money separate

As an attorney, you must keep the adult's money and other property separate from your own, unless it belonged to you and the adult jointly, before the EPA is made.

Non-disposing of property which adult left to someone in his/her Will

As per the law, an attorney cannot dispose of any of adult's property that is known subject to a specific gift in adult's Will, till it does in order to comply with other duties as an attorney. It is in the adult's interest to make the attorney aware of specific gifts included in their Will.

Use of adult's money for benefit of others and making gifts/loans

An attorney's duty is to manage the adult's financial affairs for the adult's benefit. There are some situations where an attorney can use the adult's finances for the benefit of others. In certain situations, the attorney can use the adult's money to fulfill their legal obligation to financially support their minor children.

Rights of Attorney

Accessing information

An attorney has the right to the same information and records as the adult has a right to, in case of his/her bank statements till these relate to the attorney's area of authority or to the adult and his/her incapability.

Receiving delivery of the adult's property

An attorney will need to know about and should have control of adult's financial affairs for which they are responsible. As per the Power of Attorney Act, anyone who has custody or control of property which belongs to the adult should deliver the property promptly as requested by the adult's attorney.

The attorney may not be entitled to receive the adult's Will. The adult may have given instructions to a lawyer or notary public or included instructions in their Will that it must not be delivered to the attorney.

Being paid for out-of-pocket expenses

An attorney has a right to a refund for reasonable expenses resulting from carrying out duties. He/she can document all expense claims and payments. As per Power of Attorney Act, an attorney cannot be paid a fee for acting as an attorney till it is spelled out in theEPA document.

Getting help and advice

An attorney can ask for and hire help and advice to carry out responsibilities. He/she might need the advice of an accountant to help filing adult's taxes which is different from delegating decision making power.

Being protected from liability

An attorney may not be liable for any loss or damage to the adult's financial affairs, as long as he/she follow his/her duties as an attorney and any specific requirements stated in the adult's EPA.

1.3.3 Legal Secretaries in Law House

The role of legal secretaries, also known as administrative assistants and legal assistants, has evolved in the past two decades. As technology continues to transform the law office, legal secretaries have exceeded traditional roles of typing and answering phones to performing high-value activities once reserved for professional and managerial staff such as selecting vendors, managing client relationships and drafting legal documents.

A legal secretary plays an important role in everyday workings of a law office. They need extensive knowledge of legal proceedings and documentation. It is not uncommon for the most experienced and high performing legal secretaries to go on to be promoted to paralegal positions within a law firm.

Legal secretary is a particular category of worker in the legal profession who help by preparing and filing legal documents like appeals or motions. It is not unusual for big firms to place managerial duties on a particular legal secretary. Similar to paralegal, a legal secretary is responsible for locating relevant information for cases.

Legal secretaries are involved in doing clerical duties at law firms and other legal offices. Just like office secretaries, legal secretaries need extensive knowledge of legal proceedings and documentation. They are different from paralegals or legal assistants in that they need to have a firm grasp on legal proceedings and a strong background in law documentation.

Duties

Legal secretaries often prepare documents which include legal briefs, court subpoenas, spreadsheets and other office-related letters. Many legal secretaries also organize and maintain all legal files kept on-site. Some legal secretaries also maintain electronic-filing databases.

Legal secretaries often provide lawyers with direct assistance, such as helping with research for cases, gathering necessary documents for trials and submitting paperwork to courthouses. Other duties may include scheduling client appointments, answering calls, taking notes during legal meetings and maintaining the firm's legal research references.

Legal secretaries can work in many types of office environments such as:

- legal firms
- corporate legal offices
- nonprofit organizations
- government offices

Many legal secretaries converse directly with attorneys, clerical personnel, courtroom staff members, clients, expert witnesses and commercial vendors. Legal secretaries can also teach new lawyers and paralegals about protocols for filling out and submitting courtroom documents.

Skills

Since many law firms and legal offices deal with multiple clients at the same time, a legal secretary requires the skills to multitask effectively. Strong organizational skills and attention to detail are also essential for this career. Computer skills are required since many legal documents are created and altered electronically. Good communication skills are also necessary to instruct staff members and to address clients. Legal secretaries need to be familiar with legal terminology and government regulations. Some of the skills required by legal secretary include the following:

Technology Skills

Many attorneys have neither the time nor expertise to operate law office technology. They rely on tech-savvy legal secretaries to perform a variety of computer-based tasks such as: creating spreadsheets, preparing presentations, entering time for billing purposes, creating and typing documents, maintaining calendars and tracking deadlines. Hence, legal secretaries who are proficient in a variety of computer software applications will have the most promising career opportunities.

Interpersonal Skills

Legal secretaries interact daily with attorneys, paralegals, staff, clients, opposing counsel, judicial personnel, vendors and other third-parties. Hence, top-notch interpersonal and communication skills are required. Apart from face-to-face interaction, legal secretaries communicate by e-mail, telephone and video conferencing systems.

Writing Skills

Legal secretaries are normally responsible for drafting routine correspondence and file memos with proofreading legal documents such as pleadings, briefs, discovery and transactional documents.

Organizational Skills

Attorneys are notoriously disorganized, hence legal secretaries are considered an attorney's right-hand, as they possess, excellent organizational skills that are essential to efficiently manage the law practice or corporate legal department. Legal secretaries also:

- maintain paper and electronic files
- manage projects
- track multiple deadlines
- maintain calendars
- schedule meetings
- organize events
- keeping things in order
- make things easily accessible

Transcription Skills

Transcription skills are the basics to secretarial practice. Along with good typing speed, keen listening skills are required to comprehend voice dictation files. Strong grammar, spelling, vocabulary, and language skills are required to understand legal terminology. Legal secretaries must be proficient in word processing applications and transcription equipment.

Attention to Detail

Attention to detail is critical in the legal profession. Legal secretaries handle the minutest of tasks in daily law practice and attention to detail is important in nearly every secretarial task from drafting and proofreading documents to scheduling meetings and calendaring deadlines.

Familiarity with Legal Documents and Terminology

Legal secretaries should be familiar with all legal terminology including terms like subpoena, pro se and voir dire so that it doesn't befuddle them. They should be able to understand the nuances of legal procedure and should know how to create and format pleadings, discovery and transactional documents.

Teamwork

Teamwork is an important attribute for legal secretaries to deliver legal services. In all practice settings right from large corporate legal department to solo practitioners, legal secretaries must team with attorneys, paralegals, secretaries, file clerks, vendors and others to deliver legal services effectively. The most efficient legal secretaries know how to get along with co-workers and collaborate with third parties to get the job done.

Multi-Tasking Skills

Most legal secretaries work for more than one person on more than one file. Simultaneously performing multiple tasks is second-nature to a competent legal secretary. They know how to juggle multiple assignments and competing priorities and how to manage growing workloads in today's busy law offices where one person frequently performs the job of three.

Research skills

Legal secretaries perform internet research for a multitude of tasks like:

- finding directions
- gathering client information
- researching competition
- locating expert witnesses

Many legal secretaries, particularly those in small law offices, perform paralegal duties such as:

- legal research
- cite checking
- tracking down case law

Learning legal research platforms such as Westlaw or Lexis/Nexis can give them a competitive edge.

1.4 Paralegal Organizations

The paralegal profession is bound by a core set of philosophies, standards and principles, all of which are enforced and supported by a number of strong professional organizations and associations, each with a unique role to play.

Although the paralegal profession is largely unregulated by the government, a number of industry organizations are there to take up the slack and ensure the core tenets of the profession are never compromised.

At the same time, such organizations provide paralegals with an opportunity to contribute to the profession, continue to learn, and achieve long term professional goals right from professional membership associations that provide continuing education and trade publications to agencies that host conferences and events which support advancement and professional certification to national organizations for helping set and maintaining standards for education and competency.

While some paralegal associations are best known for their professional certification opportunities, others focus more on providing professional networking and career resources for both aspiring and practicing paralegals. In all cases, such organizations provide professional advocacy, promote high professional standards, and together help form the self-regulatory system that ensures the integrity of the paralegal profession.

There are a multitude of professional paralegal associations and organizations. It is generally looked upon favorably for a paralegal to be associated with at least one of these organizations.

American Bar Association (ABA):

It is the longest-standing and most well-known voluntary legal organization in the United States. The ABA provides a standard of professional and ethical practices for the legal profession. The ABA also bestows accreditation to those programs and educational facilities that meet rigid qualifications. The ABA is typically seen as an elite group in which members or those who have a degree from ABA-accredited school are recognized as legitimate and valuable. It does not provide education but does provide resources to approved facilities, schools, and courses.

National Association of Legal Assistants (NALA):

It is a large recognized organization throughout the United States which provides certification programs in conjunction with ABA standards. This organization is the only one to offer actual title of a certified paralegal (CP). For becoming certified through NALA, participants must strictly meet the eligibility requirements. It gives many continuing education courses which is required for certified paralegals.

National Federation of Paralegal Associations (NFPA):

It offers the title of registered paralegal (RP) to those who pass their Paralegal Advanced Competency Exam (PACE). Just like the NALA exam, the PACE exam given by NFPA, has strict requirements which must be met just in order to be eligible to appear for it. NFPA is also developing another paralegal competency exam for those who do not qualify for the PACE. This exam will not offer a registered paralegal title but will offer one of a slightly lower caliber. It also offers many continuing education courses for both registered paralegals and those who are not registered.

National Paralegal Association (NPA):

It is an international organization offering numerous resources to paralegals across the globe. This organization offers information to those seeking paralegal education as well as those already employed as a paralegal. NPA has a plethora of information available to individuals and companies seriously seeking it.

1.4.1 National Federation of Paralegal Associations

National Federation of Paralegal Associations (NFPA) was founded in 1974 which was the nation's first paralegal association which has 9,000+ members who drives the policy-focused professional association. The NFPA maintains strategic alliances with the American Bar Association (ABA), the American Association for Paralegal Education (AAfPE), and others. They often work together to support unity in the profession and a common set of education standards.

National Federation of Paralegal Associations (NFPA) is a national professional organization composed of individual paralegals, paralegal associations, and other organizations concerned with the interests of paralegals. Members of NFPA have varying types of backgrounds, experience, education, and job responsibilities which reflect the diversity of the paralegal profession. NFPA promotes the growth, development and recognition of the paralegal profession as an integral partner in the delivery of legal services.

NFPA recognizes that the creation of guidelines and standards for professional conduct are important for the development and expansion of the paralegal profession. In May 1993, NFPA adopted this Model Code of Ethics and Professional Responsibility to delineate the principles for ethics and conduct to which every paralegal should aspire. The Model Code expresses NFPA's commitment to increasing the quality and efficiency of legal services and recognizes the profession's responsibilities to the public, the legal community, and colleagues.

Paralegals perform many different functions, and these functions differ greatly among practice areas. In addition, each jurisdiction has its own unique legal authority and practices governing ethical conduct and professional responsibilities.

It is essential that each paralegal strive for personal and professional excellence and encourage the professional development of other paralegals, as well as those entering the legal profession. Participation in professional associations intended to advance the quality and standards of the legal profession is of paramount importance.

NFPA Certification Options

NFPA offers two main paralegal certification programs:

Paralegal CORE Competency Exam (PCCE)

The Paralegal CORE Competency Exam (PCCE), a broad certification intended for new and early-career professionals already in possession of a bachelor's degree in paralegal studies or an equivalent combination of education and experience.

Paralegal Advanced Competency Exam (PACE)

The Paralegal Advanced Competency Exam (PACE), a high-level certification intended for paralegals who are further along in their careers and want to position themselves for advancement. PACE certification requires the completion of a four-hour exam covering the administration of client legal matters, the development of client legal matters, factual and legal research, factual and legal writing and office administration.

Paralegals should possess integrity, professional skill and dedication to work towards the improvement of the legal system and should strive to expand the paralegal role in the delivery of legal services.

Paralegals Shall Achieve and Maintain High Level of Competence:

- A paralegal shall achieve competency through education, training, and work experience.
- A paralegal shall participate in continuing education to keep oneself informed of current legal, technical and general developments.
- A paralegal shall perform all assignments promptly and efficiently.

A Paralegal Shall Maintain a High Level of Personal and Professional Integrity:

- A paralegal shall not engage in any ex parte communication involving the courts or any other adjudicatory body in an attempt to exert undue influence or to obtain advantage for the benefit of only one party.
- A paralegal shall not communicate, or cause another to communicate, with a party the paralegal knows to be represented by a lawyer in a pending matter without the prior consent of the lawyer representing such other party.
- A paralegal shall ensure that all timekeeping and billing records prepared by the paralegal are thorough, accurate, and honest.
- A paralegal shall be scrupulous, thorough and honest in the identification and maintenance of all funds, securities, and other assets of a client and shall provide accurate accountings as appropriate.
- A paralegal shall advise the proper authority of any dishonest or fraudulent acts by any person pertaining to the handling of the funds, securities or other assets of a client.

Paralegal Shall Maintain High Standard of Professional Conduct:

- A paralegal shall refrain from engaging in any conduct that offends the dignity and decorum of proceedings before a court or other adjudicatory body and shall be respectful of all rules and procedures.
- A paralegal shall advise the proper authority of any action of another legal professional which clearly demonstrates fraud, deceit, dishonesty, or misrepresentation.
- A paralegal shall avoid impropriety and the appearance of impropriety. A paralegal shall serve the public interest by contributing to the delivery of quality legal services and the improvement of the legal system.
- A paralegal shall be sensitive to the legal needs of the public and shall promote the development and implementation of programs that address those needs.

- A paralegal shall support bona fide efforts to meet the need for legal services by those unable to pay reasonable or customary fees; for example, participation in pro bono projects and volunteer work.
- A paralegal shall support efforts to improve the legal system and shall assist in making changes.

Paralegals Should Preserve Confidential Information of Clients:

- A paralegal shall be aware of and abide by all legal authority governing confidential information.
- A paralegal shall not use confidential information to the disadvantage of the client.
- A paralegal shall not use confidential information to the advantage of the paralegal or of a third person.
- A paralegal may reveal confidential information only after full disclosure and with the client's written consent; or, when required by law or court order; or, when necessary to prevent the client from committing an act which could result in death or serious bodily harm.
- A paralegal shall keep those individuals responsible for the legal representation of a client fully informed of any confidential information the paralegal may have pertaining to that client.
- A paralegal shall not engage in any indiscreet communications concerning clients.

Paralegal's Title Shall be Fully Disclosed:

- A paralegal's title shall clearly indicate the individual's status and shall be disclosed in all business and professional communications to avoid misunderstandings and misconceptions about the paralegal's role and responsibilities.
- A paralegal's title shall be included if the paralegal's name appears on business cards, letterhead, brochures, directories, and advertisements.

Paralegal Shall Not Engage in Unauthorized Practice of Law:

- A paralegal shall comply with the applicable legal authority governing the unauthorized practice of law.

Paralegal Avoid Conflicts of Interest and Disclose Possible Conflict to Employer/ Client:

- A paralegal shall act within the bounds of the law, solely for the benefit of the client, and shall be free of compromising influences and loyalties. Neither the paralegal's personal or business interest, nor those of other clients or third persons, should compromise the paralegal's professional judgment and loyalty to the client.

- A paralegal shall avoid conflicts of interest which may arise from previous assignments whether for a present or past employer or client.
- A paralegal shall avoid conflicts of interest which may arise from family relationships and from personal and business interests.
- A paralegal shall create and maintain an effective recordkeeping system that identifies clients, matters, and parties with which the paralegal has worked, to be able to determine whether an actual or potential conflict of interest exists.
- A paralegal shall reveal sufficient non-confidential information about a client or former client to reasonably ascertain if an actual or potential conflict of interest exists.
- A paralegal shall not participate in or conduct work on any matter where a conflict of interest has been identified.
- In matters where a conflict of interest has been identified and the client consents to continued representation, a paralegal shall comply fully with the implementation and maintenance of an Ethical Wall.

1.4.2 The Association of Legal Assistants

National Association of Legal Assistants (NALA) is the leading organization in the United States for paralegals and legal assistants. NALA is a non-profit organization that provides a variety of support services to paralegals, including continuing education, professional development, and a voluntary certification program.

While NALA may be best known for its professional certification program, this paralegal organization also provides continuing legal education opportunities and professional development programs. NALA works to provide more than 18,000 paralegals with opportunities to excel in the profession.

NALA also provides current information about the profession, continuing education programs (publications, courses and webinars), networking opportunities, professional certification programs, occupational survey reports, and publications to help paralegals excel in the workplace. NALA is a non-profit organization under section 501(c)(6) representing more than 18,000 paralegals, who are individual members or members of NALA affiliated associations.

NALA is a membership organization where the individual members are the leading force of NALA programs and policies. Through NALA, paralegals across the nation have come together to develop programs and standard setting codes to help them grow in the work place. The association is governed by a Board of Directors and maintains an office and which is headquartered in Tulsa, Oklahoma.

NALA membership is offered in four categories: Active, Associate, Student, and Sustaining. All members receive the same benefits of membership, although only active members may vote, serve on committees or become an officer or director of the association. Active members of NALA include any individual who has met criteria involving certification, education, and experience as an in-house paralegal under the supervision of a licensed attorney.

Powers of NALA Directors

By way of extension rather than limitation, directors shall be vested with following authority, discretion and powers:

- To purchase or otherwise acquire, deal in, sell, hold or dispose of for this Corporation such property, rights, interests or privileges (whether real, personal or mixed) of whatsoever nature which this Corporation is authorized or may legally do and upon such terms and conditions and for such consideration as it in its discretion shall deem fit and to the best interests of the Corporation;
- To appoint, hire, contract with, suspend, discharge, remove or otherwise deal with such subordinates, managers, assistants, agents, servants or employees, either permanently or temporarily and to determine and fix their duties and compensation and to require security from them, to determine their fitness, all upon such terms and conditions and for such consideration as it may in its discretion deem fit and to the best interest of this corporation;
- To confer by appropriate resolution upon any officer or agent the right to choose, hire, contract with, remove, suspend, discharge or otherwise deal with subordinate agents, employees or servants as it may in its discretion deem fit and to the best interests of this Corporation;
- To appoint any person or persons to accept, acquire, hold in trust, dispose of any property (real, personal or mixed) for or belonging to this Corporation or in which it shall or may be interested, and to otherwise act for any purpose and to execute and do such other duties and things which may be requisite or incident or convenient in relation to such trust;
- To create, make or authorize the creation or issuance of such checks, drafts, notes, bonds, debentures, mortgages, leases, trust agreements, instruments, contracts or agreements of whatsoever nature and type and to do each and every other act and thing necessary, incident or convenient in effectuating the same;
- To conduct business of the directors by mail or meetings. In the event of a mail vote, a majority of votes cast by the directors shall be required to approve any action thereof.

2

The Legal System

2.1 Introduction to Legal System

2.1.1. Law

Law is a word that means different things at different times. Black's Law Dictionary says that law is "a body of rules of action or conduct prescribed by controlling authority, and having binding legal force. In a nation, the law can serve to (1) keep the peace, (2) maintain the status quo, (3) preserve individual rights, (4) protect minorities against majorities, (5) promote social justice, and (6) provide for orderly social change. Some legal systems serve these purposes better than others. Although a nation ruled by an authoritarian government may keep the peace and maintain the status quo, it may also oppress minorities or political opponents (e.g., Burma, Zimbabwe, or Iraq under Saddam Hussein).

Even before legislatures met to make rules for society, disputes happened and judges decided them. In England, judges began writing down the facts of a case and the reasons for their decision. They often resorted to deciding cases on the basis of prior written decisions. In relying on those prior decisions, the judge would reason that since a current case was pretty much like a prior case, it ought to be decided the same way. This is essentially reasoning by analogy. Thus, the use of precedent in common-law cases came into being, and a doctrine of stare decisis (pronounced STAR-ay-de-SIGH-sus) became accepted in English courts. Stare decisions means, in Latin, "let the decision stand."

Most judicial decisions that don't apply legislative acts (known as statutes) will involve one of three areas of law—property, contract, or tort. Property law deals with the rights and duties of those who can legally own land (real property), how that ownership can be legally confirmed and protected, how property can be bought and sold, what the rights of tenants (renters) are, and what the various kinds of "estates" in land are (e.g., fee simple, life estate, future interest, easements, or rights of way). Contract law deals with what kinds of promises courts should enforce. For example, should courts enforce a contract where one of the parties was intoxicated, underage, or insane? Should courts enforce a contract where one of the parties seemed to have an unfair advantage? What kind of contracts would have to be in writing to be enforced by courts? Tort law deals with the types of cases that involve some kind of harm and or injury between the plaintiff and the defendant when no contract exists. Thus, if you are libeled or a competitor lies about your product, your remedy would be in tort, not contract.

The thirteen original colonies had been using English common law for many years, and they continued to do so after independence from England. Early cases from the first states are full of references to already-decided English cases. As years went by, many precedents were established by US state courts, so that today a judicial opinion that refers to a seventeenth- or eighteenth-century English common-law case is quite rare.

Courts in one state may look to common-law decisions from the courts of other states where the reasoning in a similar case is persuasive. This will happen in "cases of first impression," a fact pattern or situation that the courts in one state have never seen before. But if the supreme court in a particular state has already ruled on a certain kind of case, lower courts in that state will always follow the rule set forth by their highest court.

The power of state law has historically included governing the following kinds of issues and claims:

- Contracts, including sales, commercial paper, letters of credit, and secured transactions
- Torts
- Property, including real property, bailments of personal property (such as when you check your coat at a theater or leave your clothes with a dry cleaner), trademarks, copyrights, and the estates of decedents (dead people)
- Corporations
- Partnerships
- Domestic matters, including marriage, divorce, custody, adoption, and visitation
- Securities law
- Environmental law
- Agency law, governing the relationship between principals and their agents
- Banking
- Insurance

2.1.2 Sources of Law

In a country there are numerous sources of law such as:

- Constitutions—both state and federal

- Statutes and Agency regulations
- Judicial decisions

In international legal systems, sources of law include treaties (agreements between states or countries) and what is known as customary international law (usually consisting of judicial decisions from national court systems where parties from two or more nations are in a dispute).

As you might expect, these laws sometimes conflict: a state law may conflict with a federal law, or a federal law might be contrary to an international obligation. One nation's law may provide one substantive rule, while another nation's law may provide a different, somewhat contrary rule to apply. Not all laws, in other words, are created equal. To understand which laws have priority, it is essential to understand the relationships between the various kinds of law.

Constitutions

Constitutions are the foundation for a state or nation's other laws, providing the country's legislative, executive, and judicial framework. Among the nations of the world, the United States has the oldest constitution still in use. It is difficult to amend, which is why there have only been seventeen amendments following the first ten in 1789; two-thirds of the House and Senate must pass amendments, and three-fourths of the states must approve them.

The nation's states also have constitutions. Along with providing for legislative, executive, and judicial functions, state constitutions prescribe various rights of citizens. These rights may be different from, and in addition to, rights granted by the US Constitution. Like statutes and judicial decisions, a constitution's specific provisions can provide people with a "cause of action" on which to base a lawsuit. For example, California's constitution provides that the citizens of that state have a right of privacy. This has been used to assert claims against businesses that invade an employee's right of privacy. In the case of Virginia Rulon-Miller, her employer, International Business Machines (IBM), told her to stop dating a former colleague who went to work for a competitor. When she refused, IBM terminated her, and a jury fined the company for $300,000 in damages.

Statutes and Treaties in Congress

In Washington, federal legislature is known as Congress and has both a House of Representatives and a Senate. The House is composed of representatives elected every two years from various districts in each state. These districts are established by Congress according to population as determined every ten years by the census, a process required by the Constitution. Each state has at least one district; the most populous state (California) has fifty-two districts. In the Senate, there are two senators from each state, regardless of the state's population. Thus, Delaware has two senators and California has two senators, even though California has far more people. Effectively, less than 20 percent of the nation's population can send fifty senators to Washington.

Many consider this to be antidemocratic. The House of Representatives, on the other hand, is directly proportioned by population, though no state can have less than one representative.

Each Congressional legislative body has committees for various purposes. In these committees, proposed bills are discussed, hearings are sometimes held, and bills are either reported out (brought to the floor for a vote) or killed in committee. If a bill is reported out, it may be passed by majority vote. Because of the procedural differences between the House and the Senate, bills that have the same language when proposed in both houses are apt to be different after approval by each body. A conference committee will then be held to try to match the two versions. If the two versions differ widely enough, reconciliation of the two differing versions into one acceptable to both chambers (House and Senate) is more difficult.

If the House and Senate can agree on identical language, the reconciled bill will be sent to the president for signature or veto. The Constitution prescribes that the president will have veto power over any legislation. But the two bodies can override a presidential veto with a two-thirds vote in each chamber.

In the case of treaties, the Constitution specifies that only the Senate must ratify them. When the Senate ratifies a treaty, it becomes part of federal law, with the same weight and effect as a statute passed by the entire Congress.

State Statutes and Agencies: Other Codified Law

Statutes are passed by legislatures and provide general rules for society. States have legislatures (sometimes called assemblies), which are usually made up of both a senate and a house of representatives. Like the federal government, state legislatures will agree on the provisions of a bill, which is then sent to the governor (acting like the president for that state) for signature. Like the president, governors often have a veto power. The process of creating and amending, or changing, laws is filled with political negotiation and compromise.

On a more local level, counties and municipal corporations or townships may be authorized under a state's constitution to create or adopt ordinances. Examples of ordinances include local building codes, zoning laws, and misdemeanors or infractions such as skateboarding or jaywalking. Most of the more unusual laws that are in the news from time to time are local ordinances. For example, in Logan County, Colorado, it is illegal to kiss a sleeping woman; in Indianapolis, Indiana, and Eureka, Nebraska, it is a crime to kiss if you have a mustache. But reportedly, some states still have odd laws here and there. Kentucky law proclaims that every person in the state must take a bath at least once a year, and failure to do so is illegal.

Judicial Decisions: The Common Law

Common law consists of decisions by courts (judicial decisions) that do not involve interpretation of statutes, regulations, treaties, or the Constitution. Courts make such interpretations, but many cases are decided where there is no statutory or other codified law or regulation to be interpreted. For example, a state court deciding what kinds of witnesses are required for a valid will in the absence of a rule (from a statute) is making common law.

United States law comes primarily from the tradition of English common law. By the time England's American colonies revolted in 1776, English common-law traditions were well established in the colonial courts. English common law was a system that gave written judicial decisions the force of law throughout the country. Thus, if an English court delivered an opinion as to what constituted the common-law related to crime of burglary, other courts would stick to that decision, so that a common body of law developed throughout the country. Common law is essentially shorthand for the notion that a common body of law, based on past written decisions, is desirable and necessary.

In England and in the laws of the original thirteen states, common-law decisions defined crimes such as arson, burglary, homicide, and robbery. As time went by, US state legislatures either adopted or modified common-law definitions of most crimes by putting them in the form of codes or statutes. This legislative ability—to modify or change common law into judicial law—points to an important phenomenon: the priority of statutory law over common law.

2.1.3 Legal systems

Introduction

There are many legal systems in the world. At the global level, international law is of great importance, whether created by the practice of sovereign states or by agreement among them in the form of treaties and other accords. Some transnational entities such as the European Union have created their own legal structures. At the national level there are over 180 sovereign states in the United Nations Organization. Many of these are federal or nonfederal, and their constituent parts may well have their own law.

But, in spite of this great variety, it is important to begin by emphasizing one great division: that which is divided into religious and secular legal systems. Each side of this split holds quite different views as to law, in its source, scope, sanctions, and function. The source of religious law is the deity, legislating through the prophets.

- Secular law is made by human beings, and one of its most famous examples begins with the words 'We, the people'. It follows from this difference in their source that religious laws are perceived to be eternal and immutable, while secular rules can be changed by their makers.

- Religious law tells people what to believe as well as how to behave, whereas secular law deals with our external actions as they affect others. In a religious legal system disputes are usually adjudicated by an officer of that religion, so the same person is both judge and priest.
- In a secular system, by contrast, the office of judge is separate, and is often reinforced by guarantees of judicial independence. A further difference lies in the enforcement of the laws: in a secular system sanctions are imposed in this world, and its severest punishment amounts to forcible removal from the jurisdiction. The sanctions and rewards of a religious system may also occur in this world but are often to be felt most keenly in the next.

Nowadays there are few countries whose legal system is exclusively religious, though some aspire to this. By contrast a large number have secular systems, and this feature may be built into their legal structure, as in the 1958 French and the 1993 Russian constitutions, or the very first words of the First Amendment to the American Constitution, which came into force in 1789: 'Congress shall make no law respecting an establishment of religion'.

A number of other countries have 'dual' systems in which religious rules govern, and religious courts adjudicate on, such matters as marriage, divorce, family relationships and possibly family property, while a secular system with state courts covers the wider fields of public and commercial law. This was the position in England until the 1850s, and is the case today in Israel, India, and Pakistan, while in some African countries these more private areas are ruled by local ethnic and religious custom.

A word should be added here about the place of law in human relations, for different peoples and different epochs who have taken very different views on the matter. For some law is an aspiration, for others a blight. Some societies are proud to proclaim 'the rule of law'. Others see it as fit only for barbarians and put their trust in the ethical or customary matrix of the community. For instance, this seems to have been true of China both under the Emperors and in the years of the Cultural Revolution. What follows deals with positive legal systems, and not with the views of a given time or people as to the place of law within society. Such matters are proper to a study of comparative ideology, politics or sociology. At the same time, the reader should remember that the underlying justification for the legal system is often perceived in broader terms than mere utility.

Classification

Although each system has its own individuality, it is possible to group many of them into legal 'families'. The advantage of this is that, if successful, it saves time and energy in description or prediction. Inevitably, of course, classification depends on the criteria used. In the past, legal systems have often been grouped by geography, race, language, religion, or official ideology. Here, it seems more useful to classify it in terms of the systems' substantive features, and to devote most attention to the larger families.

The result of classification will differ greatly depending on whether we concentrate on public or private law. With the former, our criteria would be the state structure and the relations of government entities with each other and with the citizen, and the field would range from constitutional law through administrative and tax law to the penal system. The latter classification, more traditional but very useful in some respects, looks mainly at how a legal system treats the law governing relations between private persons, including matters such as their property, their testaments, marriages, contracts and so on. Thus, a country may resemble one family for private law purposes and another for those of public law.

Constitutions

Constitutions differ widely, and for good reason. Some have to provide for a federal structure, some, although unitary, include quite different legal systems within the one state. Some have to handle serious internal ethnic, linguistic, and religious differences, while others are written for a homogeneous population. Some are largely restricted to a set of justifiable rules of law, while others contain manifesto-like proclamations and show a tendency to the picturesque by, for instance, the adoption of a national animal. Some are never meant to be taken seriously.

The differences in constitutional features have two different motivations:

- ❖ A federal document will contain material absent from a unitary one.
- ❖ The existence of value preferences prompted by national history.

The constitution-makers in different countries, or at different moments in the history of any one country, have quite different preoccupations. The reason they are drafting a new constitution is a change in circumstances. Thus, all constitutions contain elements that are autobiographical and so idiosyncratic. Different historical contexts have generated different preoccupations and priorities, and these in turn have led to quite different constitutional structures.

For these reasons, only generalizations which can be reasonably be made include:

- ❖ Constitutions aspire to regulate allocation of powers, functions, and duties among various agencies and officers of government which define the relationship between these and the public.
- ❖ No constitution can protect a political system against effective usurpation.
- ❖ Holders of power ignore the constitution more or less entirely.
- ❖ Even where constitutions work, none is complete: each operates within a matrix of compromise, custom or case law.

- Many begin by identifying the constituent authority and often invoke the deity.
- Such usually separate the legislative, executive and judicial organs of state.
- Usually contain, or incorporate, a Bill of Rights.
- Provide some method for annulling laws and other instruments which conflict with the constitution, including the Bill of Rights.
- Address the international scene only in generalities and, in practice, confer wide powers on the executive.
- Deal with status of international law by either according or denying its direct internal effect.

Adoption and amendment

The idea of endowing a country with a single written constitution is relatively modern, though now widespread. Further in a large number of countries, constitutions follow some decisive event in national history which include:

- War
- Revolution
- Independence
- Federation

These ensure that methods of adoption vary widely right from the oldest and most prestigious whereas, as per agreement 13 states followed by ratification by elected conventions within them covering the Bill of Rights by State legislatures. By a seemingly similar method, but in very different circumstances of defeat of Nazi Germany, the constitution of the Federal Republic of Germany, finally approved by a Parliamentary Council and called the 'Basic Law', entered into force when notice of its ratification by representative assemblies in over two-thirds of the Laender was published on 23rd May 1949. By contrast, one of the most recent documents - that of the Russian Federation - by-passed the legislature and was voted directly by the people on 12th December 1993. According to the official returns, 54.8% of the electorate voted, of whom 58.4% were in favour. In between these two methods are many other techniques such as that of the 1958 French constitution which involved both approval by the legislature under procedure laid down by the existing constitution and then by the people in a referendum.

Both legal and political importance attach to the methods by which a constitution may be amended. They may divide the amending power among people, legislature, and executive, or between a federation and its components. They may express basic values by declaring certain features to be unamendable: the republican form of government in France and Italy, and in Germany the basic human rights and the federal structure. Some constitutions specify that matters like this may be amended only by referendum or by an entirely new constitution. In federal systems, amendments normally require special majorities in the federal legislature followed by ratification by a special majority of the states. This is the US provision, now adopted for some types of amendment by the Russian Federation.

A common method is to require a special majority in the legislature - two-thirds in Germany, three-fifths in France, with similar systems in India and other Commonwealth countries. Another parliamentary alternative is to require a second vote. Finally, some systems divide the amending power between legislature and people, by requiring a referendum either for certain types or methods of amendment or for any.

Unlike the systems just described, the constitution is indeterminate, indistinct and unentrenched with no single constitutional document. Also, many matters in written constitutions, such as the procedure on a finance bill or a vote of no confidence, are governed entirely by custom, convention and Standing Orders of the Houses of Parliament.

Federalism

In federal constitutions, listed powers are often allotted to the center, with the residue being left to the constituent parts. In practice the main powers of defense, taxation, and commerce go to the center, and federal laws override others. The constituent parts are protected, at least in theory, by representation in the upper house and by their own powers of governance in their territories. In this regard, the Russian Federation continues the USSR's system of a multi-level system of constituent parts to accommodate the polyethnic mix, though the old secession clause is gone. Broadly speaking the component entities retain the relative status accorded to them on paper when they were parts of the RSFSR which was itself within the Soviet Union: and the roots of the divisions are more a matter of geography and ethnic history than of politics.

Constitutional Features

Although constitutions vary greatly in length, usually the greatest detail is devoted to legislature and executive and the relations between them. Federal systems naturally have a bicameral legislature. But so also do many unitary systems with the lower house directly elected and the upper composed of those perhaps representing rural interests or possessing special skills. In most countries the lower house can ultimately override the upper.

Two widespread patterns are those of the presidential and those of the parliamentary system. The first fuses ceremonial and political power into one office, with its incumbent elected directly and quite separately from the legislature: it is thus quite possible for the President to be of one party and a majority of the legislature of another. It separates executive and legislative powers so that neither body can dissolve the other. The President is removable only for a grave crime, in which the legislature acts as a tribunal. The President nominates Ministers for confirmation by the legislature, but there is no collective cabinet responsibility. The President usually has a veto over legislation, which may be overridden only by special parliamentary majority. On the other hand, the crucial power to tax remains with the legislature.

The new Russian structure embodies several of these features, but expands the presidency in a number of ways. First, following a tradition going back to the Tsars, the office of the President is given wide power to rule by edict (ukaz). Apart from the need to comply with the constitution and with federal legislation, this power seems virtually unlimited. Second, the President appoints the prime minister and dismisses the government. As in the US, the Russian President may veto legislation, but can then be overridden by special majority. Finally, the President can dissolve the lower House and call new elections if it thrice rejects his or her candidate for premier, or if it passes a motion of no-confidence in the government.

In the parliamentary system, the Head of State is distinct from the head of government - called Prime Minister, Premier. The Head of State may be a hereditary monarch or directly elected President, but the Premier is not directly chosen by the electorate, but appointed from the majority or coalition group in the legislature. The Premier and other ministers have no fixed term of office but can in principle be forced to resign by parliamentary vote of no confidence in the government. This is usually balanced by executive power to dissolve the legislature and call new elections. The Premier and ministers dominate in two directions:

- ❖ First, although on paper the Head of State's powers look impressive in practice these are exercised on instructions of government.
- ❖ Second, executive controls the legislative timetable and usually has the exclusive power to introduce finance bills.

Some systems are a mixed parliamentary/presidential structure. For instance, in France the President is far from being merely a titular Head of State. Since 1962 he or she is directly elected by the people, appoints the Premier, has emergency powers, and signs the regulations emanating from the executive's very extensive lawmaking functions. In association with the government he or she can present bills to the people to enact by referendum, thereby bypassing the Parliament, and can dissolve the National Assembly and call new elections.

The Judiciary

When it comes to the judiciary, separation of powers is apparently taken quite seriously, although in England this is obscured by the fact that the upper House of the legislature has the same name as the highest court, and its Speaker is the senior judge. In many systems, judges are independent and irremovable. In Russia this is expressly stated, but is a frail novelty. In the USA and UK, it is not stated but is the case.

The only topic which merits brief discussion here is the relation between the constitution, the courts, and the legislature. The USA is virtually alone in allowing any court of general jurisdiction to decide matters of constitutionality. Normally, such questions are for a Supreme Court or special Constitutional Court. The French innovation allows bills to be referred only after they have passed through Parliament and before they are promulgated by the President. In England a court can examine the validity of a duly enacted statute unless it conflicts with the law of the European Community; the same may be true of Scottish courts, although some say they could examine UK statutes for conformity with the Act of Union 1707.

Emergency powers

The greater the constitutional commitment to a Bill of Rights, the more difficult it is to frame emergency powers. On one hand the executive must be permitted to take emergency action; on the other, the emergency power should not be capable of being used to subvert both the legislature and the Bill of Rights. The usual safeguard is to forbid the executive to use emergency powers to suspend or curtail the power of either of the other branches of government. Whether such provisions are effective in any given country is a matter of politics, not law. In the UK a permanent statute permits the government to proclaim a state of emergency, but regulations are subject to Parliamentary scrutiny. Special powers to deal with threats to security in Northern Ireland have been on the statute book for most of the twentieth century. The statutes restrict freedom of association and confer wide powers of arrest without warrant and, in Northern Ireland, limit the use of release on bail and jury trial. They are subject to annual renewal by Parliament.

Human Rights

The older pattern of constitutional protection of human rights is usually expressed by a negative: Congress shall make no law abridging the freedom of the press; the right to keep and bear arms shall not be infringed; the right to be secure shall not be violated; no person shall be deprived of life, liberty, or property without due process of law. This century has seen the addition of positive claims on the state - to education, employment and so on - and entitlements against discrimination on the grounds of gender, religion, nationality and the like. Such provisions are often declared to be entrenched and to bind legislature, executive and judiciary. To what extent these Bills of Rights are effective is more a matter of political power, than of legal technicality.

Common Law and Civil Law

Looking at the historical development and substantive features of the legal systems of the world, we can see that many of them fall into one of two families.

In the whole of human history only two peoples seem to have founded a secular, comprehensive, enduring, and widespread legal system- the Romans of the Ancient World and the Anglo-Normans of the Middle Ages. The pedigree of the civil law goes back to Ancient Rome, although the later customary family law, and the canon law of procedure have also marked the system. The Common Law world begins in England. Of course, within each family there are major differences between individual members, but each is still quite clearly not a member of the other family.

Elements of Civil and Common Law

Beginnings

The Common Law was conceived in 1066 and born of a union between older Saxon law and the custom of the Norman conquerors. The Civil Law was older then than the Common Law is now.

Nurture

The Common Law was nurtured in London law courts, by judges and barristers. The older Roman Law was developed - to an important extent - by jurists, who were not practising lawyers but public-minded citizens.

Spread

The Common Law spread only by conquest and colonization: no one ever accepted it freely. The Roman part of the Civil Law, preserved in Justinian's collection of 533AD, was rediscovered in the 11th century, embraced by the University law schools of Northern Italy, and spread from them throughout continental Europe. From there, and like the common law, it went to the New World and to parts of Africa by colonization. But, especially in the 19th century, the French and then the German versions were selected as models by countries in the Middle and Far East.

Language

Although originally written in Latin and spoken in Norman French, the language of the Common Law today is virtually only English. Wherever some version of the common law is in force, the native or official language of the country is English. The legal vocabulary, however, is likely to be markedly technical if not arcane and to contain much dead French and Latin. By contrast, the Civil Law is found in most languages.

Makers

The main creators of the Common Law are the judiciary: that is to say the matrix, the basic operating system, is laid down by caselaw. Recruited from the ranks of successful practising lawyers, the judges speak with individual and distinctive voices; they lay down the law. The great names are well known in common-law countries, and in the USA and Canada the highest court is an institution of enormous power and prestige. In civil-law systems, at least until very recently, judges played the comparatively minor role of settling the dispute in front of them.

Legislation

Modern countries of both systems produce large amounts of legislation. But that of the common-law countries tends to be piecemeal. Save for the constitution, and fiscal matters, basic principles are not enacted. The typical statute merely adjusts some detail of the rules laid down by the courts. In complete contrast, modern civil law systems tend to think of themselves as 'codified'. The word 'code' in this context means that a whole area of law is laid down in one legislative document which aims to provide a closed, coherent and consistent set of propositions which, if used in good faith, can be applied to solve any dispute in that area. The most obvious example is that of a criminal code.

Precedent

Where the basic principles are contained in an enacted code, this is the source of the law. Judicial decisions do not make law because they do not need to. So, for instance, the Austrian Civil Code 1811 - which lays down the basic rules of private law - can sensibly provide: 'Decisions in individual cases and the opinions handed down by courts in particular lawsuits never have the force of law; they cannot be extended to other cases or to other persons.' ('2) This approach is fortified by the historical fact that civil-law judges did not see their job as creating law, the professional fact that they are career civil servants, and the political fact that it is thought more democratic to entrust lawmaking to the elected representatives of the people. Common-law perceptions are quite different.

Fact

Legal disputes are as much about fact as about law. The work of the lower courts, in particular, is very largely taken up with determining issues of fact. The common law and the modern civil law both developed in territories where such matters were decided by ordeal, oath or battle. On discarding these methods, the two systems took different paths. The judges who built up the common law system were few in number, and left the hard work of fact-finding to non-lawyers; the jury, originally of neighbours who might be thought to know the background, and then of disinterested strangers empanelled to hear the evidence and decide. Similarly, there is no need for the judge to be acquainted with the case before the trial begins. The proceedings are oral, since that is the quickest and most effective way of conveying information to a number of laypersons.

Structure

One result of the above features is that in common-law countries the legal system is not organized in a coherent and clear structure. Its development tends to be incremental and casuistic, and it is not easy for the foreign lawyer to approach. Civil lawyers, on the other hand, lay great emphasis on system and structure. Furthermore, they tend to follow similar patterns in their organization of legal topics, and once these are understood it is relatively simple to locate the law on any given topic.

Incidence

Some version of the common-law is found today only in places once occupied by the British, among them Ireland, the USA, Canada, Australia, New Zealand, India, Pakistan, Kenya, Uganda, Zambia, Nigeria and Ghana. But no country which has common law seems able or willing to get rid of it.

So far, we have spoken of the Civil Law in general, comparing it to the Common Law. Within the former family, however, there are two great sub-branches. For one of them the French approach has largely been the model, for the other the German. The French have, directly or indirectly, influenced Belgium, the Netherlands, Mauritius, Quebec, Louisiana, Italy, Egypt, Algeria, Tunisia, Morocco, Sub-Saharan Africa, Spain, Latin America. The German model was followed later in such countries as Japan, Greece, Thailand, Taiwan, Portugal, Brazil.

Some systems, while recognizably those of the civil law, have rather gone their own way in the organization of their private and commercial law, for instance Austria and Switzerland. Finally, there has been much rethinking of the heart of private and commercial law in Quebec and the Netherlands and both have recently adopted an entirely new Civil Code.

Those countries of Eastern Europe which, before they became Soviet satellites, had their own civil-law systems have turned again to their earlier tradition.

Other systems

Outside the two large legal families are a number of systems, some relatively easy for a Western lawyer to understand, others much more remote.

Mixed Systems

In the first group are countries with a 'mixed' system influenced by both civil and common law. The older uncodified civil law of Holland is the basis of the Roman-Dutch law of South Africa, Zambia, Namibia, Lesotho, Swaziland, Botswana and, on the other side of the ocean, Sri Lanka; it is marked by a rich juristic literature stemming from Hugo Grotius in 17th century. But their long contacts with Britain mean that their public law and systems of court procedure owe much to the common law.

Scotland, Louisiana, Mauritius and Quebec are examples of a private law based on older civil and customary rules struggling to endure in a common-law environment.

Israel has a system of its own, where the older Ottoman and British mandate layers are now overridden by a modern system. It has no single constitutional document, but much of the modern law combines the broad legislative simplicity of the great codes of civil law with the careful transparency of the common-law judgment.

Socialist law

Until recently, the USSR and its satellites proclaimed that their socialism was producing an entirely new form of law, not to be judged by or even compared with the older systems. This view was said to be the scientific conclusion of a Marxist analysis.

The USSR's peaceful disintegration into 15 sovereign states has provoked much activity in fashioning new structures. Most of the states by now have a new democratic constitution and are drafting the rest of the legal system. Among the last acts of the old USSR was the enactment of a comprehensive framework of Basic Principles for private law. It was used in Russia as an interim instrument until the Civil Code of November 1994. In time the statute book will probably look much like those of the civil-law German-speaking countries.

From its inception in 1949, the People's Republic of China's declared aim was to attain socialism. It abrogated all earlier legislation and during the next decade much of the formal law appeared inspired by Soviet models. The pre-Cultural Revolution legal structure has been partly resurrected, and a legal framework of codes enacted. The Basic Principles of Civil Law contain many provisions that would be familiar to Western jurists. The actual functioning of the system, however, is affected by the persistent attitude that makes law subordinate to the decisions of central and local political authorities.

Islam

The number of Muslim countries is growing, but the main common feature is the Islamic religion which aims to cover all areas of life, not merely the spiritual. It thus has the features of a religious system of law, as described above. In its strongest formulation, some Islamic scholars state that law cannot exist outside religion and therefore the state has no power to legislate. But in practice the religion is found in countries with very different histories, whose formal legal systems vary from the absolute sovereignty of some Gulf states through the French and Swiss-influenced codes of Egypt and Turkey, the common-law patterns of Pakistan and India, the Soviet structures of the central Asian republics, to the revolutionary councils and tribunals of Iran.

Hindu law

Unrivalled in age and continuity, the Hindu law is contained in a literature which is vast, complex and seemingly impossible to summarize. Its laws and customs are derived from sages of the past who were themselves taught by a creator, it preaches the birth, death and rebirth of living things, and its precepts cover many more activities than does any secular legal system. In the countries mentioned, however, it governs only the personal and family relations of those involved and its family law has been codified and much amended, especially in India. Nonetheless it can affect the lives of some 450 million people.

Customary laws

In many parts of the world unwritten local or tribal custom sets the standard of behaviour and provides for conciliation and dispute settlement. Most of the countries have a formal constitutional and commercial law inspired by French, Belgian or British models but remit the relations between private individuals to the appropriate customary framework.

Criminal Law

Crimes are wrongdoings seen from the point of view of the society in which they occur: the convicted wrongdoer may be punished. Torts include the same wrongdoings seen from the point of view of their victim: the wrongdoer may be ordered to pay compensation. Sins include the same wrongdoings seen from the point of view of a faith; they call for repentance and atonement. Thus, all three systems agree in condemning the most common acts of wickedness - murder, rape, robbery, violence, theft and the like.

Nonetheless many societies attach great importance to a system of criminal justice: laws which define crimes and provide the sanctions; procedural rules for establishing guilt in a court; and a set of methods and places of punishment and rehabilitation. Furthermore, the types of actions declared to be criminal are, in all major matters, much the same everywhere.

The use of a jury is uncommon save for very serious crimes, though Russia is introducing the system. On the other hand, the first instance tribunal often comprises of one judge and two lay persons, all of whom deliberate together and decide on guilt and sentence. Another common feature is the presence of the victim as 'civil plaintiff', so that the same court can convict the accused, assess the victim's injury or damage, and order the accused to pay compensation.

Countries of the 'common-law' world began from the English criminal law but, unlike England, we now normally have a comprehensive and coherent penal code. A typical feature of these 'common-law' systems is that, for all save relatively minor offences, the decision on guilt or innocence is taken by a jury of lay-persons selected for that case: this has a profound effect on the conduct of a trial and the presentation of evidence. Another feature is that the victim who seeks compensation must start another lawsuit before another court.

Whatever their origin, most legal systems agree on certain basic premises. First, that no one can be guilty of a crime unless the offence is defined as such beforehand, and the conviction arrived at by a lawful procedure. Inherent in this is the requirement of clarity in criminal law, a prohibition against its retrospective effect, and certain notions of 'fair trial' and the availability of legal representation. Second, that no one can be prosecuted twice for the same thing. Third that deliberately criminal conduct can be punished although it did not succeed - it is a crime to attempt a crime, or to conspire with others to commit one.

Private Law

Private law is the name commonly given to that vast area dealing with the legal relations between persons. It covers matters of pure status; matters involving assets of some sort; and commercial activities in the wider sense. Its essential feature is that the participants are presumed to be juridically equals so that one cannot give orders to another, unless so authorized under some previous contractual or family arrangement. Its essential technique is that much of it is not automatically binding but serves to cut down the cost of legal transactions by providing a set of patterns which citizens may use if they wish. For instance, the intestacy rules operate only if a person dies without having made a will. The rules on sale, lease, loan, partnership and so on are there as models which can be adopted in full, or modified if the parties so desire.

In countries of the Civil Law group these three areas of status, assets, and business may be dealt with in separate codes of Family Law, Civil Law and Commercial Law. In the common-law world the basic system is laid down by caselaw, although there are many modern statutes which often re-state and systematize the work of the judges.

Despite the many differences on the surface and in particular detailed rules, the overall structure of private law in both civil and common-law systems can be stated quite simply in a formula derived ultimately from the Roman jurists: private law deals with persons, property, obligations and liability.

Persons

Private law defines who counts as a person able to enter into legal relations and deals with their legal capacity. Since the abolition of slavery, all human beings count as persons. Furthermore, these natural persons may set up other 'artificial' legal persons such as associations, foundations, and most important - business corporations.

Property

All these persons may own property and hold it for its own sake (house, clothes etc.) or as a business or investment. Only the socialist systems attempted to prevent this second function of property by forbidding private persons to own 'the means of production'. The property involved may be tangible, and is often divided for legal purposes into immovable and movable. It may also be intangible, such as debts in the hands of a creditor, stocks and shares, copyrights, patents and so on. If the owners have full legal capacity, they may normally deal with their property as they please, subject of course to rules of public policy, zoning regulations and the like. They can deal with their property during their lifetime or by will, although many systems ensure that some of the deceased's property goes to near relatives.

Obligations

Persons may incur obligations voluntarily by entering into a contract - for instance to get a job, buy a house, borrow on the security of a mortgage, take out an insurance policy. They also - whether they like it or not - incur the obligation imposed by law to compensate others for unjustified harm caused by them deliberately or carelessly. Likewise imposed by law are the duties which stem from family relationships.

Liability

The structure of private law is sealed by the following rule, now almost universal: a person must answer with his or her property for performance of all obligations. So, if the worst comes to the worst, most of a debtor's assets can be taken by a process of execution. Human beings can be made bankrupt, and corporations liquidated.

2.2 Legal and Ethical Environment of Business

2.2.1 The Law

A different viewpoint is legal realism, which is the belief that the law itself is far less important than the consideration of who is in the position to enforce the law. Like positivists, legal realists believe that law is the product of human making. However, unlike positivists, they believe that the outcome of any issue that arises under law is dependent on the person, such as a judge, who is in the position to exercise power under the mantle of the law.

Natural law is the idea that humans possess certain inalienable rights that are not the products of human-made law. Therefore, we can say that natural law differs from both positivism and realism in this important respect. Humans are able to reason, and therefore they are able to discover moral truths on their own. They are not automatons who require a sovereign power to tell them right from wrong.

2.2.2 The Court System

Supreme Court is a well-known institution today, but it wasn't always that way. When the Court first met, many of the justices couldn't travel in time for the Court's opening day, so the session was dismissed. For the first three years of its existence, the Court heard no cases of any importance. John Jay, the first chief justice, traveled to Europe while he was chief justice to negotiate the Jay Treaty with Great Britain.

The Supreme Court did not even get its own building until 1932, years after the nation's capital was established in Washington, DC. Before then, it met in the basement of the old Senate building to hear cases. When William Taft became Chief Justice, he persuaded Congress to appropriate funds, and the Court finally got its own building in Washington DC.

Judicial review means that any federal court can hold any act of the President or the Congress to be unconstitutional. It is a power that rests with each of the more than eight hundred federal judges, from the trial courts through the appellate courts. It is an extraordinary power in a democracy, as an unelected life-tenured person or group of persons overturns the acts of a popularly elected branch of government. Rather than give rise to judicial tyranny, however, our system of checks and balances ensures that the other two branches also play a critical role in "checking" the judiciary.

In truth, the majority of a judge's work has nothing to do with politics. Even at the Supreme Court level, most of the cases heard involve conflicts among circuit courts of appeals or statutory interpretation. In a small minority of cases, however, federal judges are called on to interpret a case involving religion, race, or civil rights. In these cases, judges are guided sometimes by nothing more than their own interpretation of case law and their own conscience. This has led some activists to claim that judges are using their positions to advance their own political agendas.

Judicial conservatives, also known as originalists or strict constructionists, believe that the Constitution should be interpreted strictly, in light of its original meaning when it was written. They believe that societal change, especially the creation of new civil rights, should come from the political process rather than the judicial process. Judicial liberals, also known as judicial activists, believe that judges have a role to play in shaping a more perfect union. They believe that the outcome of a case is paramount over other considerations, including past precedent. Judicial activists are more likely to find new civil rights in the Constitution, which they believe should be broadly interpreted in light of modern society's needs. The right to privacy is a good example of the difference between judicial conservatives and judicial liberals, and it is seen as a test to determine what philosophy a judge subscribes to. After a long period of stability, membership in the Supreme Court has changed substantially in the last three years with three new members. The Court remains closely divided between judicial conservatives and judicial liberals, with conservatives poised to control the Court's direction.

Trial and Appellate Courts

In many cities, you can find both a state and a federal courthouse. These courts hear different types of cases, involving different laws, different law enforcement agencies, and different judicial systems. The rules governing the procedures used in these courts are known as civil procedure or criminal procedure and are sometimes so hard to understand they confound experienced attorneys and judges. Nonetheless, as future business professionals, it's important to understand the general boundaries between state and federal courts.

Most people forget that there are actually fifty-one separate legal systems in the United States: one federal and fifty in the states. Within each legal system is a complex interplay among executive, legislative, and judicial branches of government. The foundation of each of these systems of government is a constitution. Some state constitutions are actually older than the federal Constitution, while others are relatively new.

In some states, state constitutions remain vibrant and provide civil protections beyond the federal Constitution. Several state supreme courts, for example, have interpreted their various state constitutions as prohibiting treating gays and lesbians differently when it comes to marriage under their "equal protection" provisions. Other state supreme courts have interpreted their state constitutions to grant citizens the right to choose the time and manner of their own death. Since these decisions are by state supreme courts interpreting their own state constitutions, they are beyond the reach or review of the federal Congress or federal courts. This dynamic power sharing between state and federal governments is known as federalism and is a key feature of our republican form of government.

To determine which court a case belongs to, lawyers first look at what the case is about. The rules of subject matter jurisdiction dictate whether a case is heard in the federal or state court. Lawsuits involving state laws are generally heard in state courts. Most criminal laws, for example, are state laws. There may be wide differences among the states about what behavior constitutes criminal behavior. Speed limits, for example, are different from state to state. Even serious crimes such as murder or manslaughter, and possible defenses to those crimes, are defined differently by the states. Domestic issues such as divorce and family law are also handled at the state level.

Laws related to the transfer of property, vehicle or watercraft ownership registration, and the disposition of property after death are different depending on which state you live in. The laws surrounding contracts are also passed at the state level. Finally, the law of torts is state based. Torts are any civil wrong other than a breach of contract and can cover a vast array of situations in which people and businesses suffer legal injury. Some states are far friendlier toward torts than others, and the resulting patchwork of tort laws means that companies that do business across the country need to bear in mind the different standards they are held to, based on what state their customers live in.

Given the wide array of subject areas regulated by state law, it's not surprising that for most individuals and businesses, their experience with courts is with state courts. Nonetheless, cases do sometimes end up in federal court as well. Federal court subject matter jurisdiction is generally limited to cases involving a federal question—either the federal Constitution or a federal law. Cases involving the interpretation of treaties to which the United States is a party are also subject to federal court jurisdiction. In fact, any case involving the United States as a party is properly litigated in federal court. Finally, in original jurisdiction cases, lawsuits between states can be filed directly with the Supreme Court.

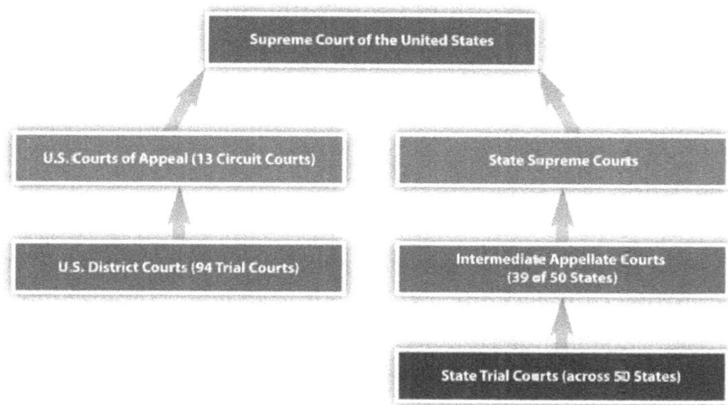

Fig State and Federal Court Systems

Sometimes it's possible for a federal court to hear a case involving a state law. These cases are called diversity jurisdiction cases, and they arise when all plaintiffs in a civil case are from different states than all defendants and the amount claimed by the plaintiffs exceeds seventy-five thousand dollars. Diversity jurisdiction cases allow one party who feel it may not receive a fair trial where its opponent has a "home court" advantage to seek a more neutral forum to hear its case, a process called removal. The figure above shows the "State and Federal Court Systems" where U.S. Supreme Court is the highest court in the country, and all courts are bound to follow precedent established by the U.S. Supreme Court through the doctrine of stare decisions.

From the above figure, in all fifty states, a trial court of general jurisdiction accepts most types of civil and criminal cases. Such courts are called by different names like superior court, circuit court or district court. Contrarily, trial courts are called supreme courts. There may be other courts of limited jurisdiction at the state level, such as traffic court, juvenile court, family court, or small claims court. Increasingly, states are also experimenting with specialized drug courts to treat drug abuse as a health problem rather than a criminal problem. State judges may be either appointed by the governor or elected by the public. Similar to federal counterparts, state trial courts hold trials, and most preserve a trial record for review by an appellate court. In thirty-nine states, a party that loses at trial can file an appeal with an intermediate court of appeals. The remaining states are smaller and therefore don't maintain this level of appeal, in which case appeals are filed directly with the state supreme court. In states with an intermediate court of appeals, the party losing the appeal can typically file one more time with the state supreme court, although state supreme court rules vary on whether appeals are a matter of right or discretion. Finally, in cases involving the federal constitutional right, a party that loses at state supreme court level can appeal to the Supreme Court for review. These cases are typically criminal and involve the application of the Constitution to criminal procedure, evidence collection, or punishment.

Litigation

Litigation is an inevitable part of a business's activities. Lawsuits, trials, and appeals can be ruinously expensive for some companies, especially small- and medium-sized enterprises. Learning about our litigation system would equip you with the skills and comfort you need, should your company find itself in litigation. As future business professionals, your responsibility to your company, your company's stakeholders, and to yourself is to avoid ever seeing the inside of a courtroom. Acting ethically and legally, and identifying the legal pitfalls that you may encounter by mastering the elements of this course, will help you achieve this goal. Agreeing to arbitration for parties that you have a preexisting relationship with, such as your customers, suppliers, or employees, will also help you stay away from a courtroom. In spite of such planning, however, many companies still find that litigation is sometimes unavoidable. Whether litigation is initiated against parties you don't have a contract with or by parties you don't have a contract with, litigation may be the only dispute-resolution mechanism available.

The federal rules of civil procedure make it easy for parties in a lawsuit to identify and join other relevant parties and to make legal claims against each other. The goal of civil litigation is to find the truth. Litigants typically rely on lawyers to assist them in litigation. An attorney's highest duty is to the administration of justice. Lawyers are ethically bound to represent their clients with zealous advocacy. A grand jury acts as a body of citizens to prevent abuse of discretion by prosecutors. A petit jury sits in trials as the trier of fact to ascertain the truth through their observations of the presented evidence.

Standing and Personal Jurisdiction

Standing is a constitutional requirement that requires a plaintiff prove that he or she is the right person to bring a lawsuit and that he or she is bringing the lawsuit at the right time. Taxpayers lack standing to sue the government just by being taxpayers. Legal injury does not have to be monetary based; environmental harm, for example, may be sufficient to demonstrate standing. Standing has nothing to do with the merits of the underlying case. Courts must have personal jurisdiction over a defendant before litigation can proceed.

Personal jurisdiction, a constitutional requirement, requires minimum contacts with the state such that substantial notions of fair play and justice are not offended. Once personal jurisdiction is established, service of process can occur, where a copy of the summons is delivered to the defendant. If the defendant lives out of state, a long-arm statute prescribes the method for service to occur. A web site creates personal jurisdiction in any state where it reaches out for customers through a shopping cart function.

Pretrial Procedures

After issues related to subject matter jurisdiction, standing, and personal jurisdiction are sorted and parties have hired counsel to represent them, then a dispute can proceed to the pretrial stage. In civil cases, litigation begins with the filing of a complaint by the plaintiff. The complaint is a simple document setting forth who the parties are, the facts of the case, and what specific laws the defendant has violated. The complaint ends with a prayer for relief. The plaintiff may be seeking damages, specific performance in certain kinds of contract cases, or a temporary or permanent injunction. It is much easier to get a temporary injunction in the early stages of litigation, because courts don't want to see the defendant take some action that may result in irreparable harm.

Litigation commences with the filing of a complaint by the plaintiff. If the plaintiff wishes to represent many others with the same claim against the same defendants, the plaintiff may try to certify the lawsuit as a class-action suit. Frivolous cases are prohibited in litigation, but it is relatively easy to argue that a case is not frivolous. The defendant files an answer to the complaint or risks a default judgment. Most civil and criminal cases must be brought within the prescribed statute of limitations. During the discovery phase of litigation, parties share and exchange information about each other's cases so that neither side is surprised during the trial. There are four methods for conducting discovery: interrogatories, requests for production, requests for admissions, and depositions.

The complaint is filed with the clerk of the court where the suit is to be heard. Every court has a clerk's office to handle administrative matters relating to litigation. Even though the court system is a public service, there is usually a fee associated with filing a complaint to cover some of the court's costs.

At any point in litigation, either party may file motions with the court. The motions are designed to short-circuit the litigation and lead to an early end to the lawsuit. Litigation is so time consuming and expensive that either party would be gratified if the judge would simply cut the lawsuit short and declare a winner. One such motion is the motion to dismiss for failure to state a cause of action. In this motion, the defendant argues that even if it admits everything in the complaint is factually true, that doesn't lead to any legal liability. In other words, the defendant's conduct has not broken any laws. A similar motion is the motion for judgment on the pleadings. In this motion, one party asks the judge to decide the case based simply on the answer and complaint.

In support of any motion, a party may submit an affidavit. Affidavits play an important role in pretrial procedure because they are an effective way for parties to tell their side of the story to the judge. They are limited, however, because even though they are given under oath, they may raise more questions and are not subject to examination by the other side.

After pleadings are filed, the litigation moves into the discovery phase. Discovery is a process in which each side finds out information about the other's case. Let's assume, for example, that you buy a new car and within a few weeks, a tire falls off suddenly while you're driving. You would rightly conclude that there's something wrong with the car, so you sue the manufacturer. At this point, you have no idea what's wrong with the vehicle. Was the design flawed? Was there something wrong with the manufacturing of your specific vehicle? All you know is that new cars should not experience this sort of failure. After you file a lawsuit against the manufacturer, discovery allows you to find out more information about the vehicle so that you can effectively proceed with the lawsuit. You could find out what engineers did when they designed the vehicle and review records of similar accidents or factory records from the day your vehicle was produced.

There are four types of discovery:

- Interrogatory: These are written questions addressed to the other party. The questions tend to be simple and straightforward, dealing with uncontroversial matters such as a company's structure or the names and addresses of relevant witnesses.
- Production request: In such form of deposition, a party can request the other party to produce written communications like internal company reports, e-mails, product manuals, and engineering specifications. In many cases, physical evidence is produced.
- Admission request: It is noted that a complaint has series of claims the plaintiff is making against the defendant with answers as series of denials of claims. As each party finds more information about the other's case in discovery, one party may ask the other to admit that one of the contested claims is true. Doing so narrows the issues for trial because it is one less thing which the jury needs to decide. Asking a party to give up a contested claim can be done at any time during litigation. If not done as a formal method of discovery, it may be done as a stipulation instead.

- Deposition: Deposition is a sworn oral statement which is in response to questions given by potential witness in trial to attorneys in the case. A deposition hearing is attended by the witness being deposed and lawyers from both sides with court a reporter who keeps a written transcript of the entire deposition.

The Trial and Appeal

On final discovery and assuming that neither side is successful in short-circuiting litigation through motions, the case is finally scheduled for a trial. In civil litigation, it is an unusual development, as over 90% of cases filed are resolved or settled before a trial. If a case actually goes to trial, it means there are genuine issues of fact that the parties cannot resolve, and both sides are determined to see their side win. It is noted that a trial is a fact-finding process by which the trier of fact attempts to show what had happened. The trier of fact applies the facts to applicable law as instructed by the judge and determines guilt or innocence in a criminal case, or liability or no liability in a civil case. The first step in this process is to seat a jury.

At any given day in a courthouse, several citizens may be called by a judge as potential jurors in a case. If a jury needs twelve members, it's not unusual for a judge to begin with a pool of more than fifty or sixty potential jurors to narrow down to a dozen. The process of selecting a petit jury is called voir dire which started with jurors filling out a written questionnaire that ask the jurors to find their occupation, work or occupational conflicts and potential conflicts of interest with the case. The process continues with attorneys quizzing each potential juror in turn. During this questioning, attorneys ask each juror if he/she has any biases against upholding the law and whether he/she can keep an open mind during the trial.

Once the jury has been selected and sworn in, the trial begins where plaintiff or prosecution begins with delivery of an opening statement that is preview of a trial where attorneys explain the facts of the case to the jury and highlight about the witnesses to be called. Here the attorneys will not make any arguments at the time of the opening statement, but simply lay out what jurors can expect from the trial ahead. Once the plaintiff has delivered an opening statement, the defendant will deliver the defense opening statement. In a criminal case, the defense has the right to reserve delivering the opening statement until after the prosecution has rested its case.

The process of selecting a jury is called voir dire in which every side is allowed to question a potential juror and excuse that juror for any reason through a peremptory challenge or good reason for causing challenge. A trial begins with opening statements where the parties lay out the essential facts of their case. After this, the witnesses are called to give testimonial evidence. The side calling the witness conducts a direct examination, while the opposing side conducts a cross-examination. After all witnesses are called, the parties make closing arguments to the jury, which then deliberates and applies the law as outlined in the jury instructions. The burden of proof in a criminal case is "beyond a reasonable doubt," while the burden of proof in a civil case is "preponderance of evidence." A jury's verdict must be converted into a legal judgment by the trial judge. Once all appeals are settled, res judicata prevents the case from being tried again.

Alternative Dispute Resolution

A common method of dispute resolution that avoids many of the challenges associated with litigation is alternative dispute resolution. Alternative Dispute Resolution (ADR) is a term that encompasses many different methods of dispute resolution other than litigation. ADR involves resolving disputes outside of the judicial process, though the judiciary can require parties to participate in specific types of ADR, such as arbitration, for some types of conflicts. Moreover, some ADR methods vest power to resolve the dispute in a neutral party, while other strategies vest that power in the parties themselves. See Figure 4.1 "A Continuum of Different ADR Methods" for a continuum of different ADR methods based on where power to solve the dispute is vested.

Common methods of ADR include negotiation, mediation, and arbitration. Lesser used methods of ADR include minitrials, hybrid forms of mediation-arbitration (with elements of both), and collaborative goal-oriented processes. ADR is often used to resolve disputes among businesses, employers and employees, and businesses and consumers. ADR can also be used in many other types of conflicts. For instance, ADR strategies can be used in domestic law cases, such as divorce, or in international legal issues, such as issues relating to transboundary pollution. This chapter limits its focus to the use of ADR methods in business. Particularly, we will examine the common methods of ADR, including the benefits and drawbacks to each. We will also examine potential consequences to parties that have unequal bargaining power. Additionally, we will examine the use of ADR methods in situations where ADR may not be the most appropriate method of dispute resolution, such as civil rights violations.

ADR methods are used outside of the courtroom, but that does not mean that they are outside of the interests of our legal system. Participation in ADR has important legal consequences. For instance, parties that have agreed by contract to be subject to binding arbitration give up their constitutional right to bring their complaint to court. The Federal Arbitration Act (FAA) is a federal statute under which parties are required to participate in arbitration when they have agreed by contract to do so, even in state court matters.

Negotiation

One of the first strategies that you and your supplier are likely to employ is negotiation. Negotiation is a method of Alternative Dispute Resolution (ADR) that retains power to resolve the dispute to the parties involved. No outside party is vested with authoritative decision-making power concerning the resolution of the dispute. Negotiation requires the parties to define the conflicts and agree to an outcome to resolve those conflicts. Often, this can take the form of a compromise. Note that a compromise does not mean that anyone "loses." Indeed, if both parties are satisfied with the result of the negotiation and the business relationship can continue moving forward, then both parties will be very likely to consider this as a "winning" situation.

Benefits of negotiation as a method of ADR include its potential for a speedy resolution, the inexpensive nature of participation, and the fact that parties participate voluntarily. Drawbacks include the fact that there are no set rules, and either party may bargain badly or even unethically, if they choose to do so. In a negotiation, there is no neutral party charged with ensuring that rules are followed, that the negotiation strategy is fair, or that the overall outcome is sound. Moreover, any party can walk away whenever it wishes. There is no guarantee of resolution through this method. The result may not be "win-win" or "win-lose," but no resolution at all. Also, generally speaking, attorneys are not involved in many negotiations. This last point may be seen as a drawback or a benefit, depending on the circumstances of the negotiation.

Negotiation is a skill often developed by people who are charged with settling existing disputes or with creating new agreements. Since we are focusing on dispute resolution in this chapter, we will limit our discussion to the resolution of disputes rather than the negotiation of new contract terms, but keep in mind that these activities essentially draw on the same skills.

Negotiation is a method of Alternative Dispute Resolution (ADR) in which the parties retain the power to decide on a resolution of the issue themselves, without relying on a neutral decision maker. Negotiation is also used between parties entering into agreements, when there is no legal dispute. Negotiation is often the first method of dispute resolution attempted, because it is inexpensive and relatively fast. Additionally, parties that wish to continue working together in the future often employ negotiation as a friendly method to resolve disputes. Negotiation between parties with unequal bargaining power can result in the stronger party being heavy-handed at the negotiation table, which can result in unfair outcomes for the weaker party. Since negotiation does not follow an externally imposed set of rules, parties may negotiate as their conscience dictates. However, negotiation is often considered a dispute-resolution option that can result in a win-win situation for all parties.

Mediation

Mediation is a method of ADR in which parties work to form a mutually acceptable agreement. Like negotiation, parties in mediation do not vest authority to decide the dispute in a neutral third party. Instead, this authority remains with the parties themselves, who are free to terminate mediation if they believe it is not working. Often, when parties terminate mediation, they pursue another form of ADR, such as arbitration, or they choose to litigate their claims in court. Mediation is appropriate only for parties who are willing to participate in the process. Like negotiation, mediation seeks a "win-win" outcome for the parties involved. Additionally, mediation is confidential, which can be an attractive attribute for people who wish to avoid the public nature of litigation. The mediation process is usually much faster than litigation, and the associated costs can be substantially less expensive than litigation.

Unlike in many negotiations, a third party is involved in mediation. Indeed, a neutral mediator is crucial to the mediation process. Mediators act as a go-between for the parties, seeking to facilitate the agreement. Requirements to be a mediator vary by state. See Note 4.23 "Hyperlink: Mediators" to compare the requirements between states. There are no uniform licensing requirements, but some states require specific training or qualifications for a person to be certified as a mediator. Mediators do not provide advice on the subject matter of the dispute. In fact, the mediators may not possess any subject-matter expertise concerning the nature of the dispute. However, many mediators are trained in conflict resolution, and this allows them to employ methods to discover common goals or objectives, set aside issues that are not relevant, and facilitate an agreement into which the parties will voluntarily enter. Mediators try to find common ground by identifying common goals or objectives and by asking parties to set aside the sometimes emotionally laden obstacles that are not relevant to the sought-after agreement itself.

In business, mediation is often the method of ADR used in disputes between employers and employees about topics such as workplace conditions, wrongful discharge, or advancement grievances. Mediation is used in disputes between businesses, such as in contract disputes. Mediation is also used for disputes arising between businesses and consumers, such as in medical malpractice cases or health care disputes.

Like other forms of dispute resolution, mediation has benefits and drawbacks. Benefits are many. They include the relative expediency of reaching a resolution, the reduced costs as compared to litigation, the ability for parties that are unable to communicate with each other to resolve their dispute using a non-adversarial process, the imposition of rules on the process by the mediator to keep parties "within bounds" of the process, confidentiality, and the voluntary nature of participation. Of course, the potential for a "win-win" outcome is a benefit. Attorneys may or may not be involved, and this can be viewed as either a benefit or a drawback, depending on the circumstances.

Arbitration

Arbitration is a method of ADR in which parties vest authority in a third-party neutral decision maker who will hear their case and issue a decision, which is called an arbitration award.

An arbitrator presides over arbitration proceedings. Arbitrators are neutral decision makers who are often experts in the law and subject matter at issue in the dispute. Their decisions do not form binding precedent. Arbitrators may be members of the judiciary, but in arbitrations they are not judges. Arbitrators act in an analogous capacity to judges in trials. For instance, they determine which evidence can be introduced, hear the parties' cases, and issue decisions. They may be certified by the state in which they arbitrate, and they may arbitrate only certain types of claims. For instance, the Better Business Bureau trains its own arbitrators to hear common complaints between businesses and consumers (B2C).

Arbitration awards can be binding or nonbinding. Some states, like Washington State, have codified the rule that arbitration decisions are binding when parties voluntary submit to the arbitration procedure. In binding arbitration, the arbitration award is final; therefore, appealing an arbitration award to the judicial system is not available. In many states, an arbitration award is converted to a judgment by the court, thereby creating the legal mechanism through which the judgment holder can pursue collection activities. This process, called confirmation, is contemplated by the FAA and often included in arbitration agreements.

Arbitration can be more expensive than negotiation or mediation, but it is often less expensive than litigation. The costly discovery phase of a trial is nonexistent or sharply reduced in arbitration. However, arbitration is not necessarily inexpensive. Parties must bear the costs of the arbitrator, and they typically retain counsel to represent them. Additionally, in mandatory arbitration clause cases, the arbitration may be required to take place in a distant city from one of the disputants. This means that the party will have to pay travel costs and associated expenses during the arbitration proceeding. The Circuit City Court also noted that mandatory arbitration clauses avoid difficult choice-of-law problems that litigants often face, particularly in employment law cases.

Arbitration is faster than litigation, but it is not as private as negotiation or mediation. Unlike mediators, arbitrators are often subject-matter experts in the legal area of dispute. However, as is true for mediators, much depends on the arbitrator's skill and judgment.

A common issue that arises is whether mandatory arbitration is fair in certain circumstances. It's easy to imagine that arbitration is fair when both parties are equally situated. For example, business to business (B2B) arbitrations are often perceived as fair, especially if businesses are roughly the same size or have roughly equal bargaining power. This is because they will be able to devote approximately the same amount of resources to a dispute resolution, and they both understand the subject under dispute, whatever the commercial issue may be. Moreover, in B2B disputes, the subjects of disputes are commercial issues, which may not implicate deeper social and ethical questions. For example, contract disputes between businesses might involve whether goods are conforming goods or nonconforming goods under the Uniform Commercial Code (UCC). No powerful social or ethical questions arise in such disputes. Indeed, resolving such disputes might be seen as "business as usual" to many commercial enterprises.

Arbitration is a form of ADR in which parties vest authority to decide a dispute with a third-party arbitrator, who hears the evidence and issues an arbitration award. Arbitration may be binding or nonbinding, and it may be mandatory or voluntary. Arbitration awards issued by arbitrators can be confirmed to judgments by judges. Issues of fairness arise in arbitration when disputants possess unequal power, such as arbitration in employment or consumer disputes. Questions concerning the appropriateness of mandatory arbitration arise in cases involving issues of civil rights violations. The Federal Arbitration Act requires enforcement of mandatory arbitration clauses in contract disputes involving commerce where mandatory arbitration clauses exist. The Arbitration Fairness Act of 2009 would resolve several issues of unfairness, but this act has not yet been passed by law.

Methods of ADR other than negotiation, mediation, and arbitration are available to disputants. For example, minitrials, med-arb, private judging, and summary jury trials are common alternatives, as are in-house programs like ombudsmen, anonymous ethics hotlines, and open-door policies. Benefits and drawbacks to these methods exist relative to other methods of ADR and to litigation.

Contract

Contracts are an integral part of business. Without contracts, promises would not be enforceable, which would wreak havoc on our financial stability, both individually and professionally. The law presumes that people who sign contracts have read the contract and understood its terms. Of course, contract language includes many terms of art, and simply reading a contract alone may not be enough to fully understand its implications.

Contracts for important matters should be reviewed and explained by attorneys, so that parties who enter into contracts do not do so without understanding the agreement. It's important to understand the implications of making promises. If those promises carry legal duties, then, barring a defense, the promise will need to be performed so that the obligation or duties arising under that promise can be discharged. If the promise is not performed, and if there are no defenses, then the contract has been breached. Breach is an actionable claim, with the goal of recovering the loss and placing the non-breaching party back to the position that he or she would have been in if the contract had not been breached.

Recognizing fundamental elements of contracts and how to incorporate considerations important to you when entering into them can go far toward ensuring business success. Likewise, the failure to recognize the traps and tricks that can be incorporated into contracts can derail a good business idea.

Torts

Tort is a civil wrong other than breach of contract which arises out of conduct or non-conduct that violates societal norms determined by judicial system. Similar to contracts and crimes, torts do not need legislative action, but can protect certain expectations related to right to travel freely and right to enjoy our property. There are three primary areas of tort law which are classified as per level of intent. Also, tort is any legally recognizable injury that appears from conduct of persons or corporations. Further, the other area of civil law which corporations have to be concerned about is contract law. There are several key differences between torts and contracts.

More than any other area of law, tort law is a reflection of societal values. It is seen that contracts are enforced as they protect the expectation that our promises are enforced. Criminal law is the result of elected legislatures prohibiting behavior that the community finds offensive or immoral. Tort law is generally not the result of legislative debate or committee reports, but every tort case arises out of different factual situations where a jury of peers decides whether or not the tort feasor has violated certain societal norms or not. Additionally, we expect that when an employee is working for the employer's benefit and commits a tort, the employer should be liable. Under the respondent superior policy, employers are really liable, unless they can demonstrate that the employee was on a play and diversion at the time he/she committed the tort.

The norms that society protects make up the basis for tort law. For example, we have an expectation that we have the right to move freely without interference unless detained pursuant to law. If someone interferes with that right, he or she commits the tort of false imprisonment. We have an expectation that if someone spills a jug of milk in a grocery store, the store owners will promptly warn other customers of a slippery floor and clean up the spill. Failure to do so might constitute the tort of negligence. Likewise, we expect that the products we purchase for everyday use won't suddenly and without explanation injure us, and if that happens then a tort has taken place.

It has been said many times that tort law is a unique feature of American law. In Asian countries that follow a Buddhist tradition, for example, many people have a belief that change is a constant part of life and to resist that change is to cause human suffering. In United States, the tradition is one of questioning and inquiry when accidents happen.

Emergency

It is observed that the other way to look at duty is to consider whether or not the plaintiff is a foreseeable plaintiff. In such case, when the risk of harm is foreseeable, then the duty exists. As seen, the emerging area in tort law is whether or not businesses have a duty to warn or protect customers for random crimes committed by other customers. As seen, crimes are random and therefore not foreseeable, but in certain cases, it is determined that when a business knows about, or should know about, a high likelihood of crime occurring, in such case, businesses must warn or take steps to protect its customers.

Businesses owe a duty to exercise a reasonable degree of care to protect the public from foreseeable risks that the owner knew or should have known about. There are many foreseeable ways for customers to be injured in retail stores, from falling objects improperly placed on high shelves, to light fixtures exploding or falling due to improper installation, to customers being injured by forklifts in so-called warehouse stores.

Once duty has been established, negligence plaintiffs have to show that the defendant breached that duty by showing how the defendant failed to act reasonably, when compared with a reasonable person. It's important to keep in mind that this reasonable person is hypothetical and does not actually exist. In reality, once a duty has been established, the presence of injury or harm is usually enough to satisfy the "breach of duty" requirement.

Also, the other element of negligence is causation. In deciding whether there is causation, courts have to consider the courts query as to whether there is causation in fact which is known as but-for causation which can be proved in the defendant's actions, whether the plaintiff has been injured or not. Further, the element of negligence is legally recognizable injuries, in which, if someone has been injured, then damages may be awarded to compensate for those injuries. Such damages take the form of money, as there is nothing tort law can do to bring back the dead or re-grow lost limbs, and also, the tort law will not allow for incarceration. Money is therefore the only appropriate measure of damages, and it is left to the jury to decide how much money a plaintiff should be awarded.

Award damages in Tort Law

There are two types of award damages in tort law:

Compensatory damages

It seeks to compensate the plaintiff for his/her injuries. Compensatory damages can be awarded for medical injuries, economic injuries, pain and suffering. They can also be awarded for past, present, and future losses. While medical and economic damages can be calculated using available standards, pain and suffering is a far more nebulous concept. Juries are often left to their conscience to decide what amount of money can compensate for pain and suffering, based on the severity and duration of the pain as well as its impacts on the plaintiff's life.

Punitive damages

In this, the jury is awarded a sum of money not to compensate the plaintiff but to discourage the defendant from ever engaging in similar conduct. The idea behind such damages is that, the compensatory damages may be inadequate to discourage future bad conduct, so extra damages are required to make sure that the defendant corrects his/her ways to prevent future injuries. Punitive damages are available in cases where the defendant acts with willful and wanton negligence, which is the higher level of negligence as compared to ordinary negligence.

Business Organizations

Business exists so as to make profit for its owners. In economy, a business that fails to make a profit will finally ceases to exist or be overtaken by creditors and competitors. The need to make a profit is truism which binds all businesses together and further, it's hard to draw generalizations about its operations. The business world is varied as human experience that ranges from neighborhood kids, neighborhood restaurant, to small tool-and-die factory, to multinational corporation with thousands of employees scattered across the globe. Many businesses make things in factories, other businesses sell things that other businesses make, and still other businesses exist to help makers and sellers make and sell better. Certain businesses don't make things at all, and instead profit by selling their services or by lending money at a higher rate of interest than it can borrow.

Many economists and public policy officials think that economy is a key anchor to society and values. Private enterprise and profit motive allow innovation and entrepreneurship to flourish, leading to prosperity and peace. Underlying the strength of business enterprises is a flexible and easy-to-manage legal system which allows business owners many options in selecting to organize their operations. Business organizations are an important part of business's structure as they provide different advantages and disadvantages in:

- cost creation
- simplicity
- ongoing maintenance requirements
- dissolution and continuity
- fundraising
- managerial control
- public ownership
- tax planning

- limited liability

This type of business being conducted has less to do with business organization where business is conducted. Many business organizations take the form of separate legal entities, which the law recognizes as nearly like persons for purposes of legal rights.

Sole Proprietorships

Sole proprietorships are common way of doing business. Legally, there is no difference or distinction between the owner and the business. The legal name of the business is the owner's name, but owners may carry on business operations under a fictitious name by filing a d.b.a. filing. Sole proprietors enjoy ease of start-up, autonomy, and flexibility in managing their business operations. On the downside, they have to pay ordinary income tax on their business profits, cannot bring in partners, may have a hard time raising working capital, and have unlimited liability for business debts.

Partnerships

A partnership is formed when two or more persons agree to share profits and losses in a joint business venture. A general partnership is not a separate legal entity, and partners are jointly and severally liable for the partnership's debts, including acts of malpractice by other partners. Income from a general partnership flows through to the partners, who pay tax at the ordinary personal income tax rate. In many countries, general partners can also bring in limited partners, creating a limited partnership. Limited partnerships must be formed in compliance with state statutes. Limited partners enjoy limited liability but generally cannot participate in day-to-day management of the business.

Corporations

A corporation is a separate legal entity in which the owners are known as shareholders who can be from few closely held corporations to millions in publicly held corporations. Shareholders of corporations have limited liability, but most are subject to double taxation of corporate profits. Certain small businesses can avoid double taxation by electing to be treated as S corporations under the tax laws. State law charters corporations. Shareholders elect a board of directors, who in turn appoint corporate officers to manage the company.

Limited Liability Entities

The limited liability company represents a new trend toward business organization. It allows owners or members to have limited liability just like corporations. Similar to corporations, LLCs can avoid double taxation by choosing to be taxed like a partnership or sole proprietorship. Unless a business wishes to become publicly traded, LLC is probably the most flexible, affordable and compatible form for doing business. The limited liability partnership is similar to the LLC, except it is designed for professionals such as accountants or lawyers who do business as partners.

2.3 Business Law and the Legal Environment

2.3.1 Business Law

Business law is sometimes called mercantile law or commercial law and refers to the laws that govern the dealings between people and commercial matters. There are two distinct areas of business law; regulation of commercial entities through laws of partnership, company, bankruptcy, and agency and the second is regulation of the commercial transactions through the laws of contract. The history of these types of laws dates back to several centuries and can be seen in the peace-guilds where members would pledge to stand by each other for protection.

Business law normally appears outside of a courtroom. There may be a few hearings here or there before boards or regulatory committees to seek approvals. However, there are very few long, hard days on the spot in an adversarial courtroom. When conflicts occur, a company may not use their business lawyer to handle it. Instead, they might refer the matter to a litigator with years of experience in a courtroom setting.

As business law focuses on transactions, it's a great choice for lawyers who don't care for high-pressure courtroom situations. With business law, a lawyer can have a full and complete practice without ever setting foot in the courtroom for an adversarial proceeding. Lawyers who pay attention to detail thrive in business law. Helping a company draft a policy, complete a filing, make a contract or come to terms on a business transaction often comes down to minute details. Lawyers who can focus on such details flourish in a business law setting.

Business law involves dealing with and preventing different problems which can hurt the business or can cause legal disputes such as:

Business formation

Business law starts with setting up of a business. In the eyes of the law, each business has its own legal entity. Starting a new business normally begins with filing the paperwork that establishes that the business formally exists, as mandated by the government.

Many types of business entities are similar throughout the country, but the exact entities that a new business can select from varies by state. The process of filing paperwork to establish the business also varies from state to state.

Business lawyers help decision makers weigh the pros and cons of each entity when they're starting a business. They help in educating business founders in law so as to help them in selecting the entity which are in their best interests. In such scenario, they help them in filing the paperwork in order to formally start the business.

Employment considerations

Once a business is set and run, it needs employees. Businesses need legal advice to help them understand how to hire and fire employees. They need to know how to handle employee disputes and discipline. Businesses need to know what they need to offer employees in terms of pay and benefits. There are also mandatory payroll taxes and deductions. Business lawyers educate their clients on the rules and best practices for managing employees.

Immigration law

Business law and immigration law often intersect. Businesses may want employees from other countries. They may want international employees on a full-time basis, they may need temporary workers, or they may need to bring in a worker just for a short period of time for a special event. Knowing how to navigate federal immigration laws is an important aspect of business law as It would help companies in acquiring manpower they require to succeed.

Sales of consumer goods

Buying and selling isn't as easy as it sounds. There are regulations that govern how companies can make products and how they can sell them. From working conditions in a factory to distribution requirements to price controls, there are all kinds of laws and rules that might regulate how a company makes and sells its products.

One of the main influential documents for business operations is Uniform Commercial Code. It's a model code that outlines recommendations for commercial transactions. It covers topics such as:

- statute of frauds
- contracts
- leases
- sales
- credit
- bulk sales
- secure transactions

Business lawyers help their clients identify the laws that a business needs to follow, and they help ensure the company's compliance with the laws.

Contract drafting and negotiations

Businesses are involved with with preparing and negotiating contracts which can be anything from lease agreement to purchase agreement or an agreement involving third-party selling vendor. A lot of contract law comes from common law which isn't written down anywhere. Rather than, it's principles of law and rules which were developed by courts over time where lawyers have to not only understand the elements of contract law from both statutes and common law, but also appreciate the nuances that might impact enforcement of contract. They must work with their clients in order to skillfully negotiate and draft contracts that are in the client's best interests.

Anti-trust

Most businesses want to control a large share of the market since they want to grow and expand. Companies who want to increase their profits and market share needs to ensure that they do so in legally sanctioned ways. Companies that employ deceptive or unfair practices in order to cut out competitors or avoid competition might find themselves the subject of allegations of anti-trust violations. Business attorneys help their clients identify conduct that might amount to anti-trust before the behavior has the chance to create problems for their business.

Intellectual Property

When a business invents a new product, they need to make sure they protect their ability to profit from their invention. Making sure a business gets to exclusively keep and use their own products falls under intellectual property and copyright law. Intellectual property is technical and complicated. Lawyers need to have a scientific background in order to formally practice it before the U.S. Patent and Trademark Office. Intellectual property work is critical to helping companies profit from their novel work.

Similarly, copyright laws help companies profit from their creative work. Business lawyers help companies register copyrights and enforce them. This process is critical to making sure that a business retains control of its work in order to commercialize it for a profit.

Taxes

Businesses pay taxes. There are estimated taxes, employee taxes and deductions which one needs to be aware of. In addition to helping a business comply with tax requirements, a business lawyer helps their client take legal steps to minimize their tax burden. They may help the business apply for special tax forgiveness or waivers that might be available in a certain location or for certain industries.

Bankruptcy

Lawyers help businesses in both good times and bad. When businesses go through financial difficulties, they need lawyers to help them determine their options. Filing bankruptcy might be the only option or the best option for a struggling business.

Making the decision to file for bankruptcy is just the beginning. There are many different types of bankruptcy filings available to businesses. They have different requirements, and there might be a reason that a business should choose one type of filing over another. Business lawyers can give their clients advice on the pros and cons of different actions. Once the business makes a plan, lawyers can help the company complete the filing accurately and stay in compliance with the associated requirements.

2.3.2 Legal Business Environment

The Legal Environment of Business involves the role of law and legal system in managerial decisions. Business managers operate their businesses and make their decisions within the constraints of legal system and government regulations. Such managers, businesses, and stakeholders strive to operate to legally protect their rights. They face potential legal liability and legal consequences from their decisions and actions. They should understand the legal environment of business which covers the legal system and its processes along with the sources of law in the society. It involves studying and comparing the business-related legal rules of tort law, criminal law, contract law, and government regulatory mechanisms. Business operators or managers must realize the ethical implications of their decisions on society and its corresponding perspective the law brings in formulating the ethical decisions in the society.

2.4 Federalism

2.4.1 Definition

Federalism is a system of government where a written constitution divides the power among the central government and regional or sub-divisional governments. Both types of government act directly upon the people through their officials and laws.

Federalism can be seen as a compromise which exists among extreme concentration of power and loose confederation of independent states for governing different people normally in large expanse of territory. It has the virtue of retaining local pride, traditions and power, while allowing a central government that can handle common problems.

Although the Constitution sets up the federal system, nowhere does it define what federalism is. However, the framers of the Constitution were determined to create a strong national government and address shortcomings of Articles of Confederation, which allowed the states too much power. In terms of the balance of power between the federal government and the states, the Constitution clearly favors the federal government.

2.4.2 Forms of federalism

Dual federalism:

- ❖ Federal role limited to enumerated powers as per Constitution while all other powers are vested with the state
- ❖ It is also called as layer cake model where each level of government is supreme in its domain of responsibility
- ❖ Separation of powers among national and state governments
- ❖ Federal and state governments are competitive in their relationships
- ❖ It is the state centered

Cooperative federalism

- ❖ Federal powers deal with the aftermath of the Great Depression
- ❖ It is called as marble cake model where the Federal role is to allot resources
- ❖ Sharing of powers among national and state governments
- ❖ Federal and state governments are cooperative in relationships
- ❖ It is nation-centered

Creative federalism

- ❖ Federal role deals with sub-national local governments by provision of categorical grants, bypassing states
- ❖ It is known as picket fence model. Here federal government deals with local governments in specific policy categories like housing, transportation, health, poverty reduction, etc.
- ❖ It is creative due to its provision of grants-in-aid directly to local governments that are categorical as these are specified by federal government, states and local governments so as to use money for specific purposes
- ❖ It forms a direct link between federal and local governments
- ❖ It results in weaker states

Competitive federalism

- ❖ Federal decision on policies curtailed by converting categorical grants to block grants where states and local governments have more discretionary power to use funds

- It is called as pineapple upside down cake model where federal government deals directly with local governments with state and local governments having more degree of discretion
- It is competitive due to competition among state/ local governments for jobs and workers
- Governments are competitive in their relationships
- It results in competitive governments

2.4.3 Powers of Federalism

The federal government determines foreign policy, with exclusive power to make treaties, declare war, and control imports and exports. The federal government has the sole authority to print money. Most governmental responsibilities, however, are shared by state and federal governments and these include taxation, business regulation, environmental protection, and civil rights.

Regardless of the types of federalism, the Constitution provides certain specific powers to both states and federal government which include:

- Delegated Powers – These are the powers that are specifically assigned to the Federal Government. The national government has very specific enumerated powers including the regulation of interstate and international trade, coinage and currency, war, maintenance of armed forces, postal system, enforcement of copyrights and power to enter into treaties.
- Reserved Powers – These are the powers that are not specifically delegated to Federal Government, but are reserved or saved for State Governments. Such powers include power to establish schools, local governments and police.
- Concurrent Powers – These powers are for both, federal and state governments, for example the power to tax, maintain courts and the ability to construct and maintain roads.
- Implied Powers – These are powers which are not particularly delegated in the Constitution but are understood or allowed. The necessary and proper clause of the Constitution states that Congress has power to make all laws that shall be necessary and proper for carrying into execution foregoing powers.

Problems of Federalism

- Federal-state relations: Supremacy of national laws vs autonomy of states
- State-state relations: Coordination between states
- State-local government relations: State preferences vs local autonomy
- Local government to local government relations: Coordination between local governments

2.5 Systems of Law

2.5.1 Introduction

The laws are expected to cover almost every aspect of the legal system. These laws are a list of codified set of rules that are constantly updated and specify all matters that can be brought to the court. The codes are used as acreference guide to state what is unlawful and to punish law breakers. There is little room for alternation and assumption. These codes do not require the judges to look to previous cases for passing judgment on the current case. The judge would refer to the book of laws to be informed about the proper process regarding the criminal activity and the corresponding punishment for it

2.5.2 Types of Legal Systems

There are two basic types of legal systems used in the Western World, which are Common Law System and Civil Law System. Common Law System was developed in England and used by its territories and colonies while Civil Law System originated with Romans and evolved with French and Spanish influences.

Common law

It was developed in Northern Europe during the middle ages by Germanic and Nordic people. It was brought to England by conquerors. In modern times England has spread common law around the world, especially to the many places that were settled or colonized by the English.

In a common law system, the judges play a bigger part in creating laws as well as altering and modifying laws based on old preceding cases. In a common law justice system, the laws of a country depend on the rulings or decisions of courts or other tribunals, where it is believed justice prevailed. Common Laws are laws that have come about and been enacted based on court rulings. These laws are developed based on rulings that have been given in older court cases. Common laws are also known as case law or precedent. These rules can be written as well as unwritten.

The general principal of this system is that similar cases with similar facts and issues should not be treated differently. If there is a dispute between laws, the authority or precedent looks to past cases and must provide the same reasoning and decision that was provided in the first case. The laws can also be altered and evolved based on the circumstances. The judges also have the authority to create new laws or alter and interpret older laws. Once the law has been altered or changed during the ongoing case, the law will then be enforceable on all other cases henceforth with similar evidence and situations. Many countries adhere to common law systems or mixed systems. In a common law court, a jury is set up to hear the case and then determine if the defendant is guilty or not guilty. On the basis of this decision, the judge then determines the best punishment for the guilty based on older proceedings.

Civil law

It began with the Romans. The Byzantine Emperor Justinian, a Roman himself, assembled a team of experts who condensed and simplified the Roman law into one single body of law. The Byzantine system spread through southern Europe and then northward. Today nearly all of Europe uses civil law.

Comparison

A comparison of two types of law systems:

	Common Law Systems	**Civil Law Systems**
Origins	Common law systems have evolved primarily in England and its former colonies, including all but one US jurisdiction and all but one Canadian jurisdiction. For the most part, the English-speaking world operates under common law. The tradition began with the Norman Conquest in the 11th century.	Civil law systems, conversely, are in place throughout the vast majority of the non-English speaking world, and are also found in Louisiana and Quebec. Civil systems owe their existence to the Napoleonic Code, which revolutionized the law by establishing methodical administration of justice based on extensive, written rules.
Type of argument and role of lawyers	Adversarial. Lawyers ask questions of witnesses, demand production of evidence, and present cases based on the evidence they have gathered.	Inquisitorial. Judges, not lawyers, ask questions and demand evidence. Lawyers present arguments based on the evidence the court finds.
Sources	Law comes from three sources: (1) statutes, enacted by legislatures, (2) precedents, drawn from court opinions in prior cases, and (3) administrative rules promulgated under authority of statute. Statutory language is often open to broad interpretation, and is not as extensive in reach as in civil law systems. Legal interpretation relies on the doctrine of stare decisis, to influence the law's application in cases before a court. As such, judges are viewed as the "sages" of the law.	Law comes, primarily, from a statutory code, and judges apply code language strictly. Court opinions do not carry the precedential effect that common law opinions do. Rather, the specific wording of statutory text is applied to individual cases. Because precedent is merely informative, rather than binding, scholars & academicians are considered the experts on legal interpretation.

Role of judges	Judges decide matters of law and, where a jury is absent, they also find facts. Most judges rarely inquire extensively into matters before them, instead relying on arguments presented by the parties in a case. As common law systems are adversarial, the judge is understood to be a neutral party, taking a position on a factual matter only when no jury is present and then, only at the conclusion of a case. For guidance in deciding a matter of law, judges rely primarily on precedent, and to a far lesser extent, academic treatises. Generally, only highly experienced lawyers become judges, and they are respected as high-level officials.	Judges in civil law systems act as inquisitor, interpreter of code language, and finder of fact, in many instances sitting on juries themselves. They rely less on precedent than on commentary by legal scholars. Civil system judges often join the bench soon after becoming licensed as attorneys in many ways, they are mere hearing officers, and are viewed as bureaucrats, rather than important officials.
Role of juries	Juries comprises of laypersons and in practice, only rarely lawyers and are rarely employed to decide non-criminal matters outside the United States. Their function is to weigh evidence presented to them, and to find fact. In criminal matters, they are often asked to determine the severity of an offense in determining a sentence.	Juries are present almost exclusively in criminal cases, and are virtually never involved in civil actions. They widely include judges, to ensure that their decisions are guided more by law than passion.
Service of process	Service of process is viewed very liberally and can often be effected by any adult non-party to a case. Although sheriffs and their deputies can be used, laypersons are often involved — particularly professional private process servers.	Service of process is generally a sovereign function, so its execution is reserved to judicial officers, such as bailiffs known as "hussiers de justice"or "deurwaarders". Private process servers are virtually unknown.
Evidence taking	Widely understood to be a necessary part of the litigants' effective pursuit or defense of a claim. Litigants are given wide latitude in US jurisdictions, but more limited outside the US. In any event, the litigants and their lawyers undertake to ask questions and demand evidence.	Evidence demands are within the sovereign inquisitorial function of the court not within the lawyers' role. As such, "discovery" by foreign attorneys is dimly viewed, and can even lead to criminal sanctions where the court's role is usurped.

Further readings

"Commerce Clause: Past, Present, and Future." 2003. Arkansas Law.

"Congressional Power in the Shadow of the Rehnquist Court: Strategies for the Future." 2003. Indiana Law Journal.

"Conservative Judicial Activism." 2002. University of Colorado Law.

"Federalism and Rights." 2002. Human Rights.

"Perspectives: Federal Jurisprudence, State Autonomy." 2003. Albany Law.

Boyer, Paul S. 2001. Oxford Companion to United States History. New York: Oxford Univ. Press.

Burke, Edmund. 1989. Reflections on the Revolution in France. Garden City, N.Y.: Doubleday.

Cardozo, Benjamin N. 1921. The Nation of the Judicial Process. New Haven, Conn.: Yale Univ. Press.

Corpus Juris Secundum. 2002. St. Paul, Minn.: West.

Dorsen, Norman. 1994."How American Judges Interpret the Bill of Rights." Constitutional Commentary.

"Federalism—Clear Congressional Mandate Required to Preempt State Law: Gregory v. Ashcroft." 1991.

McManamon, Mary Brigid. 1993. "Felix Frankfurter: The Architect of 'Our Federalism.'" Georgia Law Review 27 (spring).

Oxford Companion to American Law. 2002. New York: Oxford Univ. Press.

Savage, David G. 1995. "The Supreme Court Goes Back to Work."

Tanielian, Matthew J. 1995. "Separation of Powers and the Supreme Court: One Doctrine, Two Visions."

Vause, W. Gary. 1995."The Subsidiarity Principle in European Union Law—American Federalism Compared."

Wiessner, Siegfried. 1993. "Federalism: An Architecture for Freedom."

3

Sources of Law

3.1 Where Does Law Come From?

3.1.1 Introduction

Laws are obtained from federal and state parliaments, court decisions and adoption of Charter of Human Rights and Responsibilities Act. These laws regulate all aspect of daily life. There are many sources from which law occurs such as:

- Parliament in which politicians make laws.
- Judges make law by their decisions in court cases.
- Local councils and public servants make and administer laws.
- Range of people like Police, Centrelink officers, Council by-laws officers and Transport police, administer and enforce laws.

3.1.2 Making the Law

Parliament-made law

Much of the laws are made by the parliament. The process to make laws is similar in both the federal and state parliaments. Laws made by parliaments are statutes, acts or legislation. A draft act is known as Bill that are debated by parliamentarians and on passing with majority results in an act.

Along with acts of parliament, there are laws that cover administrative details or other matters that are not easily dealt with in the acts. Parliament delegate the power to make regulations, rules, ordinances or local laws to public authority, local council, minister controlling a government department or public servant. Such types of laws are delegated legislation.

It is noted that the precise meaning of words and phrases in acts and legislation is sometimes difficult to understand, so in such scenarios, Courts gets involved in deciding the meaning of particular parts or words of an act. The court's interpretation of sections and words in an act will then become part of t law.

Normally, judges cannot overrule or challenge an act till the act is unconstitutional. This means it was beyond the power of the Commonwealth or State Parliament to make that law in the first place. In such case, the court will declare the act or parts of it invalid and without an effect. The High Court further resolves the dispute where Commonwealth and state laws clash.

If the government is not in agreement with the court's decision and a judge's interpretation of an act, in such case, the parliament will pass an act particularly to overturn such decision or interpretation. Parliament will also add rules to judge-made law. With such reason, parliament made law by stating all the rules for that area. From time to time, parliament will repeal or amend an act and is not restricted by earlier acts, and can change laws as desired.

Set of rules developed by judges will help in interpreting acts as the rule of interpretation, which states that an act is governed by their ordinary meaning until it leads to absurdity. When an act says that a minister can do this or that, in such case, it is noted that the minister has a discretion to do something. If an act says that a minister shall do something, it means that the minister must do something. Such rules will help people to use an act, as they give some certainty to the meaning of commonly used words, especially in cases where the meaning of an act is unclear and court decision is not helpful in clarifying the meaning. When this occurs, the law is difficult to state one way or the other.

Process of Law made by Parliament

Policy development

The first stage in the legislative process is developing an idea for new or changed laws. Ideas can be generated from a number of sources, including election commitments, lobby groups, public opinion, the media and public service.

Drafting of Bill

This stage involves converting the policy idea into draft legislation that will eventually be placed before the Parliament as a Bill. For the Government, the technical details of each clause is drafted by the Office of the Chief Parliamentary Counsel. Private Members must draft their own Bills, unless approval is given by the Premier for OCPC to draft the Bill on their behalf. Once the Member or Minister is happy with the draft Bill, it can be introduced into the Parliament.

Parliamentary process

A Bill can be introduced in either House but must be passed by both Houses before it can become a law. In each House, the Bill passes through a number of stages known as readings.

- First Reading: The introduction is a formal stage at which the Member introducing the Bill reads the long title of the bill. At this stage, the Bill is still confidential and is not available in hard copy or on the Parliament's website.

- Second Reading: The Clerk announces the Bill by reading its short title and the Member moves that it be read a second time. The Member then makes the second reading speech outlining the Bill's intentions. Following the second reading speech, debate on the bill is adjourned to give Members time to study the Bill. When the Bill is on for debate, members can make speeches in support or against the Bill. At the conclusion of the second reading debate, members vote on the Bill. If the Bill is supported by a majority of members, it proceeds to the next stage.
- Third Reading: There may be some debate at the third reading stage but normally most of the debate will have already taken place. Once a Bill passes its third reading, it has passed through all stages in the House.

Royal Assent

Once a Bill has been passed by both Houses of Parliament in the same form, it is presented to the Governor of Victoria for Royal Assent.

Commencement

Some Bills come into operation immediately after they have received Royal Assent. Other Bills do not become operational until the commencement date, which is a future date specified in the Bill. Other Bills come into operation 'on a day to be proclaimed', which is a future date decided by the Governor, acting on advice of the responsible Minister.

Judge-made law

Judges decided each case as it came to court by writing the reasons for their decisions which are called as judgments. The important judgments were published in books known as law reports. Judges were bound by a strong tradition to decide each similar case along with lines of earlier decisions. If facts of earlier cases were not exactly similar, in such case, judge would still compare the situations and apply common principles or develop new, reasonable principles for new facts. It is known as doctrine of precedent. The principles and rules contained in the collection of judgments and court procedures became known as the common law.

The following are certain rules that direct the conduct of court cases and court-made law:

- A judge's decision in each case is binding on those who are involved in such case. On agreeing to court sorting the dispute, it is hard to seek changes in the rules of court once the case has been fought. Every party in a court case accepts the authority of judge and must do whatever the judge orders to be done after the case is over.
- If an appeal is not made in the time limits, the matter is finalized and the case cannot be re-opened. Occasionally, fresh evidence in a criminal case

can be used as a reason to re-examine a court's verdict.

- ❖ If one of the parties appeals to a higher court, the higher court can either agree with the lower court's decision or make a new decision. The higher court's decision will bind the parties, till an appeal is lodged in the time limits to an even higher court.
- ❖ The decision of the highest court in the court structure is final and no further appeals are possible.

Doctrine of precedent shows that judges in lower courts should follow decisions of high courts and single judge of court should follow a decision with more than one judge in that court.

The decisions of courts will not bind on city court, although these decisions can assist the courts to make decisions on new facts or legislation.

A court, when it makes a decision, will give reasons for its decision. Another case with similar but not identical facts can be decided differently. If this happens, reasons will usually be given as to why this case should be treated differently. Each case is decided on its own facts.

The high court in the state consists of a bench of judges in which chief justice is the most senior judge. The High Court need not follow its own earlier decisions or precedents and can make new laws by deciding to change the law. For the first time, the High Court directed the legal system to recognize indigenous legal systems which existed before the settlement.

Parliament-made law over rules the judge-made law in case of similar problems. Also, judge made law applies in many areas and practice of following previous court decisions continues till date. Not only do judges continue to develop the law in areas not covered by legislation, they also have an important role in interpreting legislation when there is a dispute about the meaning or application of a section of an act. The decisions that judges make in interpreting acts become part of common law, which other courts will refer to and follow.

Steps in making a law:

- ❖ A Bill can be introduced in either house of Congress by a Senator or Representative who sponsors it.
- ❖ Once a Bill is introduced, Representatives or Senators will meet in small groups to discuss, research or make changes to it.
- ❖ The Bill is then put before the house to be voted on.
- ❖ If the Bill passes one body of Congress, it is then presented to the other body to go through a similar process to be proposed, discussed and voted on.
- ❖ Once both bodies vote to accept a Bill, it is presented to the President.

- The President then considers the Bill. The President can approve the Bill and sign it into law or not approve (veto) a Bill.
- If the President chooses to veto a Bill, in most cases Congress can vote to override that veto and the Bill becomes a law. However, if the President pocket vetoes a bill after Congress has adjourned, the veto cannot be overridden.

3.2 Kinds of Law

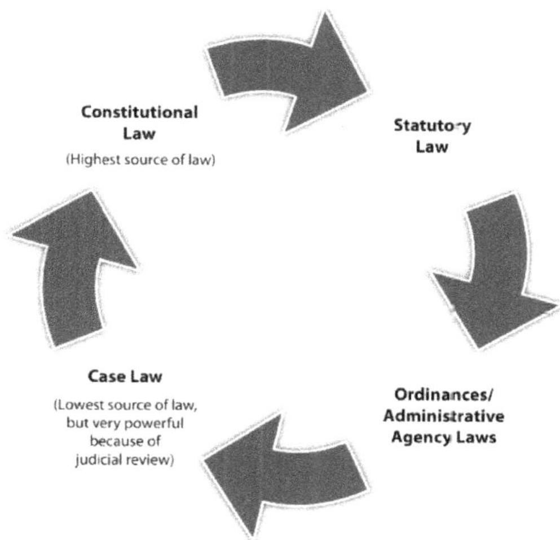

The following are the major classifications of law:

- Public and Private Law
- Civil Law and Criminal Law
- Substantive and Procedural Law
- Municipal and International Law
- Written and Unwritten Law
- Common Law and Equity

3.2.1 Public and Private Law

Public Law

It is defined as that aspect of Law which deals with relationship among the state, its citizens and other states. It is one that governs the relationship between a higher party, state and lower one. Examples of public law include:

- Constitutional Law

- Administrative Law
- Criminal Law
- International Law etc.

Private law

It is that category of the law that concerns itself with the relationship amongst private citizens. Examples include:

- Law of Torts
- Law of Contract
- Law of Trust etc.

3.2.2 Civil Law and Criminal Law

Civil law

It is defined as that aspect of Law which deals with the relationship between citizens and provides means for remedies if the right of a citizen is breached. Examples of civil law include:

- Law of Contract
- Law of Torts
- Family Law etc.

Criminal Law

It is referred to as that aspect of Law which regulates crime in the society. It punishes acts which are considered harmful to the society at large. An example of criminal law is the Criminal Code Act.

In criminal cases, standard of proof are used as proof beyond reasonable doubt. Also, the burden of proof does not shift from the prosecution. On the other hand, in civil cases, the standard of proof is on the balance of probabilities Evidence Act. In this the burden of proof shifts between both parties when they need to establish their case. Judgement normally goes in favour of the particular party that has been able to prove its case more successfully.

3.2.3 Substantive and Procedural Law

Substantive Law

It is the main body of the law which deals with a particular area of law. For example, the substantive law in relation to Criminal Law includes Criminal Code Act and Penal Code Act.

Procedural law

It is the law which deals with the process where the court follows an order to enforce the substantive law. Examples include the rules of the various courts and the Administration of Criminal Justice Act, which is procedural law in relation to Criminal Code Act and Penal Code Act.

3.2.4. Municipal/Domestic and International Law

Municipal/Domestic law

It is the aspect of law which emanates from and has effect on members of a specific state. An example of a municipal law is constitution of Federal Republic.

International law

It is the law which exists between countries. It regulates the relationship between different independent countries and is usually in the form of treaties, international customs etc. Examples of International law include Universal Declaration of Human Rights and Charter on Human and People's Rights. As per provision of the constitution, international treaties cannot have the force of law except when they are enacted by the National Assembly.

3.2. 5. Written and Unwritten Law

Written Law

A law would not be regarded as written just because it is written down in a document, and is a kind of law that is validly enacted by the legislature of a country.

Unwritten law

This type of law is not enacted by the legislature. It includes both customary and case law. Customary Law is generally unwritten while Case law though written down in documentary format would be regarded as unwritten law as per the fact that it is not enacted by the legislature.

3.2.6. Common Law and Equity

It is the English common law which is regarded as common to all parts of England. It grew over time from practices, customs and way of life of people. It is mostly unwritten. Common law was strict, formal and full of legalism such as system of writs.

3.3 Fundamental Laws

3.3.1 Constitution Law

Constitutional law is considered as the highest and should not be supplanted by either of the other two sources of law. Constitutional Law is the supreme law of the country. It stands written in the Constitution of the State. The Constitutional Law lays down the organization, powers, functions and inter-relationship of the three organs of government. It also lays down the relationship between the people and the government as well as the rights, freedoms (fundamental rights) and duties of the citizens. It can be called the Law of the laws in the sense all law-making in the State is done on the basis of powers granted by the Constitutional Law i.e. the Constitution.

3.3.2 Statutory Law

It is also called the national law or the municipal law. It is made by the government (legislature) and it determines and regulates the conduct and behaviour of the people. It lays down the relations among the people and their associations, organizations, groups and institutions. The legislature makes laws, the executive implements these and judiciary interprets and applies these to specific cases.

It is the other source of law which is inferior to constitutional law, which means that a statute cannot conflict with or attempt to supersede constitutional rights. If a conflict exists between constitutional and statutory law, the courts must resolve the conflict.

While the Constitution applies to government action, statutes apply to and regulate individual or private action. A statute is a written law that can be enacted in one of two ways. Most statutes are written and voted into law by the legislative branch of the government. This is simply a group of individuals elected for this purpose.

3.3.3 Administrative Laws and Ordinances

Administrative laws are enacted by administrative agencies, which are governmental agencies designed to regulate specific areas. Administrative agencies can be federal or state and contain not only a legislative branch but also an executive (enforcement) branch and judicial (court) branch.

Ordinances are similar to statutes, except that cities and counties vote them into law, rather than a state's legislature or a state's citizens. Ordinances usually relate to health, safety, or welfare, and violations of them are typically classified as infractions or misdemeanors, rather than felonies. A written law prohibiting jaywalking within a city's or county's limits is an example of an ordinance.

3.4 Case Law

Case Law, often used interchangeably with Common Law, refers to precedents and authority that are set by earlier court rulings, judicial decisions and administrative legal findings. It is one of the main categories of law, with constitutional law, statutory law and regulatory law.

Although statutory laws, created by legislative bodies in concurrence with constitutional law, strive to provide overall direction, guidance and rules for society at large, it is impossible to deal with all situations, legal issues and questions by this manner alone. As judicial bodies are tasked with interpreting law, in doing so, often set precedent where statutory, regulatory and even constitutional law is vague, unclear or silent. All of these precedents make up case law.

Case law is generally very jurisdiction specific. If no such previous rulings exist, one may offer precedent from a different jurisdiction, but rather than binding, this would merely be persuasive authority. There are certain features of case law:

- ❖ Case law is an important source of law in all areas, even those that are heavily legislated.
- ❖ Case law is a primary source of law and being able to identify, read and understand case law is integral to successful legal research.
- ❖ Case law is a central component to understanding, interpreting the law of a common law jurisdiction. It is the law developed over time by judges in superior courts.
- ❖ Each case or judgment delivered by these superior courts is the solution to the dispute between parties to the case.
- ❖ Once the judgment is delivered it becomes a precedent based on which future disputes would be settled or resolved.

There are also other factors in play which affect the binding authority of a specific case in common law, such as how old the decision is and how closely the material facts match in both cases. The components of a case brief are the following:

- ❖ The title, plus citation. The citation indicates where to find the case.
- ❖ The procedural facts of the case. The procedural facts discuss who is appealing and in which court the case is located.
- ❖ The substantive facts. The substantive facts discuss what happened to instigate the case.
- ❖ The issue. The issue is the question the court is examining.
- ❖ The substantive holding. The substantive holding answers the issue question and is the case law.
- ❖ The procedural holding. The procedural holding discusses what the court did procedurally with the case.
- ❖ The rationale. The rationale is the reason the court held the way it did.

3.4.1 Finding Case Law

Every reported case has a title which is usually the name of the parties involved in the action. The title is then supplemented by a citation, which helps to find the case and shows where you can find the law report. A really good place to start is entering the citation eg [1987] AC 417 or the names of the parties to check availability.

Citations

Citations normally consist of a year plus abbreviations, which lead to a page within a volume of a series of law reports. The four parts to most citations are:

- Date or year
- Volume number
- Abbreviation – for the title of the law report series
- Page number

Some cases will have multiple citations which means they have been reported in a number of different law report series. The name of the series is usually abbreviated.

Searching by subject

If you are searching for cases on a topic, you should start by using an up to date commentary where significant cases will be cited. You can then update the search by using one of the online datasets and search using case name to look for more recent cases related to that topic.

Older reports

You can find many reports published before 1865 in the English Reports, a collection of various series of reports. The easiest way to access the English Reports is to use the library.

Unreported cases

Some cases are never formally reported. Transcripts may be available and a fee is often payable to the transcriber for this service.

3.4.2 Interpreting Case Law

Definition

Interpretation is the method by which the true sense or the meaning of the word is understood. The meaning of an ordinary word of the English language is not a question of law. The proper construction of a statute is a question of law. The purpose of the interpretation of the statute is to unlock the locks put by the legislature. For such unlocking, keys are to be found out. These keys may be termed as aids for interpretation and principles of interpretation.

The conventional way of interpreting a statute is to seek the intention of its makers and apply that to the facts of the case at hand. An interpretation of the statutory provision which defeats the intent and purpose for which the statute was enacted should be avoided.

Types

Interpretation is of two kinds:

- grammatical
- logical
- Grammatical interpretation is arrived at by reference to the laws of speech to the words used in the statute; in other words, it regards only the verbal expression of the legislature.
- Logical interpretation gives effect to the intention of the legislature by taking into account other circumstances permissible according to the rules settled in this behalf. Proper construction is not satisfied by taking the words as if they were self-contained phrases. So considered, the words do not yield the meaning of a statute.

Rules

The Literal Rule

Under the literal rule, it is the work of the court to give a statute's words their literal meaning regardless of whether the result is sensible or not. The literal rule is often applied by orthodox judges who believe that their constitutional role is limited to applying laws as enacted by Parliament. Such judges are wary of being seen to create law, a role which they see as being strictly limited to the elected legislative branch of government. In determining the intention of the legislature in passing a particular statute, this approach restricts a judge to the so called black letter of the law. The literal rule has been the dominant approach taken for over 100 years.

The Golden Rule

The golden rule is an exception to the literal rule and will be used where the literal rule produces the result where the Parliament's intention would be circumvented rather than applied. As suggested, literal rule should be used first, but if it results in absurdity, the grammatical and ordinary sense of the words may be modified, so as to avoid absurdity and inconsistency, but no further.

The Mischief Rule

The final rule of statutory interpretation is mischief rule, under which a judge attempts to determine the legislator's intention about the mischief and defect that statute in question has set out to remedy and about effectively implementing the remedy through ruling. The mischief rule considered four things:

- What was the common law before the making of the Act?
- What was the mischief and defect for which the common law did not provide?

- What remedy the Parliament has resolved and appointed to cure the disease of the Commonwealth?
- The true reason of the remedy; and then the office of all the judge is always to make such construction or shall suppress subtle inventions and evasions for continuance of the mischief and pro private commodo, and to add force and life to the cure and remedy, according to the true intent of the makers of the Act, pro bono publico.

Such system of relying on external sources like common law in determining the true intention of the parliament is seen as part of a purposive approach, which is generally taken in civil law jurisdictions. Also, the literal approach has been dominant in common law systems for over a century. Here judges appear to be less bound by black letter of law and are more willing to try to determine the true intention of Parliament. The task of the judge is seen as giving effect to the legislative purpose of statute in question.

Apart from the above three rules of interpretation, there are a number of rules that are held to apply while determining the meaning of a statute:

- The statute is presumed not to bind the Crown.
- Statutes do not operate retrospectively in respect to substantive law (as opposed to procedural law).
- They do not interfere with legal rights already vested.
- They do not oust the jurisdiction of the courts.
- They do not detract from constitutional law or international law.

Hence there exists a number of intrinsic (=internal) and extrinsic (=external) aids to statutory interpretation such as:

Intrinsic (Internal) Aids to Statutory Interpretation

These are things found within the statute which help judges understand the meaning of the statute more clearly.

- The long and the short title
- The preamble
- Definition sections
- Schedules
- Headings

Extrinsic (External) Aids to Statutory Interpretation

These are things found outside of the actual statute which may be considered by judges to help them understand the meaning of a statute more clearly. These include:

- ❖ Dictionaries
- ❖ Historical setting
- ❖ Previous statutes
- ❖ Earlier case law
- ❖ Hansard
- ❖ Law Commission Reports
- ❖ International Conventions

References

Lon Fuller, The Morality of Law (New Haven: Yale University Press, 1964), p. 30.

David Hume, An Inquiry Concerning the Principles of Morals, ed. Charles Hendel (Indianapolis, Ind.: Bobbs-Merrill, 1957 [1751]).

Franz Oppenheimer, The State: Its History and Development Viewed Sociologically, trans. John Gitterman (Indianapolis, Ind.: Bobbs-Merrill, 1914 [1908]).

Robert Ellickson, "Property in Land," Yale Law Journal, vol. 102 (1993): 1315-1400.

Viktor Vanberg and James Buchanan, "Rational Choice and Moral Order," in From Political Economy to Economy to Economics and Back?, ed. James Nichols, Jr., and Colin Wright (San Francisco: Institute for Contemporary Studies, 1990).

See for example, Bruce Benson, "The Development of Criminal Law and Its Enforcement: Public Interest or Political Transfers," Journal des Economistes et des Etudes Humaines 3 (1992): 79-108.

Ibid.

Ellickson, "Property in Land," p. 1366.

Benson, "The Development of Criminal Law and its Enforcement"; "The Spontaneous Evolution of Commercial Law," Southern Economic Journal 55 (1989): 644-61; and "Law Merchant," in The New Palgrave Dictionary of Economics and the Law, ed. Peter Newman (London: Macmillan, 1998, forthcoming).

F. A. Hayek, Law, Legislation, and Liberty, vol. 1 (Chicago: University of Chicago Press, 1973), p. 51.

Benson, "The Development of Criminal Law and its Enforcement."

Ellickson, Order Without Law (Cambridge, Mass.: Harvard University Press, 1991), pp. 213-14; Hernando de Soto, The Other Path: The Invisible Revolution in the Third World (New York: Harper & Row, 1989).

Benson, "The Spontaneous Evolution of Commercial Law" and "Law Merchant."

Benson, "Customary Law as a Social Contract: International Commercial Law," Constitutional Political Economy 2 (1992): 1-27; and "Law Merchant."

See for instance, Lisa Bernstein, "Opting Out of the Legal System: Extralegal Contractual Relations in the Diamond Industry," Journal of Legal Studies 21 (1992): 115-58; Ellickson, Order Without Law; and Benson, "An Exploration of the Impact of

Modern Arbitration Statutes on the Development of Arbitration in the United States," Journal of Law, Economics & Organization 11 (1995): 479-501.

4

The Judicial System

4.1 Introduction

The judicial system is made up of courts, some of which have more power than others. Courts resolve conflicts between people, or between people and the state. Court judges base their rulings on written law (legislation) and common law – law that developed from previous judges' decisions.

Each judicial system has a number of courts of original jurisdiction, in which cases are originally filed and tried. The jurisdiction of these trial courts can be both geographically and subject matter based. Each system also has a smaller number of intermediate appellate courts. These courts hear appeals from the trial courts. An appeal is a claim by the losing party that the lower court has made a mistake of law. Usually, a losing party is entitled to one appeal as a matter of right. Each court system also has a Supreme Court, which hears appeals from the appellate courts. Appeals to the Supreme Court are usually discretionary, that is the court may choose whether or not to hear the appeal.

Law won't work without independent courts. That means courts that aren't under the thumb of the political powers-that-be. An independent judge can assure that your case will be decided according to the law and the facts—not the vagaries of shifting political currents.

Courts are required to interpret and apply the law when parties dispute. In that way, courts take law out of dry and dusty law books, and make it part of the living fabric of our lives. Courts apply the law to specific controversies brought before them. They resolve disputes between people, companies and units of government.

Often, courts are called on to uphold limitations on the government. They protect against abuses by all branches of government. They protect minorities of all types from the majority, and protect the rights of people who can't protect themselves. They also embody notions of equal treatment and fair play. The courts and the protections of the law are open to everybody.

In any state, there are not one but two distinct court systems: state courts and federal courts. The vast majority of cases are handled by the state courts. The great bulk of legal business which include traffic offenses, divorce, wills and estates, buying and selling property are handled by the state courts, as all these areas are governed primarily by state laws. With this, courts in the country are divided into:

- Trial courts, where cases start.
- Intermediate (appellate) courts, where most appeals are first heard; and
- Courts of last resort (supreme courts), which hear further appeals and have final authority in the cases they hear.

4.2 Trial Courts

Trial courts are where a case begins, where witnesses are heard and evidence is presented, sometimes to a jury and sometimes only to a judge. In the federal system, trial courts are known as District Courts. Since the country has certain judicial districts, state boundaries are used to establish district limits. Every state has a least one district with larger states having more than one. State trial courts are known by various names, such as district, superior, county, and circuit courts but despite their variations, many courts are basically the same.

A trial court of general jurisdiction is authorized to hear some type of civil or criminal case that is not committed exclusively to another court. A trial court of limited jurisdiction is authorized to hear only specified types of cases. Trial courts of limited jurisdiction may be limited in subject-matter jurisdiction or by other means, such as small claims courts in many states for civil cases with a low amount in controversy. Other trials do not take place in courts at all, but in quasi-judicial bodies or in administrative agencies with adjudicatory power created by statute to make binding determinations with simplified procedural practices, such as arbitration.

In the trial court, evidence and testimony are admitted under the rules of evidence established by applicable procedural law and determinations called findings of fact and are made based on the evidence. The court, presided over by one or more judges, makes findings of law based upon the applicable law. In most common law jurisdictions, the trial court often sits with a jury and one judge; in such jury trials, the jury acting as trier of fact. In some cases, the judge or judges act as triers of both fact and law, by either statute, custom, or agreement of the parties; this is referred to as a bench trials. In the case of most judges hearing cases through the bench trial process, they would prefer that all parties are given an opportunity to offer a vigorous and robust case presentation, such that, errors in testimony, procedures, statutes, etc., do not grow "crab legs" -- meaning compounded errors -- and are remanded or returned to their court on appeal.

Appeals from the decisions of trial courts are usually made by higher courts with the power of appellate review. Most trial courts are courts of record, where the record of the presentation of evidence is created and must be maintained or transmitted to the appellate court. The record of the trial court is certified by the clerk of the trial court and transmitted to the appellate body. Most appellate courts do not have the authority to hear testimony or take evidence, but instead rule solely on matters of law.

Functions

The trial court has original statewide jurisdiction in all civil and criminal actions within district boundaries. With judicial districts and district court judges, a family court division, juvenile court division, probate division, conciliation court division, and a traffic and ordinance violations bureau exist in district court. In support of these functions, trial courts are implementing the following strategies:

- ❖ Setting of case processing and case management standards, and institute monitoring programs for exceptions to ensure timely disposition of cases.
- ❖ Developing programs to allow litigants meaningful access to court process, e.g., court interpreter programs, free legal services for the poor, and self-help programs for persons who choose to guide their own litigation.
- ❖ Explore ways to use technology to enhance and expedite the work of the courts, including making justice more consumer oriented.
- ❖ Develop programs and technologies to provide judges the critical information needed to make timely and sound case and policy decisions.
- ❖ Delegate legal research and where possible draft decision writing to law clerks, freeing judges to spend more time hearing cases or directing the case dispositional activities.
- ❖ Review and evaluate court practices and policies to identify the need for systemic improvement through the Judicial Council and its committees.
- ❖ Explore greater integration and coordination with other justice and social service agencies.
- ❖ Develop an adequate and stable funding base, and develop a long-term allocation formula to equitably distribute state funding among the ten judicial districts.

4.3 Intermediate Appeals Courts

Intermediate appellate courts existed for more than a century in few states, but most have been established since 1960s to relieve the crowded dockets of state supreme courts. The intermediate appellate courts serve as an intermediate step between the trial courts and courts of last resort in a state.

It is known that 41 out of 50 states have at least 1intermediate appellate court. Their jurisdiction varies from state to state, but in most cases, they serve to relieve the workload of the state's highest court. Some states have more than one of these types of courts which has one intermediate appellate court for civil matters and another for criminal.

Intermediate Court of Appeals has discretionary authority to entertain cases submitted without a prior suit when there is a question of law that could be the subject of a civil action or a proceeding in the Circuit Court, or Tax Appeal Court, and the parties agree upon the facts upon which the controversy depends.

Intermediate appellate courts which resolve disputes by developing or expounding the unwritten or common law do so as a function of their exercise of power of government as per constitutional structure of state or territory from which their judicial power derives instead of courts exercising federal jurisdiction. There are occasions where such courts exercise federal jurisdiction and, as a part of certain exercise pronounce upon the common law. In the latter case, it may well be that where federal jurisdiction is being exercised in a matter, there is good reason for suggesting that the decision will be binding on all courts for same reasons as decision on Commonwealth legislation might be. Also, High Court has not gone that far and has left a freedom to depart from the intermediate appellate court's decision where the other court is convinced that it is plainly wrong.

4.4 Courts of Last Resort

The court of last resort is a legal term that refers to a court of final appeal in a jurisdiction. In simpler terms, it is the court of the highest authority. The court of last resort is a rule-making authority that assists in solving some of these dilemmas. A rule-making authority determines what state or national policy will be when it applies law to specific disputes.

A court of last resort is the highest judicial body within a jurisdiction's court system. It is a court with the highest appellate authority, meaning that its rulings are not subject to further review by another court. A court of last resort is often, but not always, referred to as a supreme court.

The rulings of courts of last resort are intended to provide clarity to lower courts. These courts also have administrative power over their jurisdiction's judicial system, overseeing lower courts and the rules of the court system. They also often oversee the ethics and conduct of the state's attorneys.

A court of last resort, is one which decides, definitely, without appeal or writ of error, or any other examination whatever, a suit or action, or some other matter, which has been submitted to its judgment, and over which it has jurisdiction. Court of Last Resort will have the following objects:

- To ask the authorities concerned in various States about details of prisoners, particularly those who have been in jail for long periods, including undertrials and convicts. The RTI Act can be used in this connection.
- To examine cases, whether of our own accord, or on the representation of someone, and find out whether injustice has been done to the person

involved, either by a delay in holding the trial or by a wrong conviction, and do the needful in this connection, including applying for bail.

- To apply for pardon, respite, suspension or reduction of sentence to the President or Governor as the case may be.
- To create awareness in the public about this gross injustice that is being done to a large number of people.
- To educate the police about this state of affairs and change their mentality.
- To approach the other authorities concerned with the aim of rectifying this injustice to a large section of people.
- To do such other acts as may be necessary for this purpose.

The supreme court is a court of last resort in all matters which legally come before it; and whenever a court possesses the power to decide without appeal or other examination whatever, a subject matter submitted to it, it is a court of last resort; but this is not to be understood as preventing an examination into its jurisdiction, or excess of authority, for then the judgment of a superior does not try and decide so much whether the point decided has been so done according to law, as to try the authority of the inferior court.

4.4.1 Supreme Court

The Supreme Court makes rules governing practice and procedure in Ohio's courts, such as the Rules of Evidence, Rules of Civil Procedure and Rules of Criminal Procedure. Procedural rules adopted by the Supreme Court become effective unless both houses of the General Assembly adopt a concurrent resolution of disapproval. The Supreme Court also exercises general superintendence over all state courts through its rule-making authority. The rules of superintendence set minimum standards for court administration statewide. Unlike procedural rules, rules of superintendence do not have to be submitted to the General Assembly to become effective.

The Court also has authority over the admission of attorneys to the practice of law in Ohio and may discipline admitted attorneys who violate the rules governing the practice of law.

The Chief Justice and six Justices are elected to six-year terms on a nonpartisan ballot. Two Justices are chosen at the general election in even-numbered years. In the year when the Chief Justice is on the ballot, voters elect three members of the Court. A person must be an attorney with at least six years of experience in the practice of law to be elected or appointed to the Court. Appointments are made by the governor for vacancies that occur between elections.

Role

The Supreme Court has a special role to play in the system of government. The Constitution gives it the power to check, if necessary, the actions of the President. It can tell a President that his actions are not allowed by the Constitution. It can tell that a law that was passed violated the Constitution and is, therefore, no longer a law. It can also tell the government of a state that one of its laws breaks a rule in the Constitution.

The Supreme Court is the final judge in all cases involving laws, and the highest law of all in the Constitution. It is far from all-powerful which is limited by other two branches of government. The President nominates justices to the court. The Senate must vote its approval of the nominations. The whole Congress also has great power over the lower courts in the federal system.

The Supreme Court is like a referee on a field where the President, State Police, and other government officials are the players. Some can pass laws, and others can enforce laws. But all exercise power within certain boundaries. These boundaries are set by the Constitution. As the referee in the system of government, it is the Supreme Court's job to say when government officials step out-of-bounds.

Powers

Original Jurisdiction

Cases which come directly to the supreme court are under its original jurisdiction and it settles disputes between Centre and State or Between States, Disputes concerning the election of the president and vice-president and the disputes arising out of the Implementation of Fundamental Rights.

Appellate Jurisdiction

It hears appeals against some decisions of the High Courts, the cases concerned to civil, criminal and constitutional matters. The Certificate of the High Court is necessary for appeals relating to civil, criminal and constitutional matters, Such certificates can be granted by the high courts on their own or on the request of the parties, In some criminal cases, the accused can directly appeal to the supreme court in case of death sentence or imprisonment of more than ten years.

Judicial Review

The Supreme Court can review any judgment given by itself and also has the power to withdraw the case if it feels an important question of law is involved. The Power of Judicial review is to decide the Constitutionality of the acts passed by the Legislatures;

- To Maintain the Constitutional equilibrium between the centre and the states.

- To establish equilibrium between the Legislature and the Executive.
- To safeguard the Fundamental Rights of the Citizens.

Guardian of Fundamental Rights

When fundamental rights of citizens are violated either by the government or any individual, the Supreme Court protects the Fundamental rights of Citizens.

Guardian of Constitution

If the government passes any law against the constitution, the Supreme Court declares it unconstitutional.

Advisory Jurisdiction

The Supreme Court gives legal advice to the president of India on matters of constitutional or legal importance.

Composition

The Supreme Court is composed of the Chief Justice, who is President of the Court, and ordinary Judges. In addition, the President of the Court of Appeal is ex officio member of the Supreme Court. The President of High Court is also an ex officio member of the Supreme Court.

The Court usually sits with a composition of three or five Judges and, exceptionally, seven Judges. When hearing cases concerning the constitutional validity of an Act of parliament, the Constitution needs that the Court has a minimum of five Judges. This need also applies when the Court is requested to give an opinion on the constitutional validity of a Bill adopted by the Parliament when referred to it by President under the Constitution. A minimum of five Judges is also required should the Court have to determine, pursuant of the Constitution, whether the President has become permanently incapacitated.

In addition to those cases in which it is required by the Constitution, a court composed of five Judges, or exceptionally seven Judges, will sit for appeals involving questions of law of particular importance or complexity. Where an insufficient number of Judges of the Supreme Court are available the Chief Justice may request any ordinary Judge of the High Court to sit as a member of the Supreme Court for the hearing of a particular appeal.

Interlocutory applications and procedural matters or issues may be determined by the Chief Justice sitting alone or another judge of the Supreme Court nominated by the Chief Justice.

5

The Legal Process

5.1 Civil Litigation

5.1.1 Definition

Civil litigation refers to a legal dispute between two or more parties that seek money damages or specific performance rather than criminal sanctions. A lawyer who specializes in civil litigation is known as a litigator or trial lawyer. Lawyers who practice civil litigation represent parties in trials, arbitrations and mediations before administrative agencies, foreign tribunals, and federal, state, and local courts. Several common types of civil litigation include environmental law, housing law, products liability, intellectual property, labor and employment, and antitrust.

Civil litigation is the process that allows individuals, businesses and other entities to use the courts to settle disputes. Unlike criminal cases in which the government prosecutes someone for violating a criminal statute with the penalty being imprisonment or fines, civil litigation cases are private disputes in which the parties are usually seeking a money judgment or some other remedy from a judge to make them whole or to end further harm.

5.1.2 Civil litigation attorney

A civil litigation professional or an attorney assumes the dispute and oppositional position faced by the hired party. As a result of this, the civil litigation professional possesses a firm knowledge of the legal matter in question and must fully understand the principles and intricacies of the underlying dispute.

A civil litigator should be well-versed in many distinct stages of civil litigation which include:

- Investigation of case
- Observation of pleadings
- Discovery stage (gathering of evidence and witness testimonies)
- Pre-trial
- Delivery and evaluation of settlement
- Appeal process

It is seen that many civil matters do not pass through each state of litigation, so majority of lawsuits will be settled prior to trial. For such civil matters which do reach a trial verdict, the majority of them are not appealed. Given the different stages and the varying subject matter involved in each case, the lifespan of a civil lawsuit may range from several months to several years—more complex civil litigation matters will often take years to pass from pre-suit investigation through trial and the subsequent settlement.

The discovery portion of civil litigation is the most labor-intensive portion of the process. As a result of this notion, the average civil litigator spends little time in the actual courtroom; the majority of resources and time are devoted to the gathering and evaluation of witness testimonies and evidence in the discovery stage.

The role and responsibilities of a civil litigation attorney can be challenging and diverse. It is an adversarial process with two or more parties pitted against each other. The attorney is his client's advocate, obligated to fight for him to achieve the best possible outcome on the client's behalf. Lawyers specializing in this field must be willing to assume oppositional positions, to embrace conflict and controversy, and to effectively act as human pit bulls in defense of their clients.

Attorneys and litigation paralegals in this field often work long hours, especially during a trial. Certain skills and knowledge are essential to litigation practice. Key legal skills include:

- Knowledge of substantive and procedural law
- Strong written and oral advocacy skills
- Analytical and logical reasoning abilities
- Ability to synthesize complex legal and factual materials
- Superior interpersonal skills
- Knowledge of legal research techniques and software
- Client development skills
- Negotiation skills

5.1.3 Types of civil litigation cases

Any case that is not a criminal prosecution is usually classified as civil litigation. Following are the five types of civil litigation cases in which the average person might be involved as either a plaintiff, the party filing the lawsuit, or as a defendant, the party against whom a lawsuit is filed:

- Personal injury or Tort
- Breach of contract
- Divorce and Family law
- Property disputes

- Landlord and Tenant disputes
- Personal injury and Tort civil litigation

A person injured as a result of the negligent conduct of another individual or entity has the right to file a lawsuit seeking compensation. Personal injury civil litigation cases may arise from motor vehicle accidents, slip-and-fall accidents, injuries caused by defective products and other cases in which negligence caused an accident in which the plaintiff was injured.

Divorce and Family law cases

Disputes and conflicts arising out of family relationships are the types of civil litigation cases that most people have had some experience with at some time in their lives. Divorce, separation, child custody, support and domestic violence are types of disputes that people resort to the courts to resolve.

Civil litigation arising from contracts

When one of the parties to a contract fails to perform its obligations under the terms of a contract, the other party has the right to file a breach of contract claim. The plaintiff in a breach of contract case could sue to recover monetary damages caused by the defaulting party, or the plaintiff might ask the court to order the defendant to perform according to the terms of the agreement. This latter remedy is referred to as specific performance.

The buyer of a home might not be satisfied with recovering monetary damages from a seller who refuses to convey title under a contract of sale if the uniqueness of the home or its location makes it one-of-a-kind. If the buyer is successful in proving breach of contract, the judge hearing the case could grant specific performance and order the defendant to sell the home to the plaintiff.

Landlord and Tenant disputes

Evictions are only one of the disputes arising between landlords and their tenants that could find their way into the courts through civil litigation. Disputes over a party's failure to comply with the terms of a lease or conflicts about services a tenant claims are lacking could end up in front of a judge as a civil litigation case.

Disputes over real property

Property line disputes, conflicts about ownership rights and title claims are civil litigation cases in which the remedy might be something more than money damages. For example, a property owner claiming trespass by an adjoining owner might ask a judge to grant an injunction to prevent future encroachments.

5.2 Alternative Dispute Resolution

5.2.1 Introduction

The concept of Alternative Dispute Resolution (ADR) mechanism is capable of providing a substitute to the conventional methods of resolving disputes. ADR offers to resolve all type of matters including civil, commercial, industrial and family etc., where people are not being able to start any type of negotiation and reach the settlement. Generally, ADR uses neutral third party who helps the parties to communicate, discuss the differences and resolve the dispute. It is a method which enables individuals and group to maintain co-operation, social order and provides opportunity to reduce hostility.

Alternative Dispute Resolution or ADR refers to any means of settling disputes outside of the courtroom. It typically includes:

- Early neutral evaluation
- Negotiation
- Conciliation
- Mediation
- Arbitration

The two most common forms of Alternative Dispute Resolution are arbitration and mediation, negotiation is almost always attempted first to resolve a dispute. It is the preeminent mode of dispute resolution. Negotiation allows the parties to meet in order to settle a dispute. The main advantage of this form of dispute settlement is that it allows the parties themselves to control the process and the solution.

Mediation is also an informal alternative to litigation. Mediators are individuals trained in negotiations, who bring opposing parties together and attempt to work out a settlement or agreement that both parties accept or reject. Mediation is used for a wide gamut of case-types ranging from juvenile felonies to federal government negotiations with Native American Indian tribes. Mediation has also become a significant method for resolving disputes between investors and stock brokers.

Arbitration is a simplified version of a trial involving limited discovery and simplified rules of evidence. The arbitration is headed and decided by an arbitral panel. To comprise a panel, either both sides agree on one arbitrator, or each side selects one arbitrator and the two arbitrators elect the third. Arbitration hearings usually last between a few days to a week, and the panel only meets for a few hours per day. The panel then deliberates and issues a written decision, or arbitral award. Opinions are not public record. Arbitration has long been used in labor, construction, and securities regulation, but is now gaining popularity in other business disputes.

Before an ADR option can be arranged, Professional Standards Branch reviews the complaint and determines whether the public interest would be best served by ADR. If the complaint is found suitable, the process begins. A complaint can be resolved through ADR only if both the complainant and the officer agree to participate. The mediator or supervisor arranges a date and venue convenient for the parties. The parties are given an opportunity to discuss the matter from their own perspective and to share how the incident has impacted them. Then the parties, with the support of the mediator or supervisor, explore how best to resolve the issues discussed. An ADR resolution must be agreed to in writing and may include the specific terms of the proposed resolution, where applicable. If the complaint remains unresolved at the end of the ADR process, the complaint is returned to the Professional Standard Branch and an investigation is initiated.

5.2.2 Need

Weight of Pendency

The need for finding alternatives arises due to the working of the present system of administration of justice, which is crumbling under the weight of the pending cases.

State fighting the citizens

Interestingly, the government is the biggest litigant in the country. According to a rough estimate, around 70 per cent of all cases are either agitated by the State, or appealed by it. The State fights cases against the citizens at the costs of citizens. Thus, directly or indirectly the State is also responsible for increasing the weight of pending cases.

Other reasons

Jurists have suggested that another reason for litigation is the reduction in number of holidays of courts, and an increase in the number of working days. At present the courts are working for 210-230 days per year, with a fairly long summer vacation. If courts work for longer hours and days, litigation can be brought under control.

Adjournments

Unnecessary adjournments also extend the life of litigation. The process of adjournment, on frivolous grounds, is one of the major reasons for increase in delay. There is a need to evolve a set of guidelines for granting adjournments, and a framework for the settlement of dispute should be designed.

5.2.3 ADR and its Types

Arbitration

When two or more persons agree that a dispute or potential dispute between them shall be decided in a legally binding way by one or more impartial persons in a judicial manner, the agreement arrived after such settlement is called 'arbitration agreement. Such process is called as arbitration and the decision when made is called the award.

Arbitration is much like a trial, in that the parties can call witnesses, present evidence, and argue the merits of their case to a neutral decision maker. In many jurisdictions, civil litigants whose claims do not exceed a certain dollar amount may be ordered to attend arbitration by the court, in an effort to keep the court's docket clear for more substantial lawsuits. Local court rules may also allow litigants to elect for their case to be sent to arbitration regardless of the dollar amount at stake. In doing so, the parties can agree that the results of the arbitration will be binding or non-binding. In non-binding arbitration, the loser can afterwards request a new trial in the civil court.

The court will appoint a well-established attorney in the local area to perform the duties of an arbitrator. This person will act as a judge at the arbitration hearing, listening to the evidence and rendering a decision. Parties may be given some amount of say in the arbitrator selection process. At a minimum, they will be allowed to strike potential arbitrators with whom they have had prior dealings.

Once a case is sent to arbitration, a conference will be held either by telephone, or in person at the arbitrator's office. Much like a pre-trial conference in civil court, this is the opportunity for the parties to give the arbitrator an overview of what the case is about, and to discuss any evidentiary issues in advance of the arbitration hearing. On the day of the hearing, the parties will meet in a conference room at the arbitrator's office or in an empty room at the courthouse. Each side will present its case over the course of several hours. Afterward, the arbitrator can render a decision immediately, or take the matter under advisement and issue a written decision in the following weeks.

Conciliation

It is the process where a third party assists the parties to resolve their disputes by agreement. A conciliator may do this by expressing an opinion about the merits of the dispute to help the parties to reach a settlement. Here, conciliation is a compromise settlement with the assistance of a conciliator.

Mediation

It is a process with which the disputes can be resolved using the aid of an independent third person which assists the parties in dispute to reach a negotiated resolution. Mediation is the acceptable intervention into a dispute of a third party that has no authority to make a decision.

Mediation is a much different type of ADR proceeding. Unlike arbitration, it does not involve an adversarial hearing, and there is no decision-making official present. Instead, the parties involved in the dispute are brought together in one location, and a neutral facilitator acts as a go-between. The job of the mediator is to help the parties reach a voluntary settlement of the case. For litigants and attorneys who have become antagonistic toward each other over the course of the litigation, or who have unrealistic expectations concerning the outcome of the case, mediation may be their only chance to avoid having to go to trial.

A typical mediation begins with everyone meeting in the same room, and each party giving a short presentation to the mediator. The purpose of the presentation is to give an overview of the facts and impress upon the mediator the relative strength of that party's case. The parties then split up into two rooms. The mediator goes back and forth between the rooms, personally relaying the parties' settlement offers and responses. Parties can share information with the mediator in confidence, and the mediator will give the parties his or her own thoughts about the case. In the end, the goal is for the parties to agree on how the case should be resolved.

Negotiation

It is a process through which parties resolve their disputes and agreed upon the course of action and bargain for advantage. They try to adopt such a creative option that serves their mutual interests. Because of its mutual advantages, people negotiate in almost all walks of life, from home to courtroom.

Lok Adalat

It is similar to people's court. It is not a court in strict sense of term, but it is a forum where voluntary efforts are made for settlement of disputes between the parties. In other words, Lok Adalat is a forum of Alternative Dispute Resolution. This system is based on Gandhian principles. It provides alternative resolution or devise for expeditious and inexpensive justice.

Gram Nyayalayas

Gram Nyayalayas is the other form of dispute resolution. It is the latest in the reforms in the structure of judiciary which provides speedy justice. It was proposed by the 114th Law Commission in 1986. Such model of adjudication is best suited for rural litigation. The Law Commission observed that such a court would be ideally suited for the villages as the nature of disputes coming before such a court require simple, uncomplicated and easy solutions. Hence such disputes should not be enmeshed in procedural claptrap.

Online ADR Mechanism

In context of Internet, where parties located in different corners of world can contract with each other at click of mouse, litigation of online disputes is often inconvenient, impractical, time-consuming and prohibitive. Providing an alternative approach to resolve online disputes might assist in redressing grievances and gaining consumer confidence in e-commerce. Alternative Dispute Resolution is an appurtenant candidate for such an approach.

5.2.4 Advantages

- It is less expensive.
- It is less time consuming.
- It is free from technicalities as in the case of conducting cases in law Courts.
- The parties are free to discuss their difference of opinion without any fear of disclosure of this fact before any law Courts.
- Last but not the least is the fact that parties know that there is no aspect of winning of losing, however they feel assured that their grievance is addressed and the relationship between the parties is restored.

5.3 Criminal Law and Criminal Procedure

5.3.1 Criminal Law

Crimes are categorized as felonies or misdemeanors as per their nature and maximum punishment that can be imposed. A felony called as high crime involves serious misconduct that is punishable by death or by imprisonment of more than one year. Most state criminal laws subdivide felonies into classes with varying degrees of punishment. Lesser crimes are misdemeanors which are misconduct punishable up to one year in prison and/or a fine.

Criminal law generally defines the rights and obligations of individuals in society. Some common issues in criminal law are the elements of specific crimes and the elements of various criminal defenses.

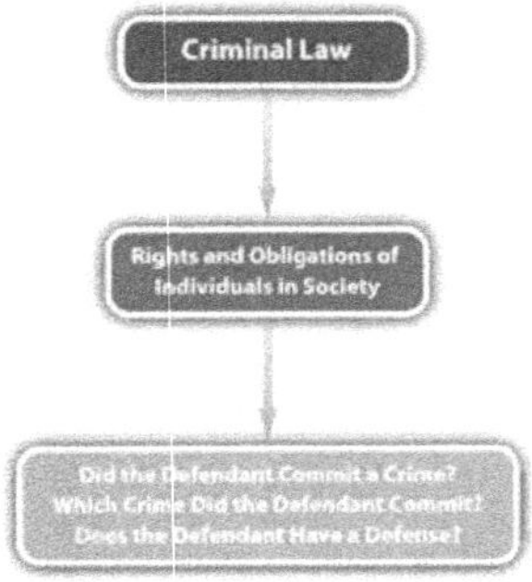

Fig Criminal Law

Criminal law is divided into two parts:

- General
- Specialized

The general part describes the rules that are common to most criminal offences, including the conditions for imposing punishment, the sanctions imposed on the guilty person and the execution of sanctions. Specialized criminal law addresses the individual penal provisions that apply to the individual criminal offence.

Criminal law appears from:

Common law

Common law, also known as judge-made law came into existence in England during 12th century. Judges created common law by ruling that certain actions were subject to punishment and defined offenses such as murder, rape, arson, and burglary as crimes against the state. Over time, British judges' law decisions produced a body of unwritten laws and customs. This law formed the basis of the legal system in the American colonies.

One of the main parts of common law is the law of precedent. Once a court makes a decision, it is binding on other courts in later cases presenting the same legal problem. The principle of stare deices relates to the law of precedent. It literally means to let the decision or precedent stand. This principle guides courts in making decisions in similar cases and ensures fairness in the judicial process.

Constitutions

The article of Constitution asserts that "This Constitution ... shall be the supreme Law of the Land; and Judges in every State shall be bound thereby, anything in Constitution or Laws of any State to Contrary notwithstanding." If any other types of law conflict with the Constitution, the U.S. Supreme Court can strike them down as unconstitutional. States make their own constitutions and all local laws are subordinate to them.

Statutes and Ordinances

Laws passed by State Legislatures make up most of criminal law. City councils also pass ordinances that compose part of criminal law. Each state has a statutory criminal code, as does the federal government. Laws defining crimes such as homicide, rape, robbery, burglary, and larceny are generally statutory. Some overlap exists between state and federal statutes. For example, some federal drug laws supplement state laws. Such laws are intended to provide added crime control in areas where local law enforcement has been ineffective.

5.3.2 Criminal Procedure

Criminal procedure generally concerns the enforcement of individuals' rights during the criminal process. Examples of procedural issues are individuals' rights during law enforcement investigation, arrest, filing of charges, trial, and appeal.

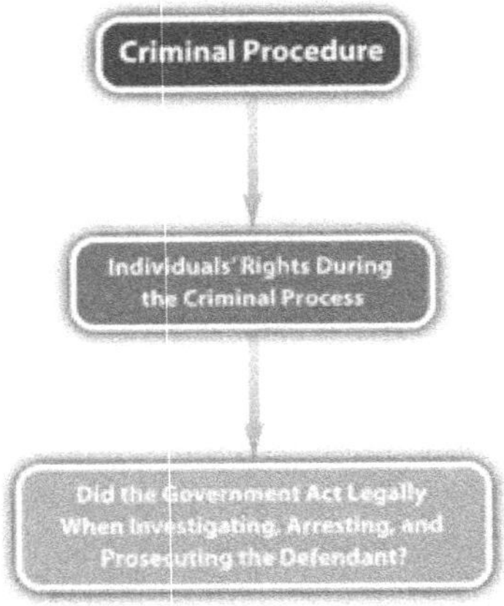

Criminal procedure focuses on the legal rules on how criminal offences are to be investigated and how penal cases must be dealt with in the legal system. It deals with the set of rules governing the series of proceedings through which the government enforces substantive criminal law. Municipalities, states, and the federal government each have their own criminal codes, defining types of conduct that constitute crimes.

Federal prosecutions follow the Federal Rules of Criminal Procedure which the Supreme Court promulgated and passed. The Federal Rules outline the procedure for conducting federal criminal trials. The Federal Rules incorporate and expound upon all guarantees included within the Constitution's Bill of Rights, such as the guarantee to due process and equal protection, the right to legal counsel, the right to confront witnesses, the right to a jury trial, and the right to not testify against oneself.

State prosecutions follow the criminal procedure code of the individual state. Although every state has its own criminal procedure code, many states choose to mimic the Federal Rules. State procedural rules may offer greater protection to a defendant in a criminal trial than the Constitution or Federal Rules, but may not offer less protection than guaranteed by the Constitution.

Criminal procedures are designed to safeguard both the innocent and the guilty from indiscriminate application of substantive criminal laws and from arbitrary or abusive treatment at the hands of law enforcement, the courts, or other members of the justice system. At the federal level these safeguards are primarily set forth in three places; the Federal Rules of Criminal Procedure to the Constitution. The rules and statutes reference each other, and both are designed to enforce and delineate in greater detail the rights established by the federal Constitution.

Steps

The criminal procedure process begins with the investigation of suspected criminal activity. During the investigation, law enforcement officers will collect the evidence needed to carry out an arrest. The accused would be taken into police custody and brought before a court for the arraignment. At the arraignment, he/she would be informed of the charges against him/her and given an attorney. He/she may also be detained and held in jail or released on bail until the next scheduled court appearance.

Before the trial is scheduled to begin, he/she may negotiate with the prosecutor. This process, known as plea bargaining, may result in a guilty plea in exchange for a more favorable sentence. If the accused is unable to reach a plea agreement with the prosecution, the case will proceed to trial. He/she may be tried before a jury, or before the judge alone. At the trial, the burden of proof is on the prosecution. This means that the prosecution must prove, beyond reasonable doubt, that the accused is guilty of the charged crimes. This means that the accused does not have to prove his/her innocence; instead, the prosecutor has to prove his/her guilt.

At the end of the trial, the jury will determine whether to convict or acquit based on the evidence presented at trial. This determination, known as the verdict, is presented to the judge, who will then enter a judgment. If found guilty of the crime, the case proceeds to the sentencing phase where the punishment is set.

The rules of criminal procedure are designed to protect an individual's civil liberties. Civil liberties are the basic personal freedoms guaranteed by the Constitution. The rules of criminal procedure strike a balance between the government's interest in punishing criminals and an individual's interest in a fair trial. If the government violates an individual's constitutional rights in the course of investigating a crime, the evidence obtained as a result of the violation may be excluded at trial. This principle is known as the exclusionary rule. The exclusionary rule is intended to deter unconstitutional government activity

5.4 The Paralegal's Role in the Legal Process

Paralegals can handle many facets of the legal process, including investigating the facts of a case; and conducting research on relevant laws, regulations and legal articles. Paralegals and legal assistants can perform many of the same duties as an attorney, but only under the supervision of the attorney by handling many facets of the legal process including investigating the facts of a case conducting research on relevant laws, regulations and legal articles; organizing and presenting the information; maintaining information related to cases or transactions in computer databases; creating reports to prepare lawyers for trials, and drafting correspondence and other documents, such as contracts and mortgages; and acquiring affidavits and other formal statements that may be used as evidence in court.

Paralegals and Legal Assistants help lawyers prepare for hearings, trials and corporate meetings. However, their specific duties may vary depending on the size of the firm or organization.

In larger organizations, paralegals most likely will work on a particular phase of a case, rather than handling a case from beginning to end.

Litigation Paralegals often do not attend trials, but might prepare trial documents or draft settlement agreements.

The paralegal provides invaluable aid to the attorney in the legal process. Paralegals are the backbone of the trial team, coordinating thousands of details that must be accomplished from the beginning of the first client interview through the trial process and post-trial procedures. The paralegal is also important to the client as they utilize time efficiently and provide the client necessary legal assistant services at a much lower rate than that of the attorney. This enables the attorney to focus on the major aspects of the case, while the paralegal gathers and collates important and necessary data.

Paralegals should in most instances utilize critical thinking skills, business managerial skills, organizational skills, general communication skills, general office skills, computer skills, and research and writing skills.

From the beginning of the client interview, under the supervision of the attorney, the paralegal will begin gathering information to assist the attorney in analyzing the client's specific legal issues through interviews with clients, witnesses and experts. The paralegal, under the attorney's direction, will also identify and evaluate alternative legal solutions; formulate logical solutions to specific problems of the case; construct logical arguments in support of the client's position; suggest potential solutions; determine which areas of law are relevant to the client's particular issues; identify interrelationships among cases, statutes, regulations, and other legal authorities; apply recognized legal authority to a specific factual situation; analyze factual situations to determine when it is appropriate to apply exceptions to general legal rules; distinguish evidentiary facts from other material and/or controlling facts; and identify factual omissions and inconsistencies.

Using organizational skills, the paralegal will sort information by category and prioritize assignments according to the client's needs, manage information manually and through computerized databases.

It is the job of the paralegal to interact effectively with clients, witnesses, experts, counsel of record, courts and other legal and business professionals. They must adapt to situations as they arise and keep the attorney informed of all new developments related to the case. They must be able to adapt to situations as they arise, and understand the need to ask questions and seek guidance from the attorney.

Legal research involves the application of critical thinking, organizational skills, and effective communication skills. The paralegal must be able to carry out legal research and analyze and categorize key facts in each legal situation. They must read, evaluate and analyze both printed and electronic sources of law and with supervision of the attorney apply that law to the facts of each case. They must not only properly cite sources, but must check the cited sources of other legal professionals to locate and formulate proper legal concepts.

One of the most important and difficult jobs of the paralegal is the drafting of legal documents. This involves understanding and application of principles of writing and rules of English grammar. The writing must be done in a way that conveys legal theory in a clear and concise manner and conforms with local, state and federal court rules. They must further locate, modify and/or customize standardized forms found in formbooks, pleadings files, form files, or on computer data banks according to the facts of each potential case.

The paralegal must have a well-rounded knowledge of the legal system, the various court procedures and the law and how it applies to the various legal matters at issue for each client. They are critical members of the legal support team and when used effectively assist in providing the client with the appropriate legal representation at a more efficient price.

5.4.1 Calendaring

It's important to follow documentary standards as a case progresses through the court system, but keeping on top of important dates and managing time of key lawyers and witnesses will be the most important factor in trial management. Just about every other mistake a legal team can make can be fixed up or patched over, but a missed deadline is just missed.

Paralegals are often keepers of calendar and organizers of schedules during trials, coordinating with opposing counsel, court clerks, outside resources, and other staff in firm to make sure that preparation time is being used efficiently and that filings and appearances happen at the appropriate times.

Part of managing the calendar is managing witnesses. It's one thing to get an attorney from your own firm to court on time as they have a vested interest in being there. But dealing with witnesses who may be indifferent or outright hostile to the case can require a whole new set of skills to motivate, prepare, and compel them to appear.

Some best practices for law office calendaring include:

Calendaring events listed on docket sheets received from the Court

When you work in a busy law office, you might receive several notices from the Court each day about new filings, deadlines, and scheduled hearings. Hence having a system for dealing with these notices in order to ensure that newly schedule events are accurately placed on the calendar is a must. You should have a clear, office wide policy regarding who is authorized to open mail from the Courts, what they should do about any deadlines or hearings mentioned in the correspondence, and how to accurately provide a check on the system. For example, having the person who opens the mail add items to the calendar, initial the correspondence as calendared, and then drop the notice in another individual's inbox for them to double check.

Calculating and Calendaring deadlines

Deadlines, not calculated for you by the Court, must be figured by someone familiar with the laws concerning the number of days provided in each particular situation and how to count those out, considering relevant exclusionary days such as weekends and holidays. Anyone who calculates and calendars a deadline should include their initials in the entry, so that everyone can be held accountable for their math and calendar entries.

Scheduling appointments with Clients, Potential clients, and Other attorneys

Appointment scheduling in some offices might be easier than in others, but when you work for an attorney who goes a lot to court, like in family law or litigation, you might want to consider setting aside specific days and/or times for appointments, as well as other times for the attorney to work in the office without interruption.

Calculating and Scheduling travel time to out of county meetings and hearings

Because out of county meetings generally take much more time than hearings a few blocks away, you should have a system in place that provides plenty of travel time to and from other counties, when the need arises. For example, requiring all out of county appointments or hearings have the county listed clearly on the calendar and that nothing be scheduled for an hour before the meeting or two hours after its expected end time.

Synchronizing firm calendars

When using more than one calendar in an office, there should be a clear procedure for matching them up. Everyone in the office should know whose responsibility synchronizing the calendars is, when it should be done, and who will do it if the elected person is out of office on any given day. If your office is using software to synchronize calendars, the software should be checked regularly to ensure it is properly doing its job.

5.4.2 Basics of E-Filing

With the advent of technology, every piece of life is going digital. Credit cards no longer have to be swiped, banking and blogging can be done from cell phones, so with such technological development, it only makes sense that industries are taking advantage of such technologies. With the rise of Web or Internet, interacting and sharing of information becomes common in personal matters as there are newer, faster ways of adding information. By use of electronic filing or e-filing of legal documents, it seems, that the law related cases are gaining momentum as the county and state courts are offering such services for getting work done faster.

E-filing is the process of filing legal documents with the court electronically. Documents are uploaded into a court database. In most courts, an email is sent to you when the document has been received, and another email is sent to which let you to know whether the document has been accepted or rejected. This process started in 2001 in bankruptcy courts, but now Federal District courts follow this whereas appellate courts offers e-filing. Once the Federal Courts started offering e-filing, more than 99% of Federal Courts have gone to requisite e-filing. As per administration office of the courts, almost 32 million cases have been filed online since federal e-filing began, with over 400,000 attorneys registered in federal e-filing system. Case Management/Electronic Court Filing is the federal system for submitting and managing electronic documents. E-filing is not just limited to Federal Courts, though that is where it is most prevalent. Many state courts and county courts have begun to make the transition to electronic filing. The courts are realizing the benefits to all parties involved that electronic filing presents.

Benefits of e-filing

The three main benefits of e-filing are time, money and ease. Initially, when you file a document electronically, an automatic email confirmation from the court is received, giving you an easy way to determine when a document was filed. In many courts, you can file documents until 12 p.m. on the day of deadline, which gives you extra hours after courts have closed to file documents. Some judges, however, set filing curfews or deadlines for when documents need to be filed. For filling, the paralegal should be aware about the rules of court where they are e-filing, as they can differ from court to court. Most courts require that your attorney at the very least sit through a training before they are allowed to e-file. Even if an attorney has been successfully e-filing in one court, they may have to complete the training at a different court. Ask your attorney if you can attend these training sessions with him or her, so that you are aware of the variations in each court.

Apart from this, e-filing saves money for the firm, especially if you have been running around to submit important documents to the court house to file, you will save on time and money. If you have been hiring a courier service to do these tasks, you will save money by no longer needing that service. You also save money on postage and the cost of materials, such as toner and paper, by e-filing. Instead of having to print and file large documents, you can simply save them as PDFs on your computer. By using less paper, you are also helping the environment and creating a greener work space. Speaking of the environment, another benefit e-filing has is that, in the unfortunate event of a natural disaster, such as a hurricane or tornado, you don't have to worry about losing all your files or paperwork. On a more positive note, the same system that keeps your files safe during disaster also allows you and your attorneys to access case files around the clock from any location with Internet access. Also, with all court documents in an electronic format, you can easily search through hundreds of pages of documents in seconds, while being able to access your court files from a laptop anywhere.

Offices greatly benefit from e-filing. When searching for new paralegals, many law firms now require experience with e-filing. A quick search of paralegal and e-filing on various popular job-search websites returned job leads for paralegals with e-filing experience. It is important to understand and have experience with e-filing for professional growth and development. Continuing education classes can bring you up to date on e-filing. While it may seem daunting at first, a good training course will teach you a lot of what you need to know about e-filing, including how to scan documents, save documents as a pdf, and how to access the documents that have already been uploaded.

When an office begins the process of e-filing, it is important to stress that it is not just a change in policy, but also a change in culture. The whole office, including the attorneys, should understand how e-filing works and why this system is being used. Technology has to be up-to-date for e-filing to be efficient and effective.

For better or for worse, e-filing is here to stay. As a paralegal, one needs to learn to embrace the technology and encourage your law office to do the same. If your office has not yet needed to use e-filing, lead the charge and make the case for your office to at least begin to go digital. When e-filing does make it to your court system, you will be prepared for the transition.

Steps for e-Filing:

In order to assist your attorney with e-filing, motion a response or reply to papers in court, follow the tips as given below:

- Verify the e-filing deadline with the court, attorney and/or co-counsel. Be sure you know the deadline in your jurisdiction.
- Check the local court rules by knowing the jurisdiction's local rules for filing motions or responses in case of local Electronic Case Files.
- Prepare any support documents as required by attorney. There may be a motion, declaration, request for judicial notice or proposed order you can draft for your attorney's review.
- Gather and quality check all exhibits. Here the exhibits to any declarations or requests for judicial notice should be gathered in PDF format. Verify each

exhibit to assure there are no missing pages, and no annotations, comments or markings which need to be removed.

- ❖ Proofread and verify all citations to declarations, exhibits, and other supporting documents in the brief. It is important that all evidence citations be accurate. Check each citation in the brief to assure that the correct paragraph, exhibit or page number is referenced.
- ❖ Prepare appropriate proofs of service. Many courts require a proof of service showing the alternate method of service when any party has not agreed to, or is otherwise not able to accept ECF service. However, even in instances where all parties are served timely via the court's ECF system, follow your firm's or attorney's practice in preparing proofs of service for your filing.
- ❖ Prepare PDF versions of all documents to be e-filed with the court. Each document to be e-filed must be converted to PDF format, including the motion, brief, all supporting documents, and all exhibits. Further, many court ECF systems have file size limits.
- ❖ Redact for privilege or other sensitive information. If any portion of your filing contains privileged information, follow the court's instructions for filing documents under seal. If the administrative motion is granted, follow the court's instructions. Some jurisdictions have a procedure for e-filing documents under seal such that they are accessible by the court but not by counsel or the public.
- ❖ Use attorney login to upload brief, all supporting documents and exhibits to the court's ECF system. Many district courts allow an ECF User to authorize another person to file documents on his or her behalf, using his or her log-in; obviously the attorney user retains full responsibility for any document filed by another. It is helpful to have training on how to navigate the ECF system prior to filing day, as unfamiliarity with the ECF steps can cause delay. Start uploading early enough to allow for e-service in time for the filing deadline. Most courts require that your e-filing be completed by midnight local time in order for your filing to be considered timely.
- ❖ Assist your attorney in complying with any agreements among counsel regarding email or fax service of e-filed documents. Parties sometimes negotiate an agreement to email all filed documents to all parties, in addition to the electronic service provided by the court's ECF system. This may be particularly important if any portion of your filing has been redacted for privilege with a motion to file under seal, and there is an agreement in place that unredacted versions be supplied to all counsel via email.
- ❖ Comply with Local Rules and/or Judge Standing Orders regarding lodging the judge's courtesy copy of all documents filed. Many jurisdictions require that chambers' copies be submitted.

- ❖ Comply with Local Rules and/or Judge Standing Orders regarding the handling of any proposed orders. Many judges require that a Word version of any proposed order be submitted to chambers via a specified email address. In addition, some judges still require that sufficient hard copies of any proposed order must be provided for conforming, together with a self-addressed, stamped envelope.

5.4.3 Bar Association

Paralegal is a person, qualified through education, training or work experience to perform substantive legal work that requires knowledge of legal concepts and is customarily, but not exclusively, performed by a lawyer. This person may be retained or employed by a lawyer, law office, governmental agency or other entity or may be authorized by administrative, statutory or court authority to perform this work. Substantive shall mean work requiring recognition, evaluation, organization, analysis, and communication of relevant facts and legal concepts.

Paralegals can be delegated any task normally performed by a lawyer, as long as the lawyer supervises the work, except those proscribed by law. For example, paralegals can review and organize client files, conduct factual and legal research, prepare documents for legal transactions, draft pleadings and discovery notices, interview clients and witnesses, and assist at closings and trials.

Paralegals are those persons, regardless of job title or classification who are employed by a lawyer, law office, government agency, or other entity in Indiana, and working under the direction of an attorney in a capacity that involves the performance of substantive legal work that usually requires knowledge of legal concepts and who perform those duties at least 70 percent of the time.

The Affiliate Membership Committee serves to integrate paralegal in Association by informing the various types of affiliate members programs and committees that will best serve their various interests. It shall work in conjunction with Membership and Membership Benefits Committee to increase the number of affiliate members in the Association. It shall monitor the progress of the committee and report to the Membership and Membership Benefits Committee and Board of Governors as necessary.

In 1995, National Federation of Paralegal Associations adopted Paralegal as the preferred term for the profession. NFPA members identified several recent trends in the paralegal profession including court decisions awarding higher fees to attorneys employing persons called paralegal instead of legal assistant, the commission on Non-Lawyer Practice's latest report using paralegal almost exclusively, and several paralegal associations changing their names to paralegal from legal assistant.

In the practice of law, a paralegal is person who works in the legal profession, typically as an assistant to a lawyer, and who is typically responsible for researching, analyzing, and managing the daily tasks for cases. While paralegals work closely with cases, they are limited in their duties and must be supervised by a lawyer, who will be ultimately responsible for the paralegal's work. They are found in all areas where lawyers are in criminal trials, in real estate, in government, in estate planning, and so on. Many paralegals go on to law school and eventually become lawyers.

Essentially, with education and experience, paralegals are qualified to perform legal work that is customarily done by a lawyer, and for which a lawyer is ultimately accountable. Paralegals do, however, hold the responsibility of providing accurate, concise, ethical and timely work to their supervising lawyer and their clients.

5.4.4 Database and Document Management

Paralegals help lawyers preparing for trials, hearings and corporate meetings. Depending on the size of organization, a paralegal's duties vary, especially in smaller firms. In addition to reviewing and organizing information, paralegals may prepare written reports that help lawyers determine how to handle their cases. If lawyers decide to file lawsuits on behalf of clients, paralegals may help draft documents and prepare the legal arguments to be filed with the court.

Paralegals support the department's partners, associates and trainees on a wide range of cases. They may be assigned to work on specific cases with specific legal teams or required to assist with a number of ad hoc tasks on a variety of matters. The tasks delegated vary widely exposing each paralegal to a range of experiences thereby allowing them to build a rapport with a cross-section of the firm's employees.

Document management is central to the role which includes document imaging/ scanning and redacting, database entry/coding, database searching, document review and database maintenance/updating, Also, paralegals preparefor court hearings, trial, arbitration, mediations etc. including transporting and setting up files / documents as instructed and arranging for storage of documents and extra equipment as may be required.

Rather than handling a case from beginning to end, paralegals that are employed in larger organizations work mostly on a particular phase of a case. Litigation Paralegals often do not attend trials, but might draft settlement agreements or prepare trial documents.

There is an overwhelming amount of documentation and filing that paralegals are responsible for, and being exceptionally organized will make this a lot easier. Paralegals also need to be detail-oriented and efficient. Because duties can vary greatly based on the size of the firm or the supervising attorneys, a paralegal must also be very adaptable to situations and must either enjoy the organizational aspect of the job, or be willing to dedicate themselves enough to become exceptional at it.

Document Management

Effective file management provides the basis or infrastructure for timely, effective client service and appropriate management of client matters. Organization of client files may include placing contents into sub-files according to class or type of documents. Each client file may contain sub-files for:

- Communications, covering correspondence, memorandums to file or notes of conversations, meetings, or telephone calls arranged chronologically
- Substantive memorandums and investigations
- Original documents
- Retainer letter
- Firm accounts and billing information
- Legal research
- Undertakings to be satisfied
- Others, as appropriate to the file

The main work of Paralegals is to correctly organize the case files. Files which needs to be organized should be labeled consistently throughout the office, both hard and online files. It allows each person in the office from the receptionist through managing partner to pick up a file and know exactly where to look to find a document within the file. The labels you choose will be specific to the area of law that your firm practices such as:

- Attorney notes
- Client information
- Pleadings
- Discovery
- Correspondence
- Billable time and invoices
- Medical records
- Tax returns
- Electronic Files

The labeling system should be carried forward in electronic files. Having a simple protocol that all employees will use to save documents will help to keep track of computer files and avoid items being lost as everyone in the office has a different system of saving files.

Daily Filing

After having a system for document management, paralegals should make filing as a daily priority. The best system is ineffective if paralegals do not place documents in their proper place. Unfiled documents can cause problems in the case and could result in client being harmed due to avoidable mistakes.

Retention and Destruction

Just as it is imperative that paralegals have a system for organizing their files, they must have a system for storing and destroying files. Paralegals should have a uniform, reasonable and consistent policy for archiving and destroying files. The retention system should be consistent and should cover the following issues:

- Specify retention period for specific categories of files.
- Take into consideration deadlines and requirements imposed by applicable law or regulation when setting retention periods.
- Specify place for storing of files (onsite or offsite).
- Include standard procedures for retaining information unique to electronic files.
- Accounting system for moving files from active to retention status.
- Identify staff members who are responsible for managing the retention system and discussing updates to the policy with attorneys as and when needed.
- Detailed plan for organizing, cataloging and storing files so that file can be retrieved expediently when needed.
- Specify the procedure to dispose of the documents within the file when the retention period has ended.

Confidentiality

Lastly, the destruction method a paralegal will select should take into consideration the client confidentiality. Whether the paralegals chooses to shred hard files in-house or use shredding service, he/she must make sure that documents are destroyed in a confidential manner. The key to a successful document management, retention and destruction system is to keep client confidentiality as a top priority. The second priority should be a uniform system that everyone in the office uses for every document that enters the office.

Paralegals should consider storing active client files (including electronic files or client information stored on diskettes), when not in use in a:

- Location separate from where closed files are stored.
- Secure or locked cabinet or location, filed in an orderly fashion for easy retrieval.

Paralegals should store all documentation related to the client matter in the client file.

Law firms may wish to consider implementing training for all professional and office personnel focusing on the importance of client confidentiality and the inherent risks of leaving files or diskettes containing client information on a desk or in an office unattended. Paralegals should consider implementing and employing systems to:

- ❖ Document every meeting, conversation or telephone communication, including telephone messages left and received, by way of dated file notation or memo to file.
- ❖ Organize, identify and trace information, documents, evidence and property relating to each file or client matter.

In cases involving substantial number of documents or exhibits, the paralegal may wish to consider the use of an electronic document management system.

6

Substantive Areas of Law

6.1 Business Law

6.1.1 Introduction

In operating a business, it is necessary to be clear in all legalities concerning your business. Governments make laws, and different countries have different structures as well as laws varying from state to state or city to city. Some have only one level of government; others have two levels (national and state) and yet others may have more levels.

It's important for business owners, managers, and other professionals to have a basic understanding of business law to help them make better decisions. Just as there are laws that apply to people, there is a huge body of law that applies to business. Businesses need these laws for the same reasons that people do: to define unacceptable behavior, to provide certainty and stability, to protect the public, and to provide a mechanism for businesses to resolve disputes.

Business law is also known as commercial law which is a branch of law which deals with the legal rights, duties, and liabilities of parties involved in any kind of business transactions related to commerce, trade, sales and merchandising. It is a branch of civil law and includes public as well as private law. Commercial law or business law deals with legal aspects such as laws of principal and agent, carriage by sea or land, laws of indemnity and guarantee, laws of insurance (marine, fire, life, accident insurance), laws of banking, partnership and much more. Business law is a very broad term by itself and has many divisions and types of law to be studied under it.

Business law deals with the creation of new businesses and the issues that arise as existing businesses interact with the public, other companies, and the government. This area of the law draws on a variety of legal disciplines, including tax law, intellectual property, real estate, sales, employment law, bankruptcy, and others. Business law attorneys specialize in transactional work, meaning they do not represent clients in court. In fact, business lawyers are often hired for the purpose of avoiding future litigation.

To understand the role of business law within the legal system, it helps to view businesses as entities separate from their owners and employees. Just like individuals living together in society, business entities are subject to legal rules designed to give every participant in the marketplace a fair opportunity to succeed.

An enforceable system of business laws also benefits the economy as a whole and provides for more efficient transactions. For example, a supplier who sells goods on credit can be confident that the buyer will hold to the agreed payment terms. As long as the contract is drafted and executed in accordance with the Uniform Commercial Code (UCC) adopted in that jurisdiction, the supplier knows ahead of time that he/she will be able to enforce the contract against the buyer if necessary.

6.1.2 Features of Business Law

- It is the law of commerce or commercial law as it deals with all the aspects of entering into selling and purchasing agreements.
- It includes the study of the law of contract which is important in agreements or contracts that involve two or more parties buying and selling things in exchange for a consideration or purchase price.
- Business law clearly explains the rights, duties, liabilities and legal obligations of the parties involved in a contract of sales, purchase or any other kind of contract or agreement entered into in relation to any kind of business or commercial activity.
- It includes intellectual property law (patents, trademarks, copyrights, etc.) and consumer protection law.
- Business law will also apply to anyone who plans on opening or starting a business of their own.
- Business law also deals with banking law, finance law and other important civil laws.

6.1.3 Types of Business Laws:

Business Structure Laws

There are different laws for different business entities. Be certain you learn about the business laws that govern the kind of business entity that you choose to start. The major types of businesses are C, S and closed corporations, limited liability companies, and sole proprietorships.

Zoning Laws

It is essential to know about zoning laws, as certain zones are restricted in certain areas. It deals with the kind or type of business allowed in certain areas, how the land surrounding a business is used, signboards, advertisements, and parking.

Licensing Laws

In order to operate a business certain licenses are required and there are some important business laws you need to know. If a business operates without these licenses, it is illegal and the business may be dissolved or forced to close.

Trademark and Patent Laws

These are laws that deal with ownership; intellectual property rights, and inventions. They are necessary to protect the business.

Employment Laws

These are laws regarding the hiring and firing of employees, their rights, compensation, safety, work place discrimination, child labor laws, overtime pay structure, disability laws and unemployment laws.

Tax Laws

It deals with filing of tax returns and depends on the kind of business entity and the state the business operates in.. It includes franchise tax, income tax and other state and federal tax requirements of a business. These are very important business laws you need to know before starting a business.

Environmental Laws

The government enforces the environmental laws for the discharge of hazardous waste and the recycling laws pertaining to the business.

Health Department Permits

If your business deals with food products, you must get health department permits to operate your business.

Fire Department Permits and Air and Water Pollution Control Permits

There are laws that certain kinds of business entities must get permits from these departments to operate.

6.1.4 Function of Law in Business

Business laws establish guidelines for what companies can and cannot do, as well as certain things that are mandatory. Law is a broad discipline with several fields that serve important functions in business.

Taxation

Just like individuals, businesses are responsible for paying taxes on income that they earn, and tax law determines how businesses pay taxes to the government. The Internal Revenue Service lets business owners choose from one of several business structures that affect taxation. Common business types include single owner operations called sole proprietorships and multi-owner businesses called partnerships and corporations, which are businesses owned by a group of stock shareholders. Owners of sole proprietorships and partnerships report business earnings on individual income tax returns, while corporations are considered tax entities that are separate from the owners.

Competition

Antitrust law is a field designed to promote business competition by curbing anti-competitive behavior such as price fixing and monopolization. Competition is considered healthy for an economy because it tends to lead to better products and services and fairer prices. The government can potentially prevent companies from merging or force companies to split into different divisions to promote competition.

Intellectual Property

Intellectual property describes creations of the mind, like art, literature, inventions and company logos. Intellectual property law grants legal protection to the creators of various types of intellectual property, which gives creators the right to profit from their work and take legal action against anyone who copies their work without permission. Intellectual property protection allows the businesses to prevent competitors from stealing and using their ideas.

Employment

While many small businesses start out as solo operations, successful business owners often hire employees as a business grows. Employment laws govern how employers and employees interact. They require certain businesses to pay employees a minimum wage and to pay workers at a rate of one and a half times their normal pay for overtime work. The government also sets various workplace safety rules to ensure that businesses provide safe working conditions for their employees.

Environmental Law

Environmental laws establish rules that seek to limit the negative impact businesses can have on the environment. For example, laws force businesses to use certain practices to limit air and water pollution, and the government can penalize companies that don't follow environmental guidelines. Some laws require companies to obtain permits to engage in activities that release pollution into the environment. Environmental law also regulates the use of chemicals and pesticides.

6.1.5 Role of Paralegal in Business Law

A Business Law Paralegal , also known as Corporate Law Paralegal is an advanced legal assistant who specializes in legal matters which arise in a corporate or office setting. To work in the paralegal field, you work as a generalist in different law firms or can select a particular area of law which interests you the most. Business law has become a popular choice because the need for legal services in this specialty area never really declines. If you would like to learn more about what you will do as a specialist and how you can go about specializing, read on and learn exactly what you need to know.

Business can be very complex and filled with different legalities. A law firm that specializes in business law will service various types of small and large business organizations with issues surrounding employment law, contractual agreements, sales, securities, property issues, and commercial compliance. Since this practice area is so broad, you may perform several different tasks each day for the lawyer or the lawyers that you assist each day. Some of the roles which a paralegal play will include:

- ❖ Drafting legal documents and correspondence sent to clients
- ❖ Making filings for Uniform Commercial Code compliance
- ❖ Interviewing clients or interacting with other parties involved in case
- ❖ Complying with Security of State document filing requirements
- ❖ Assistance with mergers, acquisitions and dissolution
- ❖ Filing and maintaining case documents
- ❖ Keeping up with the progress of cases and scheduling court dates

6.2 Contracts

6.2.1 Introduction

Contracts come in all shapes and sizes. You enter into a contract with a broker and seller when you purchase. Businesses enter into contracts with other businesses to set prices and solidify relationships, and if you want reliable work done, you will have a contract with the contractor. Contracts can be verbal, written or combination of both. Some types of contract such as those for buying or selling real estate or finance agreements must be in writing. Written contracts consist of a standard form agreement or letter confirming the agreement. Verbal agreements rely on good faith of all parties and are hard to prove.

Contracts are legally-binding relationships. In most circumstances, a contract involves an agreement to deliver a product or service at a specified time on a specified date. Violating a contract can result in a lawsuit or some kind of settlement. While courts can be involved in this process, these situations can also be settled outside of the judicial system. Laws regarding contracts vary from state to state, so it is always important to know the contract law in your area.

For a contract to be legally binding it must contain:

- ❖ An offer
- ❖ An acceptance

- An intention to create a legal relationship
- Aconsideration (usually money)

However, it may still be considered invalid if it:

- Entices someone to commit a crime, or is illegal.
- Is entered into by someone that lacks capacity, such as a minor or someone who is bankrupt.
- Wasagreedthroughmisleadingordeceptiveconduct,duress,unconscionable conduct or undue influence.

Contract conditions are fundamental to the agreement. If the contract conditions are not met it is possible to terminate the contract and seek compensation or damages. Contract warranties are less important terms and not fundamental to the agreement. A contract cannot be terminated when the warranties are not fulfilled, however, you may be able to seek compensation for any losses incurred.

When negotiating the contract terms make sure the conditions of the contract are clearly defined and agreed to by all parties. Contracts may follow a structure that can include, but are not limited to, the following items:

- Details of parties to contract, including any sub-contracting arrangements
- Duration or period of contract
- Definitions of key terms used within the contract
- Description of goods/services that the business receive/provide, including key deliverables
- Payment details and dates, including whether interest will be applied to late payments
- Key dates and milestones
- Required insurance and indemnity provisions
- Guarantee provisions, including director's guarantees
- Damages or penalty provisions
- Renegotiation or renewal options
- Complaints and dispute resolution process
- Termination conditions
- Special conditions

Written contracts

Written contracts provide more certainty for both parties than verbal contracts. They clearly set out the details of what was agreed. Matters such as materials, timeframes, payments and a procedure to follow in the event of a dispute, can all be set out in a contract. It helps in minimizing risks as it is much safer to have something in writing than to rely on someone's word. It gives more certainty and lowers business risks by making a clear agreement at the outset.

Benefits:

- Provides proof of what was agreed between you and the hirer.
- Help to prevent misunderstandings or disputes by making the agreement clear at the outset.
- Gives you security and peace of mind by knowing you have work, for how long and what you will be paid.
- Clarify your status as an independent contractor by stating that the contract is a 'services contract' and not an 'employment contract'. This will not override a 'sham' contract, but a court will take the statement into account if there is any uncertainty about the nature of the relationship.
- Reduces the risk of a dispute by detailing payments, timeframes and work to be performed under the contract.
- Sets out how a dispute over payments or performance will be resolved.
- Sets out how the contract can be varied.
- Serves as a record of what was agreed.
- Specifies how either party can end the contract before the work is completed.
- Avoids the risks that are associated with not having a written contract.

Drawbacks:

When a contract is not written, in such case, you will expose yourself and business to number of risks which include:

- Risk that you or the hirer misunderstood an important part of the agreement, such as how much was to be paid for the job or what work was to be carried out.
- Risk that you will have a dispute with the hirer over what was agreed because you are both relying on memory.
- Risk that a court won't enforce the contract because you may not be able to prove the existence of the contract or its terms.

Written contract is essential

It is always better to have a contract in writing, no matter how small the job is. Any contract with a hirer that involves a significant risk to your business should always be carefully considered and put in writing. This is advisable even if it means delaying the start of the work. A written contract is essential:

- When the contract price is large enough to make or break your business if you don't get paid.
- Where there are quality requirements, specifications or specific materials that must be used.
- Where there is some doubt whether the hirer has enough money to pay you.
- When you must have certain types of insurance for the type of work you are doing.
- Where the contract contains essential terms, such as a critical date for the completion of work before payment can be made.
- Where you or the hirer need to keep certain information confidential.
- When it is required by your insurance company for professional indemnity purposes.
- Where there is a legal obligation to have a written contract.

Verbal contracts

Many independent contracting arrangements use verbal contracts, which only work well if there are no disputes. A handshake agreement may still be a contract and may be enforced by a court. However, verbal contracts can lead to uncertainty about each party's rights and obligations. A dispute may arise if you have nothing in writing explaining what you both agreed to do.

Partly Verbal and Partly Written contracts

It is seen that certain agreements may be only partly verbal. As there may be supporting paperwork such as quote or list of specifications which forms part of the contract, so it is advisable to write the main points which will be agreed with the hirer so as to avoid relying on memory. File and organize any paperwork associated with the contract. The paperwork can later be used in discussions with the hirer to try to resolve a problem. If the dispute becomes serious, it may be used as evidence in court. The most important thing is that each party clearly understands what work will be done, when it will be completed and how much will be paid for that work.

If the contract is only partly written or terms of work are set out in a number of separate documents, it is for your benefit to make sure that any formal agreement you are being asked to sign will cover certain documents. At least, make sure that the contract does not have a term to the effect that the formal document is the entire agreement.

Standard form contracts

Standard form contract is a pre-prepared contract where many terms are set in advance and little or no negotiation among the parties occurs. Often, these are printed with only a few blank spaces for filling in information such as names, dates and signatures. Such contracts often include a lot of legal fine print and terms which are not easily understood which tend to be one-sided documents that benefit the person who prepared the contract. If you don't understand the fine print or any other part of the contract, you should get advice. If you sign the contract, you will be required to comply with the fine print even if you didn't actually read it and understand it.

6.2.2 Classification of Contracts

Bilateral Contracts

A bilateral contract is distinguishable from a unilateral contract, a promise made by one party in exchange for the performance of some act by the other party. The party who enters into a unilateral contract whose performance is sought is not obligated to act, but if he or she does, the party that made the promise is bound to comply with the terms of the agreement. In a bilateral contract both parties are bound by their exchange of promises.

Both parties to a bilateral contract make promises. With respect to the promise in issue, the party making the promise is the promisor and the other party is the promisee. The legal detriment incurred by the promisee consists of a different promise by him or her to do something or refrain from doing something that he or she was not previously legally obligated to do or to refrain from doing. This legal detriment constitutes consideration, the cause, motive, or benefit that induces one to enter into a contract. Consideration is an essential component of a contract.

Traditionally, courts have distinguished between unilateral and bilateral contracts by determining whether one or both parties provided consideration and at what point they provided the consideration. Bilateral contracts were said to bind both parties the minute the parties exchange promises, as each promise is deemed sufficient consideration in itself. Unilateral contracts are said to bind only the promisor and do not bind the promisee unless the promisee accepts by performing the obligations specified in the promisor's offer. Until the promisee performs, he or she has provided no consideration under the law.

For example, if someone offered to drive you to work on Mondays and Tuesdays in exchange for your promise to return the favor on Wednesdays and Thursdays, a bilateral contract would be formed binding both of you once you provided consideration by accepting those terms. But if that same person offered to pay you $10 each day you drove him to work, a unilateral contract would be formed, binding only upon the promisor until you provided consideration by driving him to work on a particular day.

Modern courts have de-emphasized the distinction between unilateral and bilateral contracts. These courts have found that an offer may be accepted either by a promise to perform or by actual performance. An increasing number of courts have concluded that the traditional distinction between unilateral and bilateral contracts fails to significantly advance legal analysis in a growing number of cases where performance is provided over an extended period of time.

Suppose you promise to pay someone $500.00 to paint your house. The promise sounds like an offer to enter a unilateral contract that binds only you until the promisee accepts by painting your house. But what constitutes lawful "performance" under these circumstances? The act of beginning to paint your house or completely finishing the job to your satisfaction?

Most courts would rule that the act of beginning performance under these circumstances converts a unilateral contract into a bilateral contract, requiring both parties to fulfill the obligations contemplated by the contract. However, other courts would analyze the facts of each case so as not to frustrate the reasonable expectations of the parties. In neither of these cases are the legal rights of the parties ultimately determined by the courts by applying the concepts of unilateral and bilateral contracts.

In still other jurisdictions, courts have simply expressed a preference for interpreting contracts as creating bilateral obligations in all cases where there is no clear evidence that a unilateral contract was intended. The rule has been stated that in case of doubt an offer will be presumed to invite the formation of a bilateral contract by a promise to perform what the offer requests, rather than the formation of a unilateral contract commencing at the time of actual performance. The bottom line across most jurisdictions is that as courts have been confronted by a growing variety of fact patterns involving complicated contract disputes, courts have shifted from rigidly applying the concepts of unilateral and bilateral contracts to a more ad hoc approach.

Mutuality of obligation must exist in an enforceable bilateral contract, and this involves the concept of reciprocity. A cannot enforce B's promise unless A's promise entails a legal detriment, and B can enforce A's promise only if B's promise involves a legal detriment.

If a minor enters a bilateral contract with an adult that is unenforceable due to the minor's age, the adult party cannot assert absence of mutuality as a defense if the minor sues to enforce the contract. This principle applies to any situation where the law grants a particular party a privilege to avoid a contract because of his or her status.

Unilateral Contracts

A unilateral contract is a legally enforceable promise - between legally competent parties - to do or refrain from doing a specified, legal act or acts. In a unilateral contract, one party pays the other party to perform a certain duty. If the duty is fulfilled, the party on the other side of the contract is obligated to transfer the specified funds. Only this party is under obligation of the contract, whereas the acting party is not legally obliged to perform the duty.

A unilateral contract is a legally binding contract in which an offer is accepted by fulfilling or performing the relevant conduct or condition. Unlike bilateral contracts where there is an exchange of mutual promises, only one party in a unilateral contract makes an express promise (the offer) and is obligated to perform the promise.

A common example occurs when "Person A" places an advertisement that states that if someone finds their lost dog and returns it to them, then "Person A" will pay that party $100. Only "Person A" has made an express promise. If "Person B" finds and returns their lost dog, then "Person B" has fulfilled the condition posed by "Person A", thereby accepting the offer. A unilateral contract is thus formed.

Unilateral Contracts for Small Businesses:

Consumers or parties are sometimes hesitant to enter into an obligation with small businesses. However, due to the one-sided nature of the obligation, unilateral contracts have a variety of uses that can be used to assist your business.

Firstly, unilateral contracts can be used to establish loyalty of consumers through a reward system. Take Boost for example. If you get 10 points on your Boost card, Boost promises that your next Boost would be free. This common marketing technique utilizes the reward system to incentivize consumers to remain with your business or product thereby assisting in your own business' growth.

Secondly, unilateral contracts can be utilized to promote awareness for your business. A prime example today is the Killa Burger Challenge. The promise from Killa Burger Grill was that if you eat a Killa Burger (30cm wide), Wicked Chips, Killa Drink (1.25L) and a Killa Soft Serve alone in 60 minutes, you will receive some 'Killa' prizes and your name on the 'Wall of Fame'.

This promotional challenge and campaign is also a unilateral contract, with Killa Burger Grill promising the prizes to all those who complete the challenge. The awareness of Killa Burger rose exponentially as a result of this contest and it still remains as one of the most daring food challenges in Australia.

Contractual Terms

Statements made during the course of negotiations could amount to a contractual term or a representation. It is important to know whether a particular statement is a contractual term or if it is a representation as this will determine the appropriate cause of action and remedy available. If the statement amounts to a term of the contract which is not fulfilled, the innocent party may sue for breach of contract. If the statement is merely a representation which turns out to be untrue, the innocent party may bring an action for misrepresentation. In deciding whether a statement amounts to a term or representation the courts look at four factors:

- The parole evidence rule: Where the contract has been put into writing only, the terms included in the written document are terms, any verbal statements will be representations.
- Relative expertise of the parties: If the representor has greater knowledge, it is more likely to be a contractual term. Conversely if representee has more knowledge it is more likely to be a representation.
- Importance of the statement: Where the representee indicates to the representor the importance of the statement.
- Time: The longer the time lapse between making the statement and entering the contract, the more likely it will be a representation.

It is very important to understand what your obligations and commitments are as a business owner. Some of the contractual terms used in business and law are:

Acceptance - unconditional agreement to an offer. The agreement creates the contract as solid and binding on both sides. Prior to signing, any party is free to withdraw. Any conditions have the effect of a counter offer and must be accepted by the other party before being valid.

Agent - A person appointed to act on behalf of another - known as the principal. How much authority the agent has is subject to agreement between both parties. If not told otherwise third parties can assume the agent has been given full powers to deal.

Arbitration - an independent third party used to settle disputes out of court. The arbitrator must be agreed upon by both sides. Contracts can have clauses nominating arbitrators in advance in case the need arises.

Breach of Contract - failure by one party to a contract to meet all of the contract agreements. A breach makes the whole contract void and can lead to damages being awarded to the injured party.

Collective Agreement - term for agreements made between employees and employers, usually involves trade unions. These are often covered by more than one organization and can be seen as contracts but are not governed by contract law. Employment law covers these.

Comfort Letters - these have no contractual standing and are used to back up an agreement. Often issued by a parent or associate company to say they will support the smaller company to improve its trading position. They do state they are not intended to be legally binding, and are also known as letters of comfort.

Company Seal - an embossing press indicating the official signature of a company when accompanied by the signatures of two officers of the company. Since 1989 companies have been allowed to indicate agreement without using the company seal. Instead the required 2 signatures accompanying a formal declaration. However, a lot of companies still prefer to use a seal. The articles of a company can require a seal to be used and override the law if they wish.

Conditions - these are the major terms in a contract. A condition is the basis of any contract. If one fails or is breached the whole contract is breached. These are in contrast to warranties which are less important and don't usually lead to breach of contract, but rather a price adjustment or damages paid.

Confidentiality Agreement - Made to protect confidential information if it has to be disclosed to another party. This can happen during negotiations for a larger contract, if either party needs to divulge more information concerning their operations to each other. When this happens the confidentiality agreement forms a binding contract that information will not get passed on to any other party, even if the said contact is never signed. Can be known as a non-disclosure agreement.

Consideration - In a contract each side benefits in some way, they give each other some consideration. Also known as quid pro quo - see Latin contract terms page in this guide. This would usually be a price paid by one in exchange for goods supplied by the other. But anything of value to the other party can be used. The arrangement can also be negative e.g. a promise not to exercise a right of access over another person's land in return for payment. This would be a valid contract even if the person never had an intention of using the right.

Consumer - Anyone who buys goods and/or services but not as a part of their business. Companies can be consumers for contracts unrelated to its business - especially for the goods and services purchased for employees. Charities are also considered to be consumers.

Due Diligence - refers to the formal process of investigating the background of a business. This might happen prior to buying it or as another major party in a contract. Due Diligence is exercised to ensure that there are no hidden details that might affect the deal.

Employment Contract - The contract between the employer and employee. It differs from other contracts because it is governed by employment legislation and this takes precedence over normal contract law.

Exclusion Clauses - These clauses are designed to exclude one party from any liability should certain circumstances happen. There are types of exemption clauses and courts interpret them strictly, and where ever possible, in favor of the party that did not write them. In the case of customer dealings, regulations govern to make the majority of exclusion clauses useless. But the regulations do not cover the business dealings.

Exemption Clauses - these clauses are designed to try and restrict the liability of the party writing them. These can then be divided to become exclusion clauses which try to exclude liability completely for a specified outcome and limitation clauses, which try to set a maximum amount of damages to pay if some part of the contract fails. Exemption clauses are strictly regulated in consumer dealings but don't apply to those who deal in the course of their business.

Express Terms - The terms that are actually stated in the contract. It can be written or verbal and agreed before, or when, the contract is made.

Franchising - Commercial agreements allowing one business to deal in a product or service governed by another. For example, car manufacturers give a franchise to a local garage to sell their cars under the car manufacturers brand.

Going Concern – is an accounting idea that a business should be valued on the basis of continuing trade and able to use assets for the intended purpose. The break-up basis is the alternative which sets values according to what the asset could be sold for immediately. Usually much less than value if kept in use.

Implied Terms - some terms and clauses are implied in a contract by law or custom and practiced without being mentioned by any party. An example of this is in a contract to supply services there is an implied term that the services will be carried out with reasonable care and skill. Implied terms by custom and practice can always be overridden by express terms. Some implied terms can't be overridden, particularly those relating to consumers. See exemption clauses.

Incorporate - To include in, or adopt, some term or condition as part of the contract. Different from the company law definition where it refers to the legal act of creating a company.

Injunction - when a court stops a certain action from taking place. It can be used to stop another party moving to do something against the contract. Injunctions are entirely the court's decision, and the judge can refuse to issue an injunction opting to pay damages instead.

Joint and Several Liability - Where parties act together in a contract as partners and are considered to have joint and several liability. Having joint responsibility as partners, each individual is also liable for the entire contract, which means a creditor could seek to regain a whole debt from any one of the partners. That person would then need to recover the rest of the shares from other partners.

Joint Venture - An agreement between two or more independent businesses in an enterprise. Both will share costs, management, profits, or benefits arising from the venture. Exact shares and responsibilities are set out in the joint venture agreement.

Jurisdiction - This refers to the country or state that will govern the contract and where any legal action must take place. England and Scotland have different legal codes and this may need to be specified.

Liability - a business or person deemed liable is subject to a legal obligation. A business or person who commits wrongdoing or breaks a contract/trust is said to be liable (responsible) for it.

Limited Liability - In limited companies, an owner's liabilities is dependent upon the value of the shares they own. It may also apply to contracts where a valid limitation clause is included in the terms.

Liquidation - refers to the formal breaking up of a company or partnership by realizing the assets (selling or transferring to pay a debt), usually when a business is insolvent, but a solvent one can be liquidated if it no longer wishes to trade. See receivership--and the page in this guide on finance contract terms.

Misrepresentation - Where one party to a contract makes a false statement which another party relies on. The party who has been misled can seek damages for their loss. The remedy of rescission - or putting things back in the same way they were before the contact began - may be available. If this is not possible, or is too difficult, the court can award damages instead.

Non-Executive Director - Does not work directly for the company, but advises the directors of the company. Non-executive directors have the same full powers and authority of company directors and can bind the company to any contract.

Offer - an offer to contract must be made with the intention to create a legal relationship. It needs to be capable of being accepted with no impossible conditions and must be a complete offer. Meaning it does not require more information to define the offer, nor is it merely advertising.

Parent Company - if one company owns more than 50% of the voting rights of another company it is the parent company. This can occur if the parent has less than 50% but controls the board of directors of the subsidiary company. This would give the parent company the power to appoint and remove directors without referring to other shareholders.

Partnership - Where two or more people, or organizations, band together and carry on a business as a company.

Proxy - Someone acting on behalf of another person for a specific purpose. Or it can be the term referring to the form drawn up to allow the process to take place. A company shareholder can appoint a proxy (stand-in) to attend meetings and vote on their behalf for example.

Quorum - The minimum amount of people needed to run a meeting and make decisions.

Ratification - to give authority to an act already performed. A company general meeting can discuss and ratify an action taken place by a director. A principal can choose to ratify the act of an agent who may not have had the special power to perform the act or make the decision, but needed to do so under the circumstances.

Registered Office - Official company address as stated to on the Companies House Register. Documents delivered to this address are classified as having been legally served to the company.

Repudiation - Has two meanings under contract law. Firstly, this is where a party refuses to comply with a contract. This then leads to a contract breach. Secondly, where a contract is made by a minor (under 18), who then repudiates it at, or soon after, turning 18. This repudiation voids the contract rather than a breach being caused.

Restrictive Covenant - often included in long-term contracts and contracts of employment. It stops the parties from working with competitors during an agreed period, and sometime thereafter. Unless carefully written the courts can see them as being a restriction of trade and not enforce them.

Service Contract - Directors and officers or a company usually sign different service contracts than employees. As they are not always classed as employees and the effect of employment law is different.

Shareholder's Agreement - Agreement between all shareholders stating how the company should run and how rights will be applied. This is a contract between the shareholders and the actual company is not bound by it as the company is not a party to it.

Subject to Contract - These words on the documents are exchanged by parties during negotiation denote the document is not an offer or acceptance. The negotiations are ongoing. Often the expression without prejudice is used when subject to contract is meant.

Trademark - registered name or logo protected by law. These must be granted through the patent office.

Underwriter - A person who signs as party to a contract. Now usually only applied in insurance contracts where the underwriters take all or part of the risk in return for a premium paid. Underwriters at Lloyd's of London are well known.

Unfair Terms - If terms are made unfair by legislation they will not be enforced by the courts. They could be interpreted against the person who included them into the contract. Legislation mainly protects consumers, but also applies in a business-to-business if one party is significantly more powerful than the other.

Void - A contract that cannot be performed or completed at all is void. A void contract is void from the beginning - see ab initio in the Latin contract terms in this page guide - and the normal remedy.

Warranties - Promises made in a contract which are less than a condition. The failure of a warranty results in a liability to pay damages--see page in this guide on finance contract terms. It will not result in a breach of contract like a failure of a condition would.

Without Prejudice – A term used by solicitors in dispute negotiations where an offer is made in an attempt to avoid court proceedings. If the case continues to court, none of the facts stated to be without prejudice can be used as evidence. Often misused by businesses during negotiation, when they actually mean subject to contract.

Negotiable Instruments

Negotiable instruments are document of title or evidence of indebtedness that is freely transferable in trading as substitute for money. These are unconditional orders or promise to pay, and include checks, drafts, bearer bonds, some certificates of deposit, promissory notes, and bank notes.

Principal Attributes

- An asset or property passes from the transferor to the transferee by mere delivery and/or endorsement of the instrument.
- A transferee accepting the instrument in good faith and for value obtains an indefeasible title and may sue on the instrument in his or her name.
- No notice of the transfer needs to be given to the party liable in the instrument.

Characteristics

- Writing and Signed by itsMaker
- Unconditional
- Fixed Sum of Money
- Transferable
- Absolute and Good Title
- Right to Recovery

Presumptions

- Consideration
- Date
- Time of Acceptance

- Time of Transfer
- Order of Endorsements
- Stamp
- Holder in Due Course

Kinds

- Promissory note
- Bill of exchange
- Cheque

Promissory Note

- An unconditional promise in writing made by one person (maker) to another person(payee)
- Signed by the maker
- Stamped
- Promise to pay
- On demand or at a fixed or determinable future time
- A sum certain in money
- Pay in terms of legal tender money only
- To, or to the order of, a specified person or to the bearer
- The parties i.e. the maker and the payee must be certain

Bill of Exchange

- An order in writing directing a person to pay a sum of money to a specified person
- Duly signed by its drawer
- Accepted by its drawee
- Properly stamped
- Express order to pay
- Definite sum of money
- Definite and unconditional order
- Parties to a bill must be certain

Cheque

- A bill of exchange drawn on a specified banker, and not expressed to be payable otherwise than on demand
- Includes the electronic image of a truncated cheque
- Includes a cheque in electronic form

- issued on a specified banker only
- The amount specified is always certain, and must be clearly mentioned
- The payee is always certain.
- Must bear a date
- Types -Open cheque, Crossed cheque, Bearer cheque, Order cheque

6.3 Property Law

6.3.1 Types of Properties

There are two types of property:

- Real property
- Personal Property

Most of the legal concepts and rules associated with both types of property are derived from English Common Law. Modern law has incorporated many of these concepts and rules into statutes, which define the types and rights of ownership in real and personal property.

Personal property referred to as movable property, is anything other than land that can be the subject of ownership, including stocks, money, notes, patents, and copyrights, as well as intangible property. Real property is land and ordinarily anything erected on, growing on, or affixed to it, including buildings and crops. The term is also used to declare any rights that issue from the ownership of land. The terms real estate and real property generally refer to land. The term land, in its general usage, includes not only the face of the earth but everything of a permanent nature over or under it, including minerals, oil, and gases. Residential buildings and yards are commonly referred to as premises.

Property is further classified as:

- Private
- Public

Private property is that which belongs to one or more persons while public property is owned by a country, state or political subdivision.

Personal Property

Personal property can be divided as:

- Tangible
- Intangible

Tangible property includes such items as animals, merchandise, and jewelry while intangible property includes such rights as stock, bonds, patents, and copyrights.

To have possession, an individual must have a degree of actual control over the object, coupled with an intent to possess the object and exclude others from possessing it. The law recognizes two types of possession: actual and constructive. Actual possession exists when an individual knowingly has direct physical control over an object at a given time. Constructive possession is the power and intent of an individual to control a particular item, even though it is not physically in that person's control.

In accession, the personal property of one owner is physically integrated with the property of another so that it becomes a constituent part of it, losing any separate identity. Accession can make the personal property of one owner become substantially more valuable chattel as a result of the work of another person. This occurs when the personal property becomes an entirely new chattel, such as when grapes are made into wine or timber is made into furniture.

The Law

Property law is the law that in the common law legal system governs the various forms of ownership in real property and in personal property. Property is anything that is owned by a person or entity. Property is divided into two types: "real property," which is any interest in land, real estate, growing plants or the improvements on it, and "personal property", which is everything else.

Property Rights and Rights to People

Property rights are rights over things enforceable against all other persons. By contrast, contractual rights are rights enforceable against particular persons. Property rights arise from a contract; the two systems of rights overlap. In relation to the sale of land, for example, two sets of legal relationships exist alongside one another: the contractual right to sue for damages, and the property right exercisable over the land. More minor property rights may be created by contract, as in the case of easements, covenants, and equitable servitudes.

A separate distinction is evident where the rights granted are insufficiently substantial to confer on the non-owner a definable interest or right in the thing. The clearest example of these rights is the license. In general, even if licenses are created by a binding contract, they do not give rise to property interests.

Property Rights and Personal Rights

Property rights are also distinguished from personal rights. Practically all contemporary societies acknowledge this basic ontological and ethical distinction. In the past, groups lacking political power have often been disqualified from the benefits of property. In an extreme form, this has meant that people have become "objects" of property which is legally a "thing" or chattel. These include Jews in England and married women in Western societies until the late 19th century.

The dividing line between personal rights and property rights is not always easy to draw. For instance, is one's reputation property that can be commercially exploited by affording property rights to it? The question of the proprietary character of personal rights is particularly relevant in the case of rights over human tissue, organs and other body parts.

Classification

Property law is characterized by a great deal of historical continuity and technical terminology. The basic distinction in common law systems is between real property (land) and personal property.

Before mid of 19th century, principles governing the transfer of real property and personal property on an intestacy were quite different. Though this dichotomy does not have the same significance anymore, the distinction is still fundamental because of the essential differences between the two categories. As seen, the fact that land is immovable, and thus the rules that govern its use must differ and the distinction is that legislation is often drafted employing the traditional terminology.

The division of land and chattels has been criticized as being not satisfactory as a basis for categorizing the principles of property law since it concentrates attention not on the proprietary interests themselves but on the objects of those interests. Also, in case of fixtures, chattels which are affixed to or placed on land may become part of the land. Real property is generally sub-classified into:

- Corporeal Hereditaments – tangible real property
- Incorporeal Hereditaments – intangible real property such as an easement of way

Possession

The concept of possession developed from a legal system whose principal concern was to avoid civil disorder. The general principle is that a person in possession of land or goods, even as a wrongdoer, is entitled to take action against anyone interfering with the possession unless the person interfering is able to demonstrate a superior right to do so. In England, Torts Act has significantly amended the law relating to wrongful interference with goods and abolished some longstanding remedies and doctrines.

Transfer of property

The most usual way of acquiring an interest in property is as the result of a consensual transaction with the previous owner, for example, a sale or a gift. Dispositions by will may also be regarded as consensual transactions, since the effect of a will is to provide for the distribution of the deceased person's property to nominated beneficiaries. A person may also obtain an interest in property under a trust established for his or her benefit by the owner of the property.

It is also possible for property to pass from one person to another independant of the consent of the property owner. For example, this occurs when a person dies intestate, goes bankrupt, or has the property taken in execution of a court judgment.

Priority

Different parties may claim an interest in property by mistake or fraud, with the claims being inconsistent of each other. For example, the party creating or transferring an interest may have a valid title, but intentionally or negligently creates several interests wholly or partially inconsistent with each other. A court resolves the dispute by adjudicating the priorities of the interests. According to the Indian property law, it defines the 'Transfer of property' means an act by which a living person conveys property, in present or in future, to one or more other living persons, or to himself and one or more other living persons; and "to transfer property" is to perform such act.

6.4 Family Law

Family law relates to family disputes and obligations that have grown dramatically since 1970s, as legislators and judges have reexamined and redefined legal relationships surrounding related to:

- Divorce,
- Child Custody
- Child Support

Family law has become tangled with national debates over the structure of the family, gender bias, and morality. It consists of body of statutes and case precedents that governs the legal responsibilities among individuals who share domestic connection. Such cases involve parties who are related by blood or marriage, whereas family law affects those in more distant or casual relationships.

Reasons of Family Law Cases

Divorce

In the beginning of 1960s, advocates of divorce reform called for legal recognition of no-fault divorce. With this, a divorce is granted based on the grounds related to incompatibility, irreconcilable differences, or irretrievable breakdown of marriage relationship. The court examines the condition of the marriage instead of questioning about either party faults. Such proceeding eliminates the need for one party to accuse the other on traditional ground for divorce, such as adultery, cruelty, alcoholism or drug addiction.

Child Custody

During marriage, all custodial rights are exercised by both parents which include decision making power over every aspects of upbringing, religion and education till parental decisions and conduct stay clear about neglect, abuse and dependency laws. On divorce, such power traditionally went out solely to one parent who obtained custody. In such case, the Visitation Rights given to noncustodial parent constituted little more than a possessory interest. This made the custody decision upon divorce a significant one: the relationship between the noncustodial parent and her or his children would change, as the parent would lose the ability to shape decisions affecting the children.

Child Support

In many cases, divorce decree needs the noncustodial parent normally the father, to pay child support. The failure of the parent to pay child support has important consequences. Lack of support may force the custodial parent to apply for welfare, which in turn affects government budgets and ultimately taxes. This problem has resulted in increasingly more aggressive collection efforts by the government.

Palimony

It is a substitute for alimony where the couple were not married but lived together for long period and then terminate their relationship. The main issue is whether there was an agreement that one partner would support the other in return for the second making a home and performing other domestic duties beyond sexual pleasures. Written palimony contracts are rare, but the courts have found implied contracts, in such case where a woman has given up her career, has managed the household, or assisted in man's business for longer period of time.

Same-Sex Marriage

Despite court challenges, marriage takes place only between persons of opposite sex. As gay and lesbian partners have been unable to persuade states to recognize their unions as marriage in the traditional sense, so an increasing number of states have passed laws which allows unmarried couples, including homosexual and heterosexual couples to register for partners.

Artificial Conception and Surrogate Motherhood

Modern technology has created opportunities for conceiving children through Artificial Insemination, In Vitro Fertilization, and Embryo Transplantation. Combined with these techniques is the practice of Surrogate Motherhood. These new techniques have also created legal questions and disputes new to family law.

In Vitro Fertilization and Ovum Transplantation

The technique of in vitro fertilization gained international attention with the birth of Louise Brown in England in 1978. This technique involves the fertilization of the ovum outside the womb. Where the ovum is donated by another woman, the birth mother will be treated in law as the legitimate mother of the child.

Surrogate Motherhood

In surrogate motherhood, a woman agrees to be artificially inseminated or to have a fertilized ovum inserted into her uterus, and to carry the child to term for another party. When women do this to assist members of their own family, few legal complications arise.

Areas

Before, during, and after a marriage, state law may affect families. Family law encompasses the following areas:

- Adoptions
- Alimony/Spousal Support
- Annulment
- Business Valuation
- Child Custody
- Child Visitation/Parenting Plans
- Child Support
- Contempt and Enforcement
- Division of Property
- Divorce
- Divorce Mediation
- Domestic Partners & Unmarried Couples
- Domestic Violence
- Grandparent Custody and Visitation
- Guardianships
- International Family Law
- Modification of Final Judgment
- Name Changes
- Out-of-State/Conflict of Law Issues
- Prenuptial Agreements/Postnuptial Agreements
- Paternity

- Relocation
- Restraining Orders
- Same-Sex Marriage
- Step Parent Adoption

6.5 Business and Commercial Law

Business law and commercial law are two areas of legal practice that have so many overlapping issues that most attorneys who practice one will also have expertise in the other. Commercial law focuses on the sale and distribution of goods, as well as financing of certain transactions. Business law focuses on the other aspects of business, including forming a company, mergers and acquisitions, shareholder rights, and property issues such as leasing office or warehouse space. A business that sells products will almost certainly need a lawyer with experience in both of these fields.

Business Law

Business law is regulated by both state and federal law. The federal government primarily governs stocks and investments, workplace safety and employment laws, and environmental protections. States, however, can add to these federal laws and pass their own laws in other areas, such as imposing licensing requirements for certain professions and establishing rules for forming and running a legal business.

Business law falls in two distinctive areas:

- Regulation of commercial entities by laws of company, partnership, agency and bankruptcy.
- Regulation of commercial transactions by laws of contract and related fields.

Business law touches everyday lives by every contractual dealing undertaken. A contract in the form of commercial bargain involves certain form of exchange of goods or services for a price which is a legal binding agreement made by two or more persons, enforceable by the courts. As such they may be written or oral, and to be binding the following must exist: an offer and unqualified acceptance thereof, intention to create legal relations, valuable consideration, and genuine consent. The terms must be legal, certain, and possible of performance.

Contractual relations, as base of all commercial transactions resulted in development of specific bodies of law in scope of business law regulating which include:

- Sale of goods on implied terms and conditions with effects of performance and breach of such contracts and remedies available to parties.
- Carriage of goods as national and international rules governing insurance, bills of lading, charter parties, and arbitrations.

- Consumer credit agreements;
- Labour relations determining contractual rights and obligations among employers and employees and regulation of trade unions.

Commercial Law

Commercial law is mainly regulated by Uniform Commercial Code, which is a model set of laws regarding the sales of goods, leases of good, negotiable instruments, and secured transactions. All states have adopted some form of the UCC, though each state is free to make its own modifications to the laws as it sees fit.

Commercial law is also known as corporate law or mercantile law. Mercantile law talks to the idea of merchants and traders because commercial law talks specifically to those who are dealing in a business of exchanges and transactions, whether that's for products or services. Anytime there's a sale or purchase of goods or services, commercial law would be considered an important feature along with contract law.

Commercial law must be particularly flexible and some rule can be manipulated in order to facilitate trades. Pragmatism is the key word for the interpretation of the decisions of commercial judges. But it's not just about the courts: a legislative reform of commercial law is usually preceded by a representation of the commercial community. Again, the needs of the community come first and the primary scope of the commercial law is adapting the rules to serve these requirements.

7

Knowledge about Litigation

7.1 Introduction to Civil Litigation Procedures

The litigation process comprises of:

- Determining Jurisdiction
- Statement of Claim
- Statement of Defense and Counterclaim
- Reply and Defense to Counterclaim
- Discovery Plan
- Affidavit of Documents (Documentary Discovery)
- Examinations for Discovery
- Answering Undertakings and Motions to Compel Answers
- Motions
- Mandatory Mediation
- Set the Matter Down for Trial and Pretrial Conference
- Trial

Determining Jurisdiction

The initial step in litigation process is to decide which court the action should be started in. Based on the person's claim, the action will be started as per court.

Statement of Claim

To start the litigation process, the person who has been harmed (the "Plaintiff") prepares a statement of claim. The statement of claim describes the facts and the legal reasons that the Plaintiff says he or she is entitled to compensation from the other person (the "Defendant"). The Plaintiff and the Defendant are called "parties".

It is very important to issue the statement of claim before the applicable limitation period expires. For most lawsuits, the claim must be issued within two years of the Plaintiff learning about the harm caused by the Defendant. However, there are different limitation periods for certain types of claims. In such case, the paralegal or lawyer will be in the best position to tell you when the limitation period expires after discussion about the facts.

If it is not possible to issue a statement of claim within the limitation period, the Plaintiff can issue a Notice of Action within the applicable limitation period. The Plaintiff then has an additional period of time within which he/she can file a Statement of Claim.

The statement of claim is filed with the court and the Plaintiff must then arrange to serve it on the Defendant personally.

Litigation lawyers are trained to draft Statements of Claim that best position your case, and are also able to navigate the complex court filing system quickly to ensure your claim is filed properly and on time.

Statement of Defense and Counterclaim

If the Defendant has been served in Ontario, he or she must serve the Plaintiff with a Statement of Defense within a brief window of time. Defendants served in another province or in the United States or in another country have slightly more time to serve their Statement of Defense. The Statement of Defense sets out the reasons that the Defendant says he or she should not have to compensate the Plaintiff. If the Defendant has a claim against the Plaintiff (a "counterclaim"), it is included in the same document as the Statement of Defense.

If the Defendant cannot serve the Statement of Defense within the specified time, he or she can give the Plaintiff a Notice of Intent to Defend. This Notice gives the Defendant additional time to deliver a Statement of Defense.

If the Defendant does not file a Statement of Defense within the required time, the Plaintiff can ask the court to note the Defendant in default and then obtain default judgment against the Defendant. Litigation counsel is trained to identify the appropriate legal defense to defend against the Statement of Claim.

Reply and Defense to Counterclaim

After the Plaintiff receives the Statement of Defense, he/she has chance to file a reply to allegations made in Statement of Defense. If Defendant included a counterclaim, the Plaintiff must serve the Defendant with a Defense to Counterclaim or else the Defendant can note the Plaintiff in default and then obtain default judgment against the Plaintiff for the damages described in the Counterclaim.

Discovery Plan

In this, the parties must agree to a written discovery plan within 60 days of delivery of Reply and Defense to Counterclaim, if any. The discovery plan sets out the scope of documentary discovery, names of people who will be produced for examination for discovery and timelines for completing oral and documentary discovery. The party conducting the examination must serve a notice of examination on any person being examined at least two days before the examination is to take place. This is the paralegal or lawyer's job to work with other party's lawyer to create this discovery plan.

Affidavit of Documents

The Plaintiff and Defendant must serve an affidavit of documents to the other party within the timetable established in the discovery plan. An affidavit of documents lists all documents that are in party's possession and are relevant to any matter in issue in litigation. For actions started under the simplified procedure rules, the parties must also include a list of the names of people who have knowledge of the matters described in the statement of claim or Statement of Defense.

The obligation to disclose relevant documents is ongoing throughout the litigation process. If, after preparing an Affidavit of Documents, a party comes into possession of a document that is relevant to a matter in issue in the lawsuit or otherwise discovers that the previous Affidavit of Documents is inaccurate or incomplete, the party must prepare a Supplementary Affidavit of Documents.

The importance of including all relevant documents in an Affidavit of Documents cannot be overemphasized. If a document is not listed in the Affidavit, the party may be prevented from using the document at trial. Should a party fail to include in an Affidavit a document unfavourable to his case, the court may severely penalize that party by ordering costs against that party, or even by dismissing the case.

Examinations for Discovery

The examination for discovery involves paralegal or lawyers for each party asking the other party questions related to issues in litigation. The examination takes place before an examiner who transcribes the testimony and each party takes an oath to tell the truth.

The lawyer who conducted the examination will request a transcript of the examination which can be used at trial to challenge the evidence of other party and for other purposes. Admissions made by a party can be evidence against that party.

If the lawyer for a party being examined thinks that a question is inappropriate, the lawyer will refuse to permit the client to answer the question and the examination will likely proceed without the party having to answer the question at that time. If the lawyer who conducted the examination thinks that the question is proper and wants an answer to it, the lawyer can bring a motion to the court and the court can order the party to answer the question that was asked.

Prior to an examination for discovery, your lawyer will explain the process to you and help you understand what is expected of you. Your lawyer will also explain what his or her role is at the examination.

Answering Undertakings and Motions to Compel Answers

At the time of discovery, sometimes the person being examined does not have the information needed to answer a question right away or does not have a document that is requested. If that is the case, the person being examined can agree to provide the answer to the question, or the relevant document, after the examination is completed.

If the person being examined does not provide the answer to the undertaking within a reasonable period of time, the lawyer for the other party can bring a motion to a judge asking for an order requiring the other party to provide the necessary information. If such an Order is made, the party who failed to provide the information in a reasonable time can be ordered to pay the costs to the other side for having to bring a motion to compel an answer to the undertaking. The lawyer will advise you as to whether or not a requested undertaking is reasonable and, if it is, will also ensure that undertakings are fulfilled properly.

Motions

Throughout the civil litigation process, either party may bring a motion to obtain a ruling from a judge on procedural or interim issues. For example, a party may bring a motion to exclude certain evidence from being used, or a motion to delete certain parts of the other party's pleadings.

The lawyer or paralegal will know which motions to bring and when to bring them. It is your lawyer's responsibility to use motions to find solutions to issues that may arise during the litigation process.

Mandatory Mediation

For all actions, parties are required to participate in the mediation session within 120 days of the first Statement of Defense being served. The parties can, however, consent to extend this time limit. Sometimes the parties will choose to postpone mediation in order to first carry out examinations for discovery.

Before the mediation session takes place, each party files a mediation brief with the mediator and gives a copy to the other party. The mediation brief identifies the factual and legal issues that are in dispute, sets out the party's position on each issue, and includes copies of the most important documents in the case.

At the mediation session, the parties meet with a neutral mediator who tries to help them resolve the issues in the case. The mediator cannot force the parties to accept a settlement and the mediator does not have the power to impose a decision on the parties. Discussions at the mediation session are confidential, as are any settlement offers that are made during mediation. If the parties do not reach a settlement, offers made by a party cannot be referred to during the rest of the litigation process until after a judgment is reached.

If mediation does not resolve the matters, the parties may request, or the court may order, a settlement conference. In such case lawyer or paralegal will explain how the mediation proceedings will be conducted and ensure you are comfortable knowing how the mediation works. There are rules relating to mediation that your lawyer will explain to you.

Setting Matter Down for Trial and Pretrial Conference

After the above steps are completed, a party can set the matter down for trial by asking that it be placed on the trial list. Within 90 days after the action is set down for trial, the court will give the parties notice that they must attend at a pre-trial conference. Just before the pre-trial conference, each party must file a brief containing many different items required by the judge presiding over the pre-trial conference.

The lawyers and the clients must attend the pre-trial conference. At the conference, the lawyers discuss their clients' positions and the judge who is presiding over the conference tries to help them reach a settlement. The judge may tell the parties how he or she would decide the case if he or she was trying the case. The judge's opinion on the case is not binding and the judge conducting the pre-trial conference cannot hear the actual trial if the parties decide to continue.

The judge presiding over the pre-trial conference can establish a timetable and fix a date for the trial and, if a date is set, will complete a pre-trial conference report. Although the pre-trial conference judge cannot order the parties to settle, the parties should give serious consideration to the judge's opinion on the merits of the case.

The parties should also be mindful of the costs consequences rule that applies to settlement offers. It may be advantageous to make a reasonable offer to settle. Your lawyer should explain the details of how cost allocation works when offers to settle are made.

Trial

The parties can decide to proceed with a trial if a settlement is not reached. Often, the parties will decide to settle the action before it goes to trial because the legal fees involved are quite high and there is always a risk that the party could lose at trial. Also, with the costs consequences of settlement offers, parties may be concerned that they may be liable for paying the other party's costs if they lose.

During a trial, both parties present their evidence by calling witnesses. Depending on the issues in the litigation, expert evidence may also be required. At the end of the trial, the judge will make a decision that is binding on the parties. If a party is not satisfied with the judge's decision, an appeal may be started in some circumstances.

For actions started under the simplified procedure rules, a party may request a summary trial. Summary trials have strict time limitations on presentation of evidence. The parties present their evidence by affidavit and then the person who signed the affidavit may be cross-examined by the other party's lawyer for a specified period of time. In a summary trial, a party's oral argument is restricted as well. At the end of the summary trial, the judge issues his or her decision.

7.2 Steps of litigation file

The legal papers that are filed in court at the beginning of a lawsuit are called "pleadings." Your attorney will explain pleadings to you in the particular context of your case, but the summary that follows will give you a head start in understanding some of the many documents that may become a part of your lawsuit. Filing the initial court papers is just the beginning.

Complaint/Petition

Usually the first document filed in a lawsuit is the complaint (or petition), which provides an outline of the plaintiff's case against the defendant. The complaint is a document that identifies the parties involved, sets out the legal basis for the court's jurisdiction over the controversy, states the plaintiff's legal claims, and relates the facts giving rise to the claims. The complaint will also contain a section called a demand for judgment or prayer for relief. Here the plaintiff will set forth what he or she wants the court to require the defendant to do, such as pay damages.

The purpose of the complaint is to provide the defendant with notice of the factual and legal bases of the plaintiff's claims. Generally, the facts set forth in the complaint are based on the plaintiff's own knowledge. Sometimes the plaintiff will use the phrase, "upon information and belief" before setting forth some facts. This means that the plaintiff has heard about those facts from someone else, or has formed the belief that the events described in the paragraph happened as described. Most states require that the complaint set forth a short and plain statement of the plaintiff's claims, so don't be surprised if the facts are sketchy, or if they don't seem to tell the whole story.

Summons and Service of Process

The summons is an order from the court where the lawsuit will be heard or "litigated." It notifies the recipient that he/she has been sued, refers to the complaint or petition, and sets out the time limit within which the defendant must file an answer or seek to have the case dismissed. It will also describe the consequences of failing to respond in a timely manner: the case may be decided without the defendant and he or she may be bound by the result even if he/she did not participate. Failing to respond to a lawsuit on time will cause a defendant to be "in default."

The summons is usually a form document. It will have a preprinted caption that contains the name of the court, the names of the parties and a docket number. The body of the document will tell the defendant that he or she has been sued. This language is called the "notice."

The summons will be delivered or "served" on the defendant along with the complaint, either when somebody actually confirms his or her identity and gives them the documents, or when they are mailed to the defendant. The legal term for this is "service of process." The summons, properly served, gives the court power or "jurisdiction" over the case and over the defendant. That means the court may make decisions about the controversy described in the complaint, and decisions affecting the defendant with respect to the controversy.

The defendant's response to the complaint is called an answer, though some states use a different words for this document. The answer will address each paragraph in the complaint, and each response will ordinarily take one of three forms: "admitted," "denied," "insufficient knowledge to admit or deny." An answer may also set forth various affirmative defenses, which are legal reasons why the defendant should not be held liable for the plaintiff's damages. Some of these defenses may also be the basis of a motion to dismiss.

Counterclaim

If a defendant has his or her own claim against the plaintiff, one which arose out of the same circumstances as those that led to the complaint, it should be raised in the answer in a section titled "counterclaims." The counterclaim will be written in a manner similar to the complaint.

If a defendant asserts a counterclaim in the answer, the plaintiff may respond by filing a "reply." The reply will "admit," "deny," or assert that the plaintiff lacks information, just as the original answer did. The reply also may assert defenses, just as the answer did.

Cross-claim

Cross-claims arise when there are many parties to the lawsuit and two or more, who are "aligned" as plaintiffs or as defendants, have their own dispute arising out of the transaction or occurrence. The person being sued in a cross-claim will file an answer similar to the one filed after the original complaint.

Third-party Complaint

Sometimes a defendant who has been sued will have a legal reason for passing liability off to another person. A common example is a contract in which the third party promises to pay if you the defendant is found liable in a case. This person may be brought into the lawsuit if the defendant files a Third-party complaint. Like the regular complaint, it will set forth the relevant facts giving rise to the defendant's claim against the third party, and will set forth a request for relief. The person being sued through a third-party complaint must file an answer, similar to the one filed after the original complaint.

7.3 Drafting of Pleadings and Court Documents

7.3.1 Introduction

A pleading, in legal terms, is used to explain the purpose of the documents that contain the claims or defense filed by the parties with the court. In layman's terminology, it is a formal statement that sets out the issues that have to be tried. These are short and plain statements that set the grounds upon which a party has a basis to the claim.

Pleading needs to contain three vital elements according to the Federal Rules of Civil Procedure. These elements are:

- A short statement of the grounds on which the court's jurisdiction depends
- A short statement of the claims that the plaintiff or pleader is entitled to
- The demand for judgment for the relief the plaintiff or pleader seeks

Title of the Pleading

The point of the complaint is to state enough information to inform the opposing party of the nature of the claim that is drawn against them. It does not require any conclusions or facts to establish the essentials of a cause of action. When forming a pleading, you should keep a checklist of the various claims that need to be included in the complaint and have a basis to prove each of those claims. Generally, the title of the pleading is self-explanatory as is created by the plaintiff. In case there are multiple plaintiffs or defendants represented by a separate counsel, then you would need to include the name of the party in the title to avoid confusion.

Jurisdiction and Venue

After introducing the nature of the complaint in the opening sentence, you will need to make sure that you include the jurisdiction and venue of the court in the complaint. Each court has a different jurisdiction and for the complaint to be justified, it will have to address the right court with the proper subject matter jurisdiction. The venue of the court is the geographical area in which a case can be heard and determined.

When choosing an appropriate venue, you must keep in mind several key elements such as the cost to your client, statues of limitations, choice of judges, basis to prove your client's claim or claims, allowable damages, and prospective jury pools. If you do not have the proper jurisdiction or venue, you are giving the opposing party an opportunity to have the law suit dismissed before being heard.

Organizing your Thoughts

The key to drafting a successful pleading is to make sure that you have a clear idea of what the claims are that your client is making and relevant proof for each of those claims. Then you should state the events in a chronological and logical order. Do not try and use multiple theories to prove your claim as it will create unnecessary confusion for the judge to rule in your favor. Make sure that your theory is simple so as to avoid broadening the scope of discovery in the claim which will increase your client's litigation cost. The point of pleading is to create a cause of action that is backed by a legal theory that allows the plaintiff to make an allegation with the right to judicial relief.

7.3.2 Steps

There are certain ways using which a paralegal can draft a pleading which includes:

State the facts of the case, not the law pertaining to it

The general rule of pleadings, observed in most common law jurisdictions is that pleadings should contain relevant statements of facts and material particulars. Points of law may be mentioned very briefly if absolutely necessary, but they should be kept to a minimum. Pleadings should almost never contain legal arguments. Unfortunately, quite a few lawyers tend to become excessively verbose when it comes to points of law and feel the need to insert legal arguments in between the facts of the case. This reduces readability and makes it harder to grasp the facts.

Stay relevant and on the topic

Focus is important, as is relevancy to the issues between the contesting parties which is sought to be brought to the notice of the Court. Sometimes, in explaining one fact, it is easy to go into too much background history which may not be necessary to the case. On the other hand, a little background information is always a good thing - particularly in order to explain the nature of the dispute.

Numbered paragraphs are better

Legal pleadings are often used to complement the legal arguments that are made in front of the Judge and often, the Judge can follow the pleadings far more easily if each paragraph is numbered properly. A good practice is not to state more than one important fact in a single paragraph.

When replying to a pleading, always refer to the point in dispute

In reply pleadings, it is very important to answer the opposite party's case point-by-point and denying or admitting the contentions made in the other. This is also one reason why numbered paragraphs are a good idea. It is far easier to reply to each averment by referring to the paragraph number. It also makes it easier for the Judge to understand and follow the case.

Avoid unprofessional language

Pleadings are meant to be dignified and unemotional. Using too much slang is to be avoided. It is also better to thoroughly check for spelling and grammar mistakes before finalizing the proof. Again, name calling and repeated legal threats in a pleading make little sense and is best avoided. Keep the language simple, but professional.

Coherency in narration

A pleading is a narration of facts that form the basis of a case. Pleadings should be coherent and explain the dispute in a manner that makes sense and is understandable. Unlike in literature, stylistic narrative techniques are to be avoided at all costs.

Avoid evidentiary notes

Almost as important as avoiding legal arguments. Evidence is separate from alleged facts. Any pleading should not refer to the evidence, but should stick to the facts alone. Evidence is brought out in the trial of a case, by the examination and cross-examination of witnesses and the production of supporting documents. Of course, pleadings can refer or point to any documents that are relied upon to support facts briefly, but pleadings cannot be a substitute for the actual evidence. Depending on the requirements of law, pleadings may have to contain a list of annexed supporting documents as well.

7.4 Procedures/documentation for Provincial Court and Court of Appeal

7.4.1 Court of Appeal

The Court of Appeal is the highest court in the province. It hears appeals from the Supreme Court, from the Provincial Court on some criminal matters, and reviews and appeals from some administrative boards and tribunals.

The Court of Appeal Act provides for a Chief Justice and 14 other justices, as well as for supernumerary justices. Thus, the Court of Appeal actually has more than 15 judges. The Court of Appeal has a registrar who, in addition to other administrative duties, hears matters related to the settling of orders and bills of costs.

Jurisdiction

As with other Superior Courts, some of the jurisdiction of the Court of Appeal is conferred by the Constitution and some by legislation.

Appeals in Civil Proceedings

The Court has jurisdiction to hear appeals in civil proceedings from the High Court which prior to the Thirty-Third Amendment of the Constitution would have been heard by the Supreme Court. Exceptions are those cases in which the Supreme Court has permitted an appeal to it on being satisfied that the appeal meets the threshold set out in the Constitution.

The Court can hear appeals from cases heard in the High Court about whether or not a law is constitutional. The Constitution provides that no laws may be passed restricting the Court of Appeal's jurisdiction to do this.

Appeals in criminal proceedings

Under the Court of Appeal Act, the Court of Appeal was given the appellate jurisdiction previously exercised by the Court of Criminal Appeal. Appeals by persons convicted on indictment in the Circuit Court, Central Criminal Court and Special Criminal Court now lie to the Court of Appeal. Appeals against the severity of a sentence imposed by those courts also lie to the Court of Appeal. The Director of Public Prosecutions may appeal a sentence to the Court of Appeal on grounds of alleged undue leniency under section 2 of the Criminal Justice Act 1993. In the case of an alleged miscarriage of justice, an appeal by the convicted person can be lodged under section 2 of the Criminal Procedure Act 1993. The Court of Appeal was also given jurisdiction to hear appeals by the Director of Public Prosecutions on a question of law arising out of criminal trials which resulted in an acquittal.

Courts-Martial appeals

Under the Court of Appeal Act, Court of Appeal was given the appellate jurisdiction previously exercised by the Courts-Martial Appeal Court. This means that appeals from people who have been convicted by a court-martial now lie to the Court of Appeal. The appeal is determined on a record of the proceedings at the courts-martial with power to hear new or additional evidence or to refer any matter for report to the president or the judge advocate of the courts-martial. If the appeal is against the finding and the sentence, the court may affirm or reverse the finding in whole or in part, or order a new trial or vary the sentence. If the appeal is limited to either finding or sentence, the court is confined to dealing with the matter which is the subject of the appeal. The court also has power to review a finding or sentence where new evidence shows that there has been a miscarriage of justice.

7.4.2 Provincial Court

The Provincial Court has jurisdiction to deal with the following types of cases:

- ❖ Family
- ❖ Small Claims

- Criminal
- Youth Court
- Traffic & Bylaw

The Provincial Court's criminal jurisdiction extends to most offences in the Criminal Code that may be heard by a judge sitting alone. The Provincial Court has exclusive jurisdiction in all summary conviction trials and hears all indictable matters where the accused does not choose to be tried in the Supreme Court. More than 95% of all criminal cases are dealt with in Provincial Court. In criminal cases, Provincial Court judicial justices and judges conduct bail hearings; Provincial Court Judges conduct trials where an accused person pleads not guilty and they sentence people who plead guilty or who are found guilty at a trial.

The Provincial Court has jurisdiction to hear civil lawsuits involving monetary claims from $5001 to $35,000, and from $0 to $5000 if a party files a notice of objection after a Civil Resolution Tribunal decision or the matter is refused or exempted from the Civil Resolution Tribunal. The Small Claims Act and Small Claims Rules establish procedures intended to resolve claims in a just, speedy, inexpensive and simple manner, so that people may launch and defend lawsuits without lawyers if they choose. In addition to conducting trials of civil lawsuits and hearing applications, Provincial Court judges conduct settlement conferences where Small Claims litigants are given the opportunity to settle their disputes by agreement.

When social workers remove children from their parents' care due to concerns about mistreatment or neglect, they must file a report in the Provincial Court, and the Court deals with such child protection matters under the Child, Family and Community Services Act by holding case conferences to assist in planning for the children and by conducting hearings when the parents and social workers disagree.

Sharing extensive jurisdiction with the Supreme Court under the new BC Family Law Act, the Provincial Court handles matters including guardianship, parenting arrangements, child and spousal maintenance, and protection orders. However, the Provincial Court does not deal with divorce, adoptions or the division of family property - the Supreme Court has exclusive jurisdiction in those matters. To resolve issues that arise between separated couples, Provincial Court judges hold family case conferences and conduct hearings to decide issues the parties cannot agree on. Provincial Court judicial justices conduct trials involving traffic tickets and municipal bylaw offences.

8

Regulation and Ethical Duties of Paralegals

8.1 Laws Regulating Lawyers and Paralegals

Regulation is a generic term that includes all processes granting authority for recognition to an individual or institution, and there are a number of ways to regulate any profession. Some forms of regulation specific to paralegal professions include registration, certification, and licensure. State regulation of paralegals in the United States varies greatly from state to state, from none at all to very strict regulation, and nearly everything in-between. Some states have educational and work requirements in place for paralegals, while other states have enacted Codes of Professional Responsibility along with regulations or standards for legal assistants.

Because of no across the board standard regulation, anyone may deem themselves to be a paralegal, and any lawyer may call his assistant a paralegal – whether that assistant is primarily answering the phone and making copies or performing substantive paralegal work. As a result, many lawyers have difficulty recognizing and establishing a productive working relationship with a paralegal.

Paralegals are usually regulated by voluntary or mandatory registration, statutory regulations passed by the state's bar association or legislature, or rules administered by the state bar association of the state where the paralegal is employed. All types have one common element – the terms "paralegal" and "legal assistant" are used interchangeably.

Registration involves individuals or institutions listing their names with an association or agency, and the process may be voluntary or mandatory. Education, training or bonding requirements are sometimes associated with registration.

Some voluntary registration programs also allow paralegals to take on a greater role, as in King County, Pierce County and Spokane County, Washington, where the local bar associations have created voluntary registration programs that allow qualified non-lawyers such as paralegals to perform certain "direct" legal services, such as registering with the bar or the court to present orders which will not be argued with an adverse party in court.

In some states, registration is required for certain non-lawyer direct service providers. "Legal Document Assistants" and "Unlawful Detainee Assistants" in California are subject to registration and bonding under California Business & Professions Code. To be eligible to register as one of these direct service providers, applicants must meet minimum educational or experience requirements under California law. Similarly, legal document preparers in Arizona have to meet certain minimum education requirements, experience requirements, and pass a written examination.

Currently, the decision to obtain paralegal certification is strictly voluntary, and no state has put into place a mandatory program. A paralegal in North Carolina or Texas can choose not to be certified and still perform substantive legal work under the supervision of an attorney and can use the title "paralegal" or "legal assistant." In North Carolina, paralegals must meet a minimum level of education to be eligible for certification and must have a minimum level of continuing education to remain certified under the plan. To become board certified in Texas, a legal assistant must meet several eligibility requirements, including a showing of involvement in the specific area of law for which certification is sought. The legal assistant must also have at least five years of experience, have peer reviews by professionals associated with the specialty area, pass a four-hour written examination, and sometimes undergo an oral interview as part of the certification process. Currently, there are over 320 board certified paralegals in Texas.

NALA's Certified Legal Assistant/Paralegal (CLA/CP) program was started in 1976, and more than 13,000 paralegals have earned the CLA/CP credential since then. It is a voluntary self-regulatory program that encourages the growth of the paralegal profession and a high level of achievement. The CLA/CP examination is a two-day comprehensive exam with more than 1,000 questions based on federal law and procedure, and continuing education is required to maintain certification.

NFPA's Paralegal Advanced Competency Exam (PACE), established in 1994, provides a competency evaluation of paralegals through a four-hour exam taken via a computer. An applicant who successfully passes the exam obtains the Registered Paralegal designation, and continuing education is required to maintain it.

Licensure is a process by which an agency or branch of government grants permission to persons meeting predetermined qualifications to work in a specific profession. No state currently requires that legal assistants be licensed to work in the profession or use the term "paralegal," largely because not everyone agrees on the need for mandatory regulation of paralegals. Some courts and paralegal organizations believe that consumers of legal services are adequately protected by the license of the lawyer for whom the paralegal works, and that regulation may hinder the growth of the paralegal profession.

Attorneys, on the other hand, must be licensed to practice, and are ultimately accountable for the work done by a paralegal under their supervision. For their own protection, attorneys must verify academic credentials and prior work history when considering employment of a paralegal and must ensure that their paralegals are informed of changing laws and ethical concerns.

8.1.2 Paralegal Rules

Rule 1 Citation and Interpretation

Rule 2 Professionalism

- A paralegal has a duty to provide legal services and discharge all responsibilities to clients, tribunals, the public and other members of the legal professions honourably and with integrity.
- A paralegal has a duty to uphold the standards and reputation of the paralegal profession and to assist in the advancement of its goals, organizations and institutions.
- A paralegal shall be courteous and civil, and shall act in good faith with all persons with whom he or she has dealings in the course of his or her practice.
- A paralegal who engages in another profession, business, occupation or other outside interest or who holds public office concurrently with the provision of legal services, shall not allow the outside interest or public office to jeopardize the paralegal's integrity, independence, or competence.
- A paralegal shall not allow involvement in an outside interest or public office to impair the exercise of his or her independent judgment on behalf of a client.
- A paralegal shall respect the requirements of human rights laws in force in Ontario and without restricting the generality of the foregoing, a paralegal shall not discriminate on the grounds of race, ancestry, place of origin, colour, ethnic origin, citizenship, creed, sex, sexual orientation, gender identity, gender expression, age, record of offences, marital status, family status or disability with respect to the employment of others or in dealings with other licensees or any other person.
- The right to equal treatment without discrimination because of sex includes the right to equal treatment without discrimination because a woman is or may become pregnant.

Rule 3 Duty to Clients

- A paralegal shall perform any services undertaken on a client's behalf to the standard of a competent paralegal.

- A paralegal is required to recognize a task for which the paralegal lacks competence and the disservice that would be done to the client by undertaking that task. A paralegal shall not undertake a matter without being competent to handle it or being able to become competent without undue delay or expense to the client.
- If a paralegal discovers that he or she lacks the competence to complete the task for which he or she has been retained. For the purposes of this rule, a competent paralegal is one who has and applies the relevant knowledge, skills, and attributes appropriate to each matter undertaken on behalf of a client including, knowing general legal principles and procedures and the substantive law and procedures for the legal services that the paralegal provides.
- A paralegal has a duty to provide courteous, thorough and prompt service to clients. The quality of service required of a paralegal is service that is competent, timely, conscientious, diligent, efficient and civil.
- A paralegal shall be honest and candid when advising clients.
- A paralegal shall not undertake or provide advice with respect to a matter that is outside his or her permissible scope of practice.
- A paralegal shall advise and encourage a client to compromise or settle a dispute whenever it is possible to do so on a reasonable basis, and shall discourage the client from commencing or continuing useless legal proceedings.
- The paralegal shall consider the use of alternative dispute resolution (ADR) when appropriate, inform the client of ADR options, and, if so instructed, take steps to pursue those options.
- Before providing legal services under a limited scope retainer, a paralegal shall advise the client honestly and candidly about the nature, extent and scope of the services that the paralegal can provide and, where appropriate, whether the services can be provided within the financial means of the client.

Rule 4 Advocacy

When acting as an advocate, the paralegal shall not:

- Abuse the process of the tribunal by instituting or prosecuting proceedings which, although legal in themselves, are clearly motivated by malice on the part of the client and are brought solely for the purpose of injuring the other party.
- Knowingly assist or permit the client to do anything that the paralegal considers to be dishonest or dishonourable.

- Knowingly attempt to deceive a tribunal or influence the course of justice by offering false evidence, misstating facts or law, presenting or relying upon a false or deceptive affidavit, suppressing what ought to be disclosed, or otherwise assisting in any deception, crime or illegal conduct;
- Deliberately refrain from informing the tribunal of any binding authority that the paralegal considers to be directly on point and that has not been mentioned by an opponent.
- Appear before a judicial officer when the paralegal, a partner of the paralegal, a paralegal employed by the paralegal firm or the client has a business or personal relationship with the officer that gives rise to, or might reasonably appear to give rise to, pressure, influence or inducement affecting the impartiality of the officer, unless all parties consent and it is in the interests of justice.
- Knowingly assert as true, a fact when its truth cannot reasonably be supported by the evidence or as a matter of which notice may be taken by the tribunal.
- Make suggestions to a witness recklessly or knowing them to be false.
- Endeavour or allow anyone else to endeavour, directly or indirectly, to influence the decision or action of the tribunal or any of its officials in any case or matter by any means other than open persuasion as an advocate.
- Knowingly misstate the contents of a document, the testimony of a witness, the substance of an argument or the provisions of a statute or like authority.
- Knowingly permit a witness or party to be presented in a false or misleading way or to impersonate another.
- Knowingly misrepresent the client's position in the litigation or the issues to be determined in the litigation.
- Needlessly abuse, hector, harass or inconvenience a witness.
- Improperly dissuade a witness from giving evidence or suggest that a witness be absent.
- When representing a complainant or potential complainant, attempt to gain a benefit for the complainant by threatening the laying of a criminal charge or by offering to seek or to procure the withdrawal of a criminal charge.
- Needlessly inconvenience a witness.
- Appear before a court or tribunal while under the influence of alcohol or a drug.

Rule 5 Fees and Retainers

A fair and reasonable fee will depend on:

- The time and effort required and spent

- The difficulty of the matter and importance of the matter to the client
- Whether special skill or service was required and provided
- The amount involved or the value of the subject matter
- The results obtained
- Fees authorized by statute or regulation
- Special circumstances, such as the loss of other retainers, postponement of payment, uncertainty of reward, or urgency
- The likelihood, if made known to the client, that acceptance of the retainer will result in the paralegal's inability to accept other employment
- Any relevant agreement between the paralegal and the client
- The experience and ability of the paralegal
- Any estimate or range of fees given by the paralegal
- The client's prior consent to the fee

Rule 6 Duty to Administration of Justice

- A paralegal shall encourage public respect for, and try to improve, the administration of justice.
- A paralegal shall take care not to weaken or destroy public confidence in legal institutions or authorities by making irresponsible allegations or comments particularly when commenting on judges or members of a tribunal.
- So long as there is no infringement of the paralegal's obligation to the client, the paralegal profession, the courts, or the administration of justice, a paralegal may communicate information to the media and may make public appearances and statements.
- A paralegal shall not communicate information to the media or make public statements about a matter before a tribunal if the paralegal knows or ought to know that the information or statement will have a substantial likelihood of materially prejudicing a party's right to a fair trial or hearing.
- A paralegal shall assist in preventing the unauthorized practice of law and the unauthorized provision of legal services.
- A paralegal who gives an undertaking to the Law Society to restrict his or her provision of legal services shall comply with the undertaking.

Rule 7 Duty to Licensees and Others

- A paralegal shall avoid sharp practice and shall not take advantage of or act without fair warning on slips, irregularities or mistakes on the part of other licensees not going to the merits or involving the sacrifice of a client's rights.

- A paralegal shall agree to reasonable requests concerning trial dates, adjournments, waiver of procedural formalities and similar matters that do not prejudice the rights of the client.
- A paralegal shall not, in the course of providing legal services, communicate, in writing or otherwise, with a client, another licensee, or any other person in a manner that is abusive, offensive, or otherwise inconsistent with the proper tone of a professional communication from a paralegal.
- A paralegal shall not engage in ill-considered or uninformed criticism of the competence, conduct, advice or charges of other licensees, but should be prepared, when requested, to represent a client in a complaint involving another licensee.
- A paralegal shall answer, with reasonable promptness, all professional letters and communications from other licensees that require an answer, and a paralegal shall be punctual in fulfilling all commitments.
- A paralegal shall not use any device to record a conversation between the paralegal and a client or another licensee, even if lawful, without first informing the other person of the intention to do so.
- A paralegal who receives a document relating to the representation of the paralegal's client and knows or reasonably should know that the document was inadvertently sent shall promptly notify the sender.

8.2 Duties of a Paralegal

8.2.1 Confidentiality and Privilege

A paralegal must adhere strictly to the accepted standards of legal ethics and to the general principles of proper conduct. The performance of the duties of the paralegal shall be governed by specific canons as defined herein so that justice will be served and goals of the profession attained.

Both confidentiality and privilege are calculated to encourage complete candor on the part of a client with his or her attorney. In order to effectively represent a client, a lawyer needs to know all the facts, no matter what they are. Therefore, both the law and the ethics codes have been written to ensure that a client can reveal all facts to an attorney without fear of those confidences being disclosed.

As per the conduct, a paralegal shall not reveal information relating to the representation of a client unless the client gives explicitly informed consent, or unless required by certain other limited circumstances. Privilege is a rule of evidence that permits an attorney to refuse to testify to confidential client information, and also permits a party to refuse to testify communications with his or her counsel. It also permits a party to refuse to produce documents, ESI or other evidence reflecting communications with counsel.

Confidentiality

(a) Except when permitted a paralegal shall not knowingly:

- Reveal a confidence or secret of the lawyer's client.
- Use a confidence or secret of the lawyer's client to the disadvantage of the client.
- Use a confidence or secret of the lawyer's client for the advantage of the lawyer or of a third person.

(b) Confidence refers to information protected by attorney-client privilege under applicable law, and secret refers to other information gained in the professional relationship that the client has requested be held inviolate, or the disclosure of which would be embarrassing, or would be likely to be detrimental, to the client.

(c) A paralegal may reveal client confidences and secrets, to the extent reasonably necessary:

- To prevent a criminal act that the lawyer reasonably believes is likely to result in death or substantial bodily harm absent disclosure of the client's secrets or confidences by the lawyer, or
- To prevent the bribery or intimidation of witnesses, jurors, court officials, or other persons who are involved in proceedings before a tribunal if the paralegal reasonably believes that such acts are likely to result absent disclosure of the client's confidences or secrets by the paralegal.

(d) When a client has used or is using a paralegal's services to further a crime or fraud, the paralegal may reveal client confidences and secrets, to the extent reasonably necessary:

- To prevent the client from committing the crime or fraud if it is reasonably certain to result in substantial injury to the financial interests or property of another.
- To prevent, mitigate or rectify substantial injury to the financial interests or property of another that is reasonably certain to result or has resulted from the client's commission of the crime or fraud.

(e) A paralegal may use or reveal client confidences or secrets:

- With the informed consent of the client.
- When permitted by these Rules or required by law or court order.
- If a government paralegal, when permitted or authorized by law.
- To the extent reasonably necessary to establish a defense to a criminal charge, disciplinary charge, or civil claim, formally instituted against the lawyer, based upon conduct in which the client was involved, or to the

extent reasonably necessary to respond to specific allegations by the client concerning the lawyer's representation of the client.

- ❖ When the paralegal has reasonable grounds for believing that a client has impliedly authorized disclosure of a confidence or secret in order to carry out the representation.
- ❖ To the minimum extent necessary in an action instituted by the lawyer to establish or collect the lawyer's fee.
- ❖ To the extent reasonably necessary to secure legal advice about the paralegal's compliance with law, including these rules.

(f) A paralegal shall exercise reasonable care to prevent the paralegal's employees, associates, and others whose services are utilized by the paralegal from disclosing or using confidences or secrets of a client, except that such persons may reveal information permitted.

(g) The paralegal's obligation to preserve the client's confidences and secrets continues after termination of the paralegal's employment.

(h) The obligation of a paralegal also applies to confidences and secrets learned prior to becoming a paralegal in the course of providing assistance to another paralegal.

(i) For purposes of this rule, a paralegal who serves as a member of Counseling Committee, or as a trained intervenor for that committee, shall be deemed to have a paralegal client relationship with respect to any lawyer-counselee being counseled under programs conducted by or on behalf of the committee. Information obtained from another paralegal being counseled under the auspices of the committee, or in the course of and associated with such counseling, shall be treated as a confidence or secret in terms. Such information may be disclosed only to the extent permitted by this rule.

(j) For purposes of this rule, a paralegal who serves as a member of Management Service Committee, or a staff assistant, mentor, monitor or other consultant for that committee, shall be deemed to have a paralegal client relationship with respect to any paralegal counselee being counseled under programs conducted by or on behalf of the committee. Communications between the counselor and the lawyer being counseled under the auspices of the committee, or made in the course of and associated with such counseling, shall be treated as a confidence or secret. Such information may be disclosed only to the extent permitted by this rule. However, during the period in which the paralegal counselee is subject to a probationary or monitoring order of the Court of Appeals or the Board on Professional Responsibility in a disciplinary case instituted pursuant of Rules of Court of Appeals Governing the Bar, such information shall be subject to disclosure in accordance with the order.

(k) The client of the government lawyer is the agency that employs the paralegal unless expressly provided to the contrary by appropriate law, regulation, or order.

8.2.2 Avoiding Conflicts of Interest

A conflict of interest refers to a situation where someone, such as an attorney or public official, has competing professional or personal obligations or personal or financial interests, that would make it difficult to fulfill his duties fairly.

A conflict of interest in the legal sense is the information about a client held by a member of the legal team which is an attorney, paralegal or legal secretary. The information does not have to be attorney/client privileged information, nor does it have to include actual documented facts about a client's legal matter. It only needs to be information about the client that, were it revealed to other members of the legal team, may cause some harm, injury or prejudice to the client.

Reasons of Conflict:

A conflict will occur when:

- You are working on a case where a close relative is on the other side which can be parents, children, siblings, spouses and grandparents, in such case, some states include friends, roommates and significant others.
- You have information about the client on opposite side of the case. As, prior to your current employment you worked at a firm that represents a person who is a divorcee and now your current employment has a firm's client. You know nothing about the new case but you have a great information about other party business from previous employment, thereby putting him at disadvantage, then a conflict may take place.
- You want to enter in a business relationship with a client, in such case a conflict takes place. In such case, the client must give written consent, the transaction must be fair and the client should be advised to seek independent counsel. This rule covers taking an interest in a client's business in lieu of fees.
- Your client decides to make you the beneficiary of his estate, where principles indicate that paralegals would not accept such gift but you may still receive the inheritance if the client seeks independent counsel and you have absolutely nothing to do with the drafting or signing of the documents. You must take every possible step to avoid any appearance of impropriety.
- You are changing jobs and the new firm represents a client who is on the opposite side of a case you worked on at your old firm. To avoid disqualification, your new employer may decline to hire you or request your former employer consent to your hiring and also, establish a screen that will prevent you from access to the client's file and any involvement in the case at your new firm.

The existence of a conflict may result in the disqualification of the attorney and the firm. For this reason, conflicts of interest must be identified and avoided. A Paralegal shall avoid conflicts of interest and shall disclose any possible conflict to the employer or client, as well as to the prospective employers or clients. A paralegal possesses information about a client's transactions, the attorney's strategies, thought processes, work product, and/or other client privileged information. Conflicts of interest involving paralegals usually result from personal and business relationships outside the legal environment or from legal matters handled at the paralegal's prior employment.

If a conflict of interest is not identified and disclosed to the client or supervising attorney, the firm or employer may lose considerable time and money expended in handling the client's legal matter. For paralegals who are supervised by or accountable to an attorney, the attorney is obligated to determine whether there is conflict of interest between the paralegal and the client or legal matter. In practice areas where paralegals are not supervised by or accountable to an attorney but deal directly with the clients, paralegals make those decisions.

Paralegals should abide by the decision made by the attorney. If, however, a paralegal feels uncomfortable continuing to work on a matter with which a conflict was not determined, it should be discussed with the supervising attorney or a conflicts committee within the firm or employer's structure. Finally, existence of conflict results in the disqualification of attorney and firm, hence paralegal should identify and avoid conflicts of interest.

8.2.3 Avoiding the Unauthorized Practice of Law

If paralegals breach legal ethics, serious sanctions can result, including suspension or revocation of license, a fine, loss of job, or if there was criminal activity, referral to the appropriate authorities. Legal ethics for paralegals are similar to those for lawyers. The list of activities that constitute the practice of law include:

- Abstracting and passing upon titles to real estate.
- Organizing corporations.
- Preparing or aiding in the preparation of deeds, trusts, wills or other legal documents.
- Preparing or aiding in the preparation of probate petitions and accountings.
- Preparing or aiding in the preparation of court pleadings
- Appearing in court or before any judicial or quasi-judicial body on behalf of another.

A paralegal needs to keep in mind that there are certain things only a licensed lawyer is authorized to do. To be precise, there are five things that only a licensed lawyer can do:

- Initiate a lawyer-client relationship.
- Provide legal advice.
- Any legal papers or pleadings on behalf of the client can only be signed by a lawyer.
- Carry out legal proceedings in a court of law.
- Charge a fee for these legal services.

A paralegal should also ensure that any prospective client or, for that matter, any other person he/she interact with, knows you are a paralegal and not authorized to provide legal advice. If you do provide information that could be construed as legal advice, explicitly mention the source.

Paralegals are representatives of the legal profession, so they should keep their conduct above reproach, perform all assignments efficiently, and constantly seek to improve their legal knowledge and skills. The unauthorized practice of law is illegal because a person who is not trained and licensed as an attorney may seriously harm the interests of a member of the public by providing incompetent legal services.

The unauthorized practice of law is a misdemeanor criminal offense that may be prosecuted by the local district attorney. Additionally, accepting fees for unauthorized practice of law may involve other crimes, such as false pretense, that are felonies. The State Bar may ask the courts for an injunction to prohibit a person or business from engaging in the unauthorized practice of law. Engaging in unauthorized practice of law may also expose a person to potential civil liability to a person harmed by the unauthorized practice including potential claims of fraud or unfair and deceptive trade practices.

8.2.4 Limits of Zealous Representation

Paralegals have a strict ethical responsibility to advocate zealously on behalf of their client. Zealous representation does not mean a paralegal should strive to "win" a case at all costs, if that means harming third parties and adversaries unnecessarily in the process. It means doing everything reasonable to help a client achieve the goals set forth at the outset of the representation. Therefore, a balance must be struck in strategizing -- between what is achievable within the bounds of the law, and what is reasonable in light of the impact on parties involved.

In the nature of law practice, however, conflicting responsibilities are encountered. Virtually all difficult ethical problems arise from conflict between a paralegal's responsibilities to clients, to the legal system and to the paralegal's own interest in remaining an ethical person while earning a satisfactory living.

The Rules of Professional Conduct often prescribe terms for resolving such conflicts. Within the framework of these Rules, however, many difficult issues of professional discretion can arise. Such issues must be resolved through the exercise of sensitive professional and moral judgment guided by the basic principles underlying the Rules. These principles include the lawyer's obligation zealously to protect and pursue a client's legitimate interests, within the bounds of the law, while maintaining a professional, courteous and civil attitude toward all persons involved in the legal system.

8.2.5 Competency and Malpractice

Paralegal Malpractice

Malpractice is improper conduct in the performance of duties by a professional, either intentionally or through negligence. Legal malpractice is a form of professional malpractice, based on negligence. Normally, paralegals are covered under their attorney employers' malpractice insurance, however, with more paralegals performing legal services for the public without the supervision of an attorney, claims of malpractice against paralegals may start to become more common.

Malpractice Claims:

- ❖ Substantive incompetence
- ❖ Management incompetence
- ❖ Poor communication skills and practices
- ❖ Fee misunderstandings
- ❖ Substance abuse and stress

Avoiding malpractice:

Paralegals working in normal setting under direct supervision of attorney should not worry about malpractice insurance, but as negligence on part of paralegal can get supervising attorney to take legal action against paralegals working in setting, so paralegals should follow their attorneys' instructions carefully and ask questions when they are unsure about what they are supposed to do or not do. Paralegals not working under the direct supervision of an attorney might want to consider purchasing a professional liability policy. There are certain ways by which paralegals can protect themselves and their attorney from malpractice which include:

- ❖ Following client screening procedures precisely. Weeding out potential problem clients can reduce risk of being sued. If you suspect that your firm's screening process could be modified to work better, tell your supervisor.
- ❖ Proofread the document as many clients will have no idea if their firm is doing a good job in representing them, but if letters and pleadings have typos and misspelled words, they will know that, and it could lead them to believe the rest of work the firm does is not up to par.
- ❖ Make sure that your attorney's reviews any legal documents or correspondences before you send it to a client, the Court, or another party.

- Double and triple check all deadlines that you calculate.
- Do not take on more work than you can handle. If your case load is too much, talk to your supervisor about it. If you are forced to rush through your work, you will be more likely to miss deadlines and make mistakes that could lead to a lawsuit.
- Be sure you know and follow the Rules of Professional Conduct in your state.
- Let your clients know you care. Appearances are very important, and a law firm who appears to truly care about their clients is far less likely to be sued for malpractice than a firm who does not appear to car.
- If you discover that you, your attorney, or any other staff at you firm has made a mistake in a case, tell your attorney or supervisor right away. If you practice as a freelance paralegal or legal document preparer and realize a mistake has been made, talk to your insurance agent or a malpractice attorney immediately.
- Know how your state defines the unauthorized practice of law, and avoid engaging in it. All states prohibit paralegals from forming the attorney-client relationship and giving legal advice, but it may sometimes to be difficult to distinguish advice from information.

Paralegal Competencies

Ethical and Professional Responsibilities

- Demonstrates integrity which includes honesty, meeting financial obligations, responsibility to Law Society and other licensees.
- Demonstrates civility and professionalism in dealings with others.
- Maintains appropriate professional relationships with clients, other licensees, employees and others in areas of sexual harassment, discrimination and human rights violations, respects multi-cultural issues.
- Creates and maintains an ongoing electronic or written record for each matter for which the paralegal is retained.
- Understands duties related to advising clients which could be in terms of honesty and candour.
- Demonstrates an understanding of the obligation to represent the client within the limits of the law.
- Takes appropriate steps to determine who the client is and the client's role in the matter (e.g., multiple parties, spouses/family members, business partners, corporations, authority to bind).
- Accepts only retainers that are capable of performance under the law.
- Recognizes situations that constitute a conflict of interest or potential conflict of interest.

- Understands the obligation to maintain a conflicts checking system.
- Understands the obligation to maintain reminder systems (e.g., limitation periods, important dates).
- Meets all financial obligations (e.g., obligations incurred by the paralegal, obligations incurred on the client's behalf).
- Understands the meaning and enforceability of undertakings and trust conditions, fulfils all undertakings and trust conditions, and does not give an undertaking or agree to a trust condition that cannot be fulfilled.
- Declines to act when a matter is outside the permitted scope of practice.
- Avoids becoming the tool or dupe of an unscrupulous client (e.g., proceeds of crime, evidence, fraud).
- Understands the obligation owed to clients with diminished capacity (e.g., maintain normal relationship, take appropriate steps to have a lawfully authorized representative appointed).
- Understands the obligations related to the discovery and reporting of errors or omissions (e.g., duty to disclose to client and insurer, advise client to obtain independent legal advice).
- Identifies potential conflicts of interest before acquiring confidential information.
- Recognizes and fulfils duties related to joint retainers.
- Recognizes issues related to communicating with witnesses at any time and especially when dealing with the provision of testimony.
- Identifies the instructing client (e.g., who has the authority to provide instructions).
- Avoids engaging in sharp practice (e.g., taking advantage of slips by other licensees not going to the merits or involving a sacrifice of the client's rights).
- Communicates with clients in a timely and effective manner (e.g., returns messages in a timely manner, copies the client on correspondence as appropriate).
- Manages and updates the client's expectations with respect to timeframes, results and costs.
- Takes appropriate steps to avoid problems associated with phantom clients.
- Establishes the scope of the retainer.
- Sets out and explains the basis for fees and disbursements in the retainer.
- Addresses termination issues in the retainer.
- Recognizes duties to the administration of justice.

- Understands the obligation to use technology in a competent manner.
- Recognizes the disciplinary authority of the Law Society.
- Understands the obligations related to acting as a mediator.
- Understands the obligations related to dealing with unrepresented persons.
- Demonstrates an understanding of restrictions regarding firm name, letterhead and signs (e.g., does not mislead regarding firm, paralegals employed, jurisdiction where services are offered).
- Maintains competence and quality of service, and declines to act or seeks appropriate assistance when the matter is beyond own abilities.
- Recognizes and fulfils duties related to confidentiality, including recognizing situations where disclosure is required or may be justified.
- Demonstrates an understanding of the obligations related to acting as an advocate or as a witness.
- Complies with requirements of the Law Society related to bookkeeping and preservation of client's property.
- Ensures that staff is properly trained to understand and adhere to relevant Paralegal Rules of Conduct and delegates and supervises staff appropriately.
- Takes appropriate action in situations where an actual or potential conflict of interest is identified.
- Withdraws from representation in compliance with the Paralegal Rules of Conduct or rules of tribunal.
- Understands the requirements to maintain sufficient insurance, file required documentation with the insurer, pay fees to the insurer, and cooperate with the insurer regarding any claims made against the paralegal.
- Demonstrates an understanding of the duties owed to the Law Society.
- Charges fair and reasonable fees and disbursements.
- Understands the obligation to properly open, maintain, close and store client files.
- Demonstrates an understanding of referral fees and fee splitting.

Civil Litigation

Demonstrates an understanding of:

- How to draft pleadings.
- Service of pleadings and documents.
- Purposes of settlement conferences.
- Minutes of settlement.
- Purposes of motions.

- Ex parte motions.
- Default proceedings.
- Cost awards.
- Contempt process.
- Intentional torts.

Torts

Demonstrates an understanding of:

- Elements of negligence.
- Strict liability law.
- Remedies in tort law.
- Types of damages in tort law.
- Product liability issues.

Contracts

Demonstrates an understanding of:

- Elements of a valid contract (e.g., intention, consideration, capacity, certainty).
- Principles of contract interpretation.
- Conditions, warranties and implied terms.
- Contractual defects (misrepresentation, mistake, undue influence, duress, and illegality).
- Remedies for breach of contract.
- Types of damages in contract law.
- Principles of unjust enrichment.

Criminal/Quasi-Criminal Law & Procedure

General Principles

Demonstrates an understanding of:

- Difference between criminal offences and provincial offences.
- Charter motions (e.g., section 11(b)).
- Arrest and compelling the attendance of the defendant.
- Compelling witnesses.
- Sentencing (purpose and objectives, principles of sentence, sentencing powers and restrictions).

Provincial Offences Act

Demonstrates an understanding of:

- ❖ Various procedural streams.
- ❖ Role of police, prosecution, provincial offences officers, and defendants in the provincial offences system.
- ❖ Classification of offences (i.e., men's rea, strict liability, and absolute liability).
- ❖ Common offences under Highway Traffic Act and related statutes.
- ❖ Available defences under the Highway Traffic Act and related statutes.
- ❖ Charging documents (e.g., identifying fatal defects, proof of service, filing dates).
- ❖ Provincial offences trial process.
- ❖ Plea enquiry in Provincial Offences Act matters.
- ❖ Judicial interim release or bail in Provincial Offences Act matters.
- ❖ Enforcement proceedings in Provincial Offences Act matters.

Conviction

Demonstrates an understanding of:

- ❖ Elements of a crime.
- ❖ Relevant legislation (Criminal Code, Charter, Controlled Drugs and Substances Act, Criminal Rules).
- ❖ Role of police, Crown and the accused in criminal proceedings.
- ❖ Charging documents.
- ❖ Summary conviction trial process (pre-trial conference, pre-trial motions, and applications, trials).
- ❖ Common summary conviction offences.
- ❖ Defences to summary conviction offences (e.g., procedural and substantive).
- ❖ Judicial interim release or bail in Summary Conviction matters.
- ❖ Plea enquiry in Summary Conviction matters (i.e., obtains instructions, voluntary, informed, and waiving of the trial and original charge, and consequences).
- ❖ Diversion options.
- ❖ Enforcement proceedings in Summary Conviction matters.

Administrative Law

Demonstrates an understanding of:

- Relevant primary legislation (Judicial Review Procedure Act, Statutory Powers Procedure Act, federal and provincial human rights legislation, the Charter).
- Basic principle of admin law (natural justice, fairness, discretion, bias, substantive review of public decision making).
- Who has standing to bring an action.
- Difference between courts and administrative tribunals.
- General practice and procedure before administrative tribunals (burden of proof, who hears cases, record of proceedings, documentation, and tribunal process).
- Judicial review.
- workplace safety and insurance board/ workplace safety and insurance appeals tribunal
- Nature of the employer-employee relationship.
- Practice and procedure related to Workplace Safety and Insurance Board (time limits, special categories of appeals, service requirements, parties, witnesses, evidence, types of benefits).
- Practice and procedure related to Workplace Safety and Insurance Appeals Tribunal (time limits, service requirements, parties witnesses, evidence, benefits).

Landlord and Tenant

Demonstrates an understanding of:

- Types of tenancies.
- Rights and responsibilities of tenants and landlords (quiet enjoyment, essential services, pets).
- Rules and procedures regarding tenancies (landlord and tenant applications, tenant termination, landlord termination, notice of termination).

Human Rights

Demonstrates an understanding of:

- Threshold and requirements for filing an application.
- Federal versus provincially regulated human rights matters.
- Disability and the duty to accommodate.
- Practice and procedure related to Human Rights Tribunal (time limits, service requirements, parties, witnesses, evidence, and types of remedies).

Other Specific Tribunals

Demonstrates an understanding of:

- Legislation, practice and procedure related to the Social Benefits Tribunal.
- Legislation, practice and procedure related to Financial Services Commission/Statutory Accident Benefits Schedule.
- Legislation, practice and procedure related to Municipal Board.
- Legislation, practice and procedure related to Labour Relations Board.

Problem/Issue Identification Analysis and Assessment

- Information Gathering, Case Analysis and Planning
- Recognizes urgency and takes emergency steps where necessary.
- Identifies, obtains and reviews relevant facts and documents.
- Identifies the relevant legal issues.
- Conducts research and investigations related to the matter as appropriate.
- Complies with all privacy legislation when gathering information.
- Theory of the Case
- Develops an informed theory of the case based on the paralegal's assessment of the facts and law.
- Develops an appropriate plan and strategies in consultation with the client to achieve desired results.
- Reassesses the theory as the case evolves.

Alternative Dispute Resolution

Demonstrates an understanding of:

- Various dispute resolution processes (negotiation, mediation, arbitration).
- Remedies that may be uniquely available through alternate dispute resolution (negotiation, mediation, arbitration).
- Potential implications of choosing to use or not use alternative dispute resolution and prepares the client for their informed choice.
- Obligation to encourage settlement, compromise and alternative dispute resolution where reasonable.

Litigation Process

Demonstrates an understanding of:

- Disclosure requirements.

- Advises which client of disclosure obligations related to full and complete disclosure, ensuring the preservation of relevant evidence for disclosure, confidentiality issues).
- Capacity, litigation guardians and parties under a disability.
- Meeting required timelines for trial or hearing.
- Onus and burden of proof at each stage.
- Agreed statements of facts and admissions.
- Different requirements of effective opening and closing statements.
- Own witnesses for examination.
- Cross-examination of witnesses of other parties.
- Anticipating and preparing for objections.
- Preparing submissions on penalties, remedies or disposition, where applicable.
- Conducting Trial or hearing
- Presenting admissions effectively.
- Examinations-in-chief.
- Conducting cross-examinations.
- Conducting re-examinations.
- Evidence if appropriate.
- Initiating and responding to motions/applications as appropriate.
- Direct verdict and non-suit motions.
- Revising litigation strategy as necessary.
- Considering and establishes an adequate record for purpose of submissions or appellate review.
- Raising and responding to objections appropriately on record.
- appeals
- Rules and requirements for an appeal (procedures, timelines).
- Considering need of an appeal.
- Reviewing merits and consequences of an appeal with the client.
- Obtaining client instructions regarding appeals.
- Obtaining and preparing all necessary evidence and documents for conduct of appeal.
- post disposition of matter
- Ensuring matter to be completed and documented correctly as per disposition (minutes of settlement, judgment/order issued, final releases).

- Providing final reports and accounting to clients.
- Conducting final review of file prior to closing the file.

Practice Management Issues

- Makes appropriate arrangements for practice absences and maintains appropriate powers of attorney respecting the practice.
- Makes appropriate arrangements for succession/contingency planning (e.g., death, disability, business interruption, disaster).
- Demonstrates an awareness of the ongoing costs of managing a practice.
- Complies with continuing professional development requirements.

9

Communication Fundamentals

9.1 Communication

9.1.1 Introduction

Effective communication is all about conveying your messages to other people clearly and unambiguously. It is also about receiving information that others are sending to you, with as little distortion as possible. By following, we will attain the effort from both the sender and the receiver of the message. In this process simulation, it is noted that the communication is full of errors having their messages either mixed-up by the sender or is normally misread by the recipient. If the error or fault is not found, then it will create confusion among the people which will led to wastage of effort and resources. It is found that for a communication to be successful, both the sender and receiver should properly understand same information which will give rise to the process communication.

Generally, designers are introverts and do not naturally have strong communication skills. They mostly enjoy working on their own and creating something special, but communicating with clients is a main issue that needs to be considered. There is plenty of back and forth communication for the client to the designer during the process of development of the product. For a media graphic designer, coding and creativity are a part of the everyday work, and so is communication. Clients know the details of their business that need to be considered while designing. Without effective communication, gathering this information will be difficult or impossible. With effective communication you can work with the client to create a design that suits their requirements.

As the designer, you will need certain information from the client to complete the job to the best of your ability. You'll need their initial input plus their feedback throughout the process. As the client, they depend on you to create an attractive and effective design. Due to this mutual dependence, communication is absolutely necessary to bridge the gap and to create satisfactory results from both parties. Being able to effectively communicate in a simple and understandable manner is a skill in itself that will add on to your credibility as a designer. In fact, getting new clients or even a job will be much easier with better communication skills.

Communication is the very basic need of any organization and it is so fundamental that without it, it is not possible for any organization to exist, function effectively and achieve its objectives. Communication brings people together by establishing commonness among people. It is a social need for an individual and lifeblood for an organization. We communicate 75% of our working time; an organization communicates 90% of its working time. If individuals communicate for their personal purposes, communication in an organization is for the business purposes. Thus, the role of communication is to bring all the aspects of business together - manufacturer, employees, customers, suppliers, agencies, distributors etc. That is why it is very important to understand business communication at different levels. Communication is an art of sharing meaningful ideas, information, knowledge, experience and feelings.

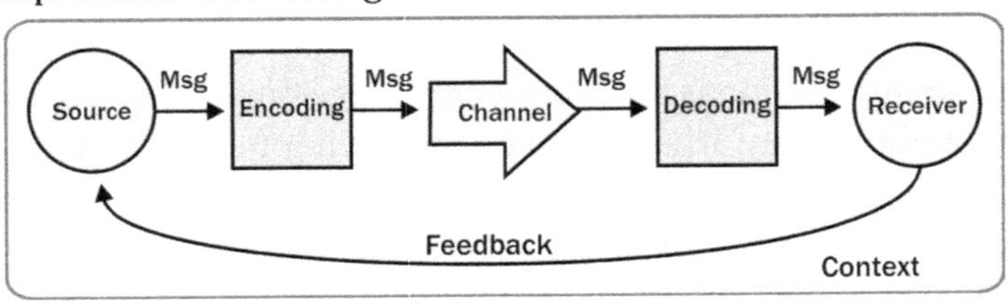

Fig. The Communications Process

The word Communication is derived from the Latin word 'communis' meaning 'Common'. It stands for a natural activity of all human beings to convey opinions, information, ideas, and feelings, emotions to others by words spoken or written, by body language or signs. George Vardman, in his book 'Effective communication of ideas' defined effective communication as - "Purposive interchange resulting in a workable understanding and an agreement between the sender and the receiver of the message".

9.1.2 Process of communication

Communication is a bilateral approach mechanism in which the transfer of ideas affinities the sender along with the receiver towards a collectively accepted course. The transmission of the sender's concepts to the receiver as well as the receiver's feedback or acknowledgment to the sender compiles the communication approach.

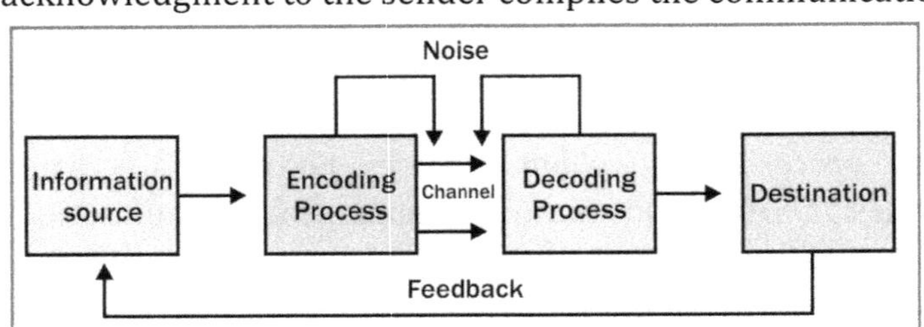

Fig Process

In place to understand the appropriate as well as effective communication, either the sender as well as the receiver hold to act in a common atmosphere or in other words, we can discuss that there should be bilateral parties for communication- one is sender as well as other is always receiver. The sender necessary has his/her ideas, attentions, emotions which he/she can carry to the receiver by any medium of expression which is called a channel. The process of communication can be understood by the given steps:

- ❖ Sender: The approach of communication commences with a sender, the person who acquires a concept and demands to convey it to the receiver. In other terms, we can say that the person with concepts to participate is called sender. On account of communication mechanism commences with the sender.
- ❖ Encoding: The alteration of the concept into message by syntactical or nonverbal mechanism is identified encoding. While encoding a message, one expects to appraise what will be analysis of the message. This mechanism of converting the analysis of the sender into message is encoding.
- ❖ Message: It exists a crucial bit of communication. Message exists the content that sender demands to deliver. A message could be syntactical or non-verbal. The conceived, idea, emotion or anything that the sender desires to deliver is identified message.
- ❖ Channel: The approach or the means of sending the message is designated channel. The desire of the medium is affected by the inter relationship between sender and receiver. It moreover depends upon the quickness of the message. Medium or channel can be aloud, written or it can be non-structural.
- ❖ Receiver: The acceptor is the person who acknowledges or abuts meaning to the dispatched message. In the better way, if it extends to the receiver that time there is no problem to the receiver to know the message correctly. In other words, we can say that the acceptor is the other group who receives the message of the sender.
- ❖ Decoding: It is a mechanism where the acquired message is changed into compassionate. It is not compulsory that the message reached to acceptor will be known by the receiver, but analysis is a process which changes the message into responsive. There are chances of misinterpretation of the message.
- ❖ Feedback: This is the final component of communication process. After acquiring the message, the receiver behaves or acknowledges to the sender. The answer can be based on the complete information of the message or it can be based on the misinterpretation or confusion of the message. This explanation from receiver to sender is identified feedback.

Feedback acquires its own criticalness as the achievement or downfall of communication is determined by feedback only.

The approach of communication commences with concept, which assigns to the development of the concept or choice of a message to be broadcast by the sender. The extent of the concept is normally disclosed by the sender's information, competence along with capability. Encoding is the former step in communication. It is the procedure of altering the information into several form of appropriate as well as coded correspondence. It describes the alternative of language, factor of communication as well as development of communication.

Transmission assigns to the stream of message higher than the selected channel. It approves the means elected for encoding furthermore preserves the communication channel ease from challenge or noise on account of that the message can reach the receiver without some exacerbation. Decoding is the approach of changing a message into calculations by analyzing it. It embodies the message, which will serve his/her concept sent by the sender too on the factor of this opinion; the receiver can give answer that is known as feedback. So feedback is an important and last part of communication process.

9.1.3 Communication Types

Communication between members of a large corporate house is very necessary for its proper functioning. It may be upward, downward, diagonal and grapevine. It is also known as dimensions or channels of communication.

Downward Communication:

Downward communication is generally found in all major organizations. It is communication in the organization which starts from higher authority to lower authority, like the board of directors-managers-assistant manager-purchase officer-executive-clerk etc. Communication passes in a down ward manner that is it moves from the top to the bottom. This type of communication is called downward communication.

Objectives:

- To give specified directions about the job being entrusted to a subordinate.
- To explain policies and organizational procedures.
- To appraise the subordinates for their performance.
- To give information to the subordinates about the rational of their job so that they understand the significance of their job in relation with the organizational goal.

Advantages:

- It is a convenient channel through which simple information can be spread easily.
- Major decisions are conveyed through this type of communication.
- It helps to assign specific duties to a newly appointed individual.
- Individual members can interact with those to whom they are accountable.
- Appreciation can be done through this type of communication.

Limitations:

Downward communication is often found either under communication or over communication, i.e. superior may either talk too little or too much about a job. Downward communication being a very long channel, transmitting information to the lowest worker is a time consuming process and in this process there is a chance of loss of information. Sometimes message can reach beyond time limit. In this process there is a chance of exaggeration, understatement, and twisting of matter due to its long time. Downward communication is an authoritarian process where subordinates do not get any opportunity to participate in the decision making process.

Upward Communication:

The communication channel which starts from the bottom level to the top level is called upward communication. For example worker conveys message to production manager, he conveys it to the director of company etc. It is a channel which passes the flow of information upward.

Advantages:

Upward communication provides the management with necessary feedback. It also provides valuable information on what the employees think of the organization and its policies. It gives an opportunity to workers to voice their problems and complaints. Upward communication is also important for workers' suggestions for the welfare of an organization. This process provides a chance to workers to take part in the decision making process which creates harmony between the workers and the management.

Limitations:

Upward communication is difficult as it moves upward against the force of 'gravity' – meaning that the workers hesitate to initiate upward communication. Workers cannot enter easily in the area of management. They are afraid of the reaction from management. At bottom level people have less power; it is very difficult for them to give their views, suggestions, and complaints to top level. There is no surety of complete communication in upward communication as there are so many barriers in its path. Workers at the lowest level are not efficient communicators so their communication oral or written may not be accurate and may not be welcomed by superiors.

Diagonal/Horizontal Communication:

Communication between departments or employees in the same organization without any hierarchy is called diagonal communication. It is the most used channel of communication. Workers communicate with other workers, clerks sharing information with one another, managers discuss some organizational problems with their colleagues, all of these are engaged in diagonal communication.

Diagonal communication is extremely important for promoting, understanding and co-ordination among various departments. It can take place among any employees of the organization. In this type of communication anybody without any hesitation can enter into this process for discussion. It most effectively carried on through oral communication. Group discussion, face to face exchange of views or a brief conversation are diagonal communication.

Grapevine:

An informal channel of communication in an organization is called grapevine. It follows no set lines or any definite rules but spreads very fast in any direction. For example people working together take interest in one another and talk about appointments, promotions, demotions or even domestic and romantic affairs of another. Though all these things are top secrets some people take great pleasure from gathering such secrets and transiting to others. This is nothing but grapevine. It is basically a channel of horizontal communication because people working at the same level can do it.

Features:

- It provides much needed release to emotions.
- Any information in the name of 'secret' spreads very fast.
- Information which cannot be transmitted to employees through official channels can be sent by grapevine.
- It provides feedback to the management. The management can tactfully spread some information through it and wait for the reaction.

Limitations:

- One of the major limitations of the grapevine is that it may spread baseless news which may harm the employees.
- Misunderstanding can take place because sometimes it transmits incomplete information.
- It can cause serious damage before management becomes aware of it.

9.1.4 Levels of Communication

The levels of communication can be described under the following heads:

- Intrapersonal
- Interpersonal
- Extra personal
- Organizational
- Mass Communication

Intrapersonal:

This communication occurs within the individual's brain in the form of internal dialogue, as one cannot stop communicating with himself. In fact when we communicate with other person, internal dialogue with oneself continues - verifying the truth, using logical reasoning etc. For example, when one gets injured, the brain gets information and then sends the feedback that he should consult a doctor or take medicine. This is nothing but intrapersonal communication.

Interpersonal:

This level of communication includes ideas or information shared by people. This can assume the form of face to face conversation, video conferencing, and telephonic talk and so on. It takes place in our day to day life. This level of communication is beneficiary as doubts can be clarified instantly and immediate feedback is possible.

Interpersonal communication depends on the chemistry, between two parties involved. The environment and cultural context also play their vital role. Besides it can be formal and informal.

Extra personal:

Extra personal communication occurs between human beings and non-human beings in which sign language is used to transmit information or to respond. For example when a pet dog feels hungry, it comes to its keeper wagging its tail; it is nothing but an extra personal communication.

Organizational Communication:

Communication between members of a big organization is organizational communication. It may be upward, downward, diagonal and grapevine. This type of communication is extremely necessary for the smooth working of any organization.

Mass Communication:

In this level of communication, information is transmitted to the public at large through media such as television, radio, internet, books, journals and newspapers. Information in the oral form requires equipments such as microphones, amplifiers and information in the written form requires electronic or print media. It plays an important role in boosting the image of the organization and attracting customers.

9.2 Effective Communication

Having excellent communication skills is critical in the paralegal profession. Much of a paralegal's day is spent communicating in writing or verbally. A paralegal's day is filled with drafting motions, writing summaries of depositions, discussing the project status with an attorney, corresponding by email, telephone calls to clients and vendors, taking notes or writing memos – the list is endless. It is an inherent part of your job, and that is why it is always listed in the requirements of all paralegal job postings.

Learning to communicate your point clearly is about more than just learning how to write grammatically correct sentences. Say, for example, that you want to convince your attorney to purchase new software that will increase the team's efficiency on cases. How do you write a request that is compelling and persuasive? Do you know how to summarize everything that the software does, the cost analysis and how you will roll it out to the team? Can you write about it or speak about it in such a way that convinces the higher-ups that it would be a good purchase? This is something that can only be learned by improving your communication skills. It is the duty of paralegal to make sure that while communicating verbally or in writing, their every communication should include following:

Clear

To be clear, try to minimize the number of ideas in each email and in each sentence within the email. Make sure that it's easy for your reader to understand your meaning. People shouldn't have to read between the lines and make assumptions on what you are trying to say.

Ask yourself: what is your purpose in communicating with this person? If you're not sure, then your audience won't be sure either.

Also, be clear about any attachments. Do not send the attachment without any explanation for what it is or why you have sent it. This may make both the email and the attachment look like spam. Make sure to note how large the attachment is—if it is very large, explain the size of the attachment so they know it is supposed to be that large, and it is not a potential virus.

Concise

As paralegals working with lawyers, we read briefs, demand letters, contracts and all kinds of other written communication that can be quite lengthy and filled with a lot of legal jargon. It can be far too easy to start developing that writing habit in your other communications, like emails and memos.

When you're concise in your communication, you stick to the point and keep it brief. Being conscious of time is especially important in the legal industry. Your audience doesn't have the time and does not want to read six sentences when you could communicate your message in three.

Unless the topic necessitates a very long email, keep your correspondence as short and to the point as possible. This might mean cleaning up long email chains, as well as whittling down what you need to say in the email to the most basic points.

You do not want your recipient to miss an important point because it was buried in long paragraphs. If it has to be a long email, then separate the topics with a topic title (underlined) and a call to action for each topic. To make your writing more concise, consider eliminating redundancy and expletive constructions. A few examples of redundancy that can be eliminated in your writing:

Redundancy	Revised Version
12 midnight	Midnight
Close Proximity	Proximity
Completely Unanimous	Unanimous
Exactly the same	the same
Final Completion	Completion
Summarize Briefly	Summarize
Surrounded on all sides	Surrounded
We are in receipt of	we have received

An expletive construction normally causes the sentence to lose energy and is unnecessary to make a sentence complete and concise. In such case, the paralegal should look for "to be" verbs to find the expletive construction such as:

- There are
- There is
- That was
- Who was
- It was
- Who is

Confident

The more confident you are when you communicate whether verbally or in writing, the more confident people will be in you. Confidence builds trust and credibility.

One way to have confidence in your communication is through research and knowing your subject matter. With adequate knowledge of a subject, you'll appear more confident when communicating.

Confidence is even more important in the legal profession. There may be a time when you have to communicate with your supervising attorney about a problem on a file or a transaction. If you have thoroughly researched how the problem occurred and potential solutions, you will be confident in your communication of the problem.

Correct

Mistakes with spelling, tone, and grammar can make you look careless. That's why it's essential to check all of your communications before you send them.

Email may not seem as formal as sending a physical letter, but it is, in many ways. This means that you should not just type out the email and send it out without reading it over. This gives you the opportunity to catch any grammar mistakes or typos, as well as to clean up the email, make sure it is formatted in a way that is easy to read, and only contains the most applicable points.

Don't rely on spell-checkers: they won't pick up words that are used incorrectly. Instead, proofread your work, and use a dictionary to look up any words that you're unsure about. Proofread the email thoroughly, at least once, before hitting send and proofread the subject, line, too. It is the first thing that is going to be read, so it should be as spotless as the rest of your email.

Credible

There are three important elements to being credible in your communication: integrity, competence and sound judgment. All three elements are necessary for credibility to exist. Think of the very competent expert witness without integrity. They may be competent, but they will lose credibility without integrity. Alternatively, think about the very competent expert witness without sound judgment. They frequently change their minds and their opinions last minute. This also loses credibility. There are certain methods which will help to increase credibility such as:

- Building a reputation for truthful and ethical behavior
- If you make a mistake, be truthful about it
- Avoiding snap judgments
- Staying current on the trends within your industry and company

Complete

In a complete message, the audience has everything they need to be informed and, if applicable, to be able to take action. It can be difficult to balance complete with concise. Concise does not mean that you leave out information. The message still has to be complete.

Courteous

Courteous communication is friendly, open, and honest. There are no hidden insults or passive-aggressive tones. Email seems like an informal method of communication, but as a paralegal, you likely already know that the emails you send are professional communication. They should be treated as such. Don't fall into the trap of letting your emotions write the email for you. If you are angry or upset about the subject of the email, type it out, save it as a draft, and come back to it the next day.

9.3 Importance of correct and current business English

9.4 Verbal and Non verbal communication

9.4.1 Introduction

Communication refers to the transfer of meaning from one person to another person. In communication we use different modes or channels to convey our experiences as well as understand and attach meaning to other people's experiences. Communication is an important element in our daily lives as most of the waking time an individual Communication can be done verbally and nonverbally, it is also frequently mixed with signals and noise.

9.4.2 Verbal communication

It refers to the spoken part of communication. It can be face to face, over the telephone, or via voice mail. The elements of verbal communication include your choice of words and phrases, sentence construction and voice tone and pitch. When combined, these elements paint a picture of who you are as a person.

Most of us do not realize that a portion of our communication occurs relevantly a non-verbal class as confronted to syntactical communication. Non-verbal communication contains relevantly eye contact, frontal expressions, body posture, tone of speech etc. It may additionally compose the manner we dress our clothes or the hush we keep. Information of non-verbal communication is considerable managers who assist as administrators of organizational "teams," for at least coupled reasons:

- ❖ To behave consequentially as a team authority the manager necessary interacts with the foreign members consummately. Non-verbal advises, when analyzed correctly; deliver him with one means to do so.
- ❖ The team members project attitudes and feelings through non-verbal communication. Some personal needs such as approval, growth, achievement and recognition may be met in effective teams. The extent to which these needs are met is closely related to how perceptive the team leader and team members are to non-verbal communication in themselves and in others on the team.

9.4.3 Non verbal communication

Non-verbal communication consists of all the messages other than words that are used in communication. In oral communication, these symbolic messages are transferred by means of intonation, tone of voice, vocally produced noises, body posture, body gestures, facial expressions or pauses.

Non-verbal communication is the message without words received through the medium of gestures, signs, bodily movements, and facial expressions, tone of voice, color, time, space, and style of writing and choice of words. Unlike animals who can communicate their deepest feelings through gestures, we human beings have God's gift of language to convey our feelings in a structured manner. Yet in our moments of excitement, we need to convey our feelings and emotions of joy, anger, sorrow, love, wonder, hatred etc. by smiling, shouting, patting or using other wordless clues. This is nothing but non-verbal communication. However some non-verbal messages go hand in hand with the verbal messages to convey the full meaning.

Basically there are two components of non-verbal (wordless messages) communication:

1. Kinesics Communication
2. Meta Communication

Kinesics Communication:

Kinesics communication is a message conveyed through non-verbal acts in the form of body movements such as gestures, winking, smiling, style of dressing and grooming. This type of communication transmits the unstated feelings, attitude and hidden intentions of the speaker. For example, when a faculty enters in the class room to deliver a lecture, his body movements tells the students whether he is a man of confidence or not. This is nothing but Kinesics communication.

Meta Communication:

Meta communication includes a message communicated not through words, but along with words. It conveys an implied meaning by the selection and tone of words. For example - when one says "work hard to become someone of eminence" This statement offers advice. But the sentence without stating implies that the concerned person is not very hard working and may be idle

9.5 Written communication skills and techniques

9.5.1 Introduction

Writing can be a pleasure if the basic purpose is clear. It proves to be tiresome and boring when the very purpose is hazy. In simple words, the goal of effective business writing is getting things done. This simple target can be attained if we write with the following two-fold approach in mind:

1. To inform the reader

2. To request the reader to take action

In written business communication the expectations regarding involvement are higher from the reader. The effectiveness of the business message can be measured in terms of the speed with which the required action is initiated and consequent results produced.

Suppose after completing the writing project, a simple question is posed by the writer, "So what?" In other words, the writer asking himself that if this business message was drafted and sent to the receiver, then what will be the inference drawn from it. What response does the message expect to get? What will be the impact on the receiver? Would he be persuaded to take prompt action? Answers to these types of questions will automatically clear the way for writing coherent and meaningful business messages

9.5.2 Stages of Writing

"Writing is a fluid process created by writers as they work. Accomplished writers move back and forth between the stages of the process, both consciously and unconsciously. Paralegals, however, benefit from structure and security of following writing process in their writing.

- ❖ Prewriting (generating ideas for writing): brainstorming; reading literature; creating life maps, webs, and story charts; developing word banks; deciding on form, audience, voice, and purpose as well as through teacher motivation.
- ❖ Rough Drafting (getting ideas on paper): writing without concern for conventions. Written work does not have to be neat; it is a 'sloppy copy.'
- ❖ Rereading (proofreading one's own work) by reading aloud and reading for sensibility.

9.5.3 Preparing Notes

Preparing notes is a tedious process and requires a high level of concentration. To prepare the notes in a systematic manner, they would necessarily follow a five-step process given below:

1. Read the text carefully.

2. Select the key words in the passage or words that communicate the main idea.

3. Construct a sentence that captures the essence of the paragraph or state it in brief. To get the gist of the paragraph it must be carefully studied. If the statement needs to be copied as it is in the original, care should be exercised while doing so, to ensure that there is no punctuation or spelling error.

4. Note down the page number.

5. Note down the bibliographical details.

If notes for letters or reports are being prepared, reference numbers are used instead of bibliographical details. This makes it easy to retrieve the information when the need arises.

9.5.4 Business Message

A written business message is one of the methods of business communication governed by the culture of the organization, values, habits, interest networks and relationships. The formation of an effective and successful written message includes planning, formulating, improving and editing the message. However, the goal is to attract the reader to read and accept the message. It is therefore important to compose a well-structured and particularly a clearly composed written message.

In modern times Email has become the preferred method of conducting business communication for many professionals because of its convenience and speed. However, because email is so quick to use, it is easy to overlook some of the attention to detail we use with traditional correspondence. Here are 10 steps to ensure your business emails reflect your company's professional reputation.

Step 1: Address your recipient by name in your salutation. Although it may be convenient to get right to your message content, do not overlook the same personal address you would use with a traditional letter. Whether you address your contact by first or last name and with the use of a title like Mr., Mrs. or Ms. will be dictated by your familiarity with the recipient. However, personalizing your message indicates your level of interest in conducting business with that individual.

Step 2: Always include a subject in your message, and make it as specific as possible. Subjects make it easier for your recipient to find your correspondence at a later date. They also reduce the likelihood that your message will get trapped in a spam filter. If your recipient is not familiar with your email address, include your name or your company name in the subject to identify your message.

Step 3: Write complete sentences. These are easier and quicker to read and comprehend. If you write sentences after full picturisation, then there will be no need for assumptions and it gives an impression to recipient that you understood the whole idea.

Step 4: Be concise. The requirement of professional's emails is short and up to date with all content. It impacts the business communication. Big messages are skimmed rather than read carefully.

Step 5: Avoid overly familiar phrasing, text messaging syntax and emoticons. One of the biggest mistakes you can make in professional email correspondence is using a style of writing that should be reserved for personal messages, forums and online social networks. Although these forms of expression may be acceptable for some interoffice messages and communication with the most familiar business contacts, abbreviations and emotion key combinations generally have no place in professional emails.

Step 6: Pay special attention to how you articulate your message while addressing sensitive issues. Because email is a strictly written form of communication, nuances like tone of voice and intonation are not expressed. This can be of special concern when your message involves conflict resolution, assessing mistakes or dealing with job performance concerns. Ideally, these issues are best addressed in person or in a phone call. However, if email must be used, take special care to articulate your concerns very specifically without pejorative phrasing. In addressing any negative issues, it is also a good idea to begin and end with more positive statements. Rather than firing off a potential damaging reply to a negative email, compose it and save as a draft. Give yourself a few hours to review it with a fresh perspective before actually hitting "Send."

Step 7: Avoid writing in all caps and using too many exclamation points. These forms of typing translate as yelling in the sphere of email communication. They also make your message much harder to read quickly since most of us are conditioned to read large bodies of text best in uppercase and lowercase type.

Step 8: Use CCs sparingly. Make sure the recipients who are kept in CC for your message are essential participants in the communication. If you feel that others need to be kept abreast of your correspondence, consider using your email software's BC feature to send a message that will be blind to the primary recipient. Never address negative issues or concerns in a CC email. Those concerns should be addressed individually. However, when replying to messages that have been CC'd, be sure to use your "Reply to All" feature so that communication remains clear between all parties.

Step 9: Check spellings and proofread before sending. Set your email software's preferences to spell-check as you type so that you can correct misspellings immediately. Also, be sure to actually read your email message before you send it to make sure its grammar and syntax are correct.

Step 10: Use a standard signature with every email. In addition to "signing" your name, set up an email signature to be used on every email that includes your name, title and company. Also make sure it includes all your contact information, your email address and your website address. This adds legitimacy to your message and ensures your recipients will always be able to contact you, even if it's not by email.

9.5.5 Style and Tone

Tone in writing is the attitude that the writer conveys to the reader. It's not necessarily what you say, but how you say it. Tone is intended to create a specific response or emotion in the reader; it creates a personality that can either engage or repel users.

The tone and the style of writing change according to the audience who is going to read it. Different types of styles and tones can be used for different occasions and purposes. Style of writing could be formal or informal. Different occasions necessitate a different style of writing. While the highly formal prose is acceptable for reports or documentation, a slightly informal style could be adopted when it comes to business correspondence.

Once again this would be dependent upon the relationship between the sender and the receiver. If styles of writing were viewed on a continuum the writer, who is extremely formal on one side and an extremely informal reader, on the other, it would be seen that almost all business writing occasion and facts cluster in between the formal and somewhat informal points of reference. This cluster could then be used to understand the tone used for communicating messages that would vary from active to passive, personal to impersonal, colorful to colorless. The choice of the tone for depicting these styles would be dependent upon the sender (who), the reader (to whom), the occasion (when and where), and the content (what). With a change in any one of these components, there is bound to be a change in the tone through which the message is expressed.

Let us consider a few examples of formal and informal words.

	Formal	Informal
1.	Subsequent to	After
2.	We trust	I hope
3.	Consulted	Checked
4.	Undertake	Handle
5.	Rearrange	Juggle

Let us take a look at the various styles that can be used to reflect different moods.

1. Active: An active tone reflects a desire to get things done at the earliest. There is also a sense of responsibility for what is being communicated. In this style, the simplest of the sentence construction is used, that is, the 'subject-verb-object (SVO) ordering. Messages are short, to the point, and use imperatives normally. The tone is commanding and succinct, active is used by people at the helm of affairs who are in the habit of voicing and issuing directives. Direct statements are used and no efforts are made to camouflage the impact of a direct utterance that could have a negative impact. For example: Project Report should be completed by 12th November 1999.

2. Passive: This is a rather soft style and is used in situations when some negative message is to be communicated and the sender does not wish to hurt the receiver. This style is also used in reports where the long sentences or statements are not universal truths but need to be studied and critically examined. Hence, words and statements such as, suppositions "maybe", "perhaps" and "possibly" are used. Nothing is stated that would communicate a feeling that this is the ultimate truth. Compared to the active style, the sentences are longer since many are cushioned in suppositions. Even the sentence ordering is reversed. It follows an object-verb-subject patterning. For example: The date for completion of the Project Report is 12th November 1999.

3. Personal: A personal style is used when an individual wishes to be personal in his communication. It is much like the spoken message and part of the personality of the communicator gets translated into it. Use of pronouns like "I", "you" is made, and the receivers are referred brief sentences to by their first names instead of their surnames. Personal references are also made that indicate ties between the sender and the receiver. Sentences, in this form of writing, are brief ones and short and the overall tone is conversational. The active voice for communication of messages is used and on occasions even direct questions can be asked to the reader, e.g. I want you to complete the Project Report immediately.

4. Impersonal: In contrast to the personal style, the impersonal style is tedious. It is withdrawn and is more pompous. Personal pronouns such as Use of "We"- a "You" are avoided and are replaced by a more passive voice; corporate word, "we". The names of receivers are not mentioned and the tone is passive. Occasionally the sentences are long and complex, making the written message complicated and heavy.

For instance, we would greatly benefit as a result of completion of the Project Report.

5. Colorful Style: Normally used for literary purposes, it increases the impact of the written message. Adjectives and adverbs are frequently made use of so as to add weight and give color to the written message. Further, concrete words or "those that add to the visual impact of the written message, adjectives and e.g., metaphors, similes and other figures of speech are used. In adverbs, the colorful style of writing, the choice of words is extremely important. As the impact of the message being transmitted is contingent upon these, proper care should be exercised in interjecting statements with appropriate words, e.g. preparing the project report is a challenging task ahead of us. If it is completed by November 12, 2016, it would be a tremendous feat accomplished.

6. Colorless style: A colorless style is a combination of an impersonal and passive style. This is a dull and monotonous way of communicating the message. It avoids concrete in favor of abstract. The passive style message is absolutely colorless

without any figures of speech such as similes, metaphors etc. In fact, it is one of the most depressing styles as there is neither vigor nor intellectual or emotional appeal in the writing.

9.6 Good Writing Skills in Workplace

Good writing skills can help you come across as more credible, more capable, than a colleague who frequently has typos and grammatical errors.

Profession

Obviously good writing skills are important when your job involves writing, be it as a journalist, paralegal or public relations professional – that goes without saying. If you are employed for your writing skills, having "good" writing skills is a job requirement. However, more professions require good writing skills than those traditionally associated with writing. Any time a profession requires written communication, writing skills become important.

Communication

With emails, notes, letters, texts and Tweets, most people spend a fair amount of time at work communicating via the written word. Whether you are messaging a colleague, writing to your manager, or crafting the company newsletter, your writing skills can boost or hinder your career easily, even if you do not have a "writing" profession. Basically, writing skills make a difference in how you come across.

Credibility

People with good writing skills are generally seen as more credible. Think to yourself how you would interpret an email from a colleague that was filled with typos and grammatical errors. At best, he was negligent in that he didn't proofread his message or use spell check; at worst, he comes across as less intelligent and less capable. Better writers tend to get higher grades and be perceived as more competent and more intelligent than their less literary counterparts.

Considerations

In the workplace, you need to make sure that you proofread everything you write, from an email to a company memo. However, just because good writing skills are a plus, you still need to pick your battles. Correcting others can work against you, in some cases even undermining you. Further, context and tone are just as important as grammar. While obvious mistakes are a no-no, such as using "their" and "they're" incorrectly, smaller errors, like confusing "who" and "whom" are less important.

9.7 Business correspondence

Apart from knowing the structures and formalities of business, a paralegal or legal assistant, must be familiar with the types of legal correspondence common to the field or practice of law in which he or she is working. The following is a list of types of correspondence that a paralegal might run across in civil litigation practice:

Transmittal Letter

Letter used to send documents or information to the client. It is relatively short and should include a description of whatever is being transmitted or sent to the client.

Confirmation Letter

Letter used to confirm information, conversations, and/or important dates to the client. Typically it will follow a conversation or meeting with the client.

Demand Letter

Letter used to outline the client's claims/demands for settlement. Typically such a letter will provide detailed information about amounts incurred, injuries sustained, damages or other information relevant to the client's claim. The letter will also outline the relevant law and the client's rights arising out of the law/legal relationship. Often a demand letter will include a dollar amount or other terms of settlement.

Notice of Termination of Relationship

Such letter is used by the lawyer to send notice to the client that he or she is no longer the attorney for the client. This may be sent after a meeting with a potential client during which the lawyer determined he or she was unable or unwilling to represent the client. It may also be used where the relationship between the lawyer and the client has broken down, and the lawyer is no longer ethically able to continue the representation.

Conflict Letter

Such letter may be used by the attorney to notify potential and/or prior clients that a potential conflict of interest exists between the clients that may impact the attorney's representation of one or both of the clients. Typically such a letter will include a waiver of the potential conflict for the parties to sign.

10

Legal Document Processing

10.1 Using MS Office Tools for document processing

Strong computer skills are essential for today's paralegals. Included in these skills are the paralegal's ability to adapt to differences in their employer's computer system, selected software programs, and the supervising attorney's personal preferences for document formatting.

A skilled paralegal must have exemplary word processing skills. These include knowing the proper format for a variety of documents and keeping track of the particular drafting preferences of their attorneys. Many paralegals struggle with correct grammar, punctuation, and word usage.

Today's legal assistants and paralegals need to be proficient in a variety of computer and technology skills. As the role of the legal professional changes and grows, a need for technology knowledge is high on the list of requirements for legal industry job positions. The more technology skills you possess, the more valuable you become as a legal assistant or paralegal. Bureau of Labor and Statistics lists the following duties that are performed by paralegals:

- Investigate and gather the facts of a case
- Conduct research on relevant laws, regulations, and legal articles
- Organize and maintain documents in paper or electronic filing systems
- Gather and arrange evidence and other legal documents for attorney review and case preparation
- Write or summarize reports to help lawyers prepare for trials
- Draft correspondence and legal documents, such as contracts and mortgages
- Get affidavits and other formal statements that may be used as evidence in court
- Help lawyers during trials by handling exhibits, taking notes, or reviewing trial transcripts
- File exhibits, briefs, appeals and other legal documents with the court or opposing counsel

- Call clients, witnesses, lawyers, and outside vendors to schedule interviews, meetings, and depositions
- Having knowledge of a wide array of technological skills will increase your career opportunities.

Word Processing, Spreadsheets and Presentation Software

Document creation is a large part of a legal professional's responsibilities. Microsoft Office, Open Office, and Google Docs are common software suites that are used in many law firms. Knowledge of one of these programs is a must for legal assistants and paralegals. As a legal professional, you will be communicating and exchanging documents with other parties. Being proficient in programs other than those used in your office is a great advantage when you are sent files with different file types created with different software systems.

Paralegals need to recognize their role in the firm as a profit center, as distinguished from an overhead staff member, and utilize the software to document accurately how each work hour is spent. Many paralegals find accounting for all of their minutes at work is difficult at first, and are surprised to see how much of their day is not accounted for. Some firms have paralegals who have sole responsibility for client conflict checks throughout the firm. However, in smaller firms, a paralegal should know how to check the database for client conflicts.

Paralegals can be particularly valuable to a firm if they have experience in the use of slide show such as Microsoft PowerPoint. These are used in a variety of ways in the mediation and litigation process. When the paralegal is familiar with the important issues and evidence of the case, as well how to create powerful visual presentations, the result is more successful and cost effective. This does not require that the paralegal be particularly artistic. Features include using appropriate color schemes, use of cropping and enlarging photographs, highlighting techniques for text documents, and subtle animation that brings the slide to life at the mouse click of the presenter. Attention to detail turns a static slide show into a persuasive presentation.

Computer Skills

There are many general computer safety issues, but three in particular that need to be understood and followed by a paralegal: Data backup, safe internet usage, and disposal of drives and disks.

Every paralegal needs to verify that there is a backup data system in place and that it is used according to the plan. One of the simplest methods for documents is built into Microsoft Word. Auto recover is accessed in Word by selecting File/Save. To the left of the Save button is a drop down menu called Tools/Save Options. One can select how often the software auto saves and where to store the files.

Each firm that has a network should have an automatic data backup system that is maintained by the technical department. However, for a freestanding PC, one should have a device that automatically backs up one's data to an external hard disk on schedule. How often one backs up is a personal choice as well as the method and selection of backing up the data. Good questions to ask are: how long it would take to redo the document? Is there data that would be lost or forgotten if not backed up immediately? The answers to these questions will help determine a suitable auto backup schedule.

Online backup programs are available for use over the Internet. Some of them are free for limited amount of data. Be sure to consider the security issues, as well as unsettled attorney-client confidentiality and privilege issues involved, if selecting this storage method.

The widespread use of laptops has created serious questions of internet safety, particularly in the use of public access Wi-Fi spots. Given the sensitive client data that can be stored on a business laptop, paralegals need to consider avoiding all public access Wi-Fi sites and using only secured internet networks. If public sites are used, be sure to turn on encryption software and consider using one of the mobile Virtual Private Networking software programs available.

Finally, when the computer dies, or is determined to have become technologically obsolete, the disposal of the hard drive becomes a sensitive issue. Some firms back up the internal drive to the new system and then dispose of the old drive by physical destruction. Some internal drives are saved and archived to be used later if necessary. An external enclosure can inexpensively create an external drive from an original internal drive. Under no circumstances should a computer be given away, even to an employee, without wiping it clean of the data. This can be done by restoring the internal hard drive to its original condition using the restore disks created when the computer was brand new.

Lastly, any CDs or DVDs created for backup purposes and no longer needed should be shredded. Many paper shredders now have the capacity to shred CDs or DVDs. Electronic data needs to be treated as sensitively as paper documents to prevent client information from being released.

Maintaining paralegal skills is a never-ending task. A well-trained paralegal must stay up to date with technology so that the firm can best represent the client both ethically and profitably. Paralegals, either in coordination with the firm's technology department or on their own, can create a structure that works well for the firm using the latest technology and observing the ethical rules.

10.2 Knowing about various legal documents

10.2.1 Introduction

Paralegals function as an assistant to lawyers. They draft, revise, finalize and keep organized almost every type of document seen by law firms and other organizations employing lawyers. One of a paralegal's most important tasks is helping lawyers prepare for closings, hearings, trials, and corporate meetings. Paralegals might investigate the facts of cases and ensure that all relevant information is considered. They also identify appropriate laws, judicial decisions, legal articles, and other materials that are relevant to assigned cases. After they analyze and organize the information, paralegals may prepare written reports that attorneys use in determining how cases should be handled. If attorneys decide to file lawsuits on behalf of clients, paralegals may help prepare the legal arguments, draft pleadings and motions to be filed with the court, obtain affidavits, and assist attorneys during trials. Paralegals also organize and track files of all important case documents and make them available and easily accessible to attorneys.

Legal Documents

Legal document is any written instrument that defines, declares, limits, or expands the legal rights or privileges of a person or entity. Legal documents are often times come from court or other government agency which defines legal rights, privileges or duties of persons named in the instrument. Courts issue orders that require or prohibit certain actions, and limit or expand legal rights, privileges, define the rights of ownership, benefits, etc. Courts issue orders, writs - which is a declarative order like a Writ of Possession in an eviction case which declares that the landlord is entitled to possession of the property. Courts also issue warrants like arrest warrants or search warrants.

Types of Legal Documents

Paralegals should have basic knowledge and information about following legal documents which covers fields such as:

Business

If you're running a business, you will require legal documents. A paralegal should have knowledge about following business forms:

- Affidavit Templates
- Demand For Payment Letter
- Non-Compete Agreement
- Toll Manufacturing Agreement

Business Formation

To form and run any business, you require a legal document which covers:

- ❖ Amendment to LLC Operating Agreement
- ❖ Articles of Incorporation
- ❖ Assignment of Partnership Interest
- ❖ Business Plan Template
- ❖ Business Purchase Agreement
- ❖ Joint Venture Agreement
- ❖ Limited Liability Company (LLC) Operating Agreement
- ❖ Partnership Agreement
- ❖ Partnership Agreement Amendment
- ❖ Privacy Policy
- ❖ Shareholder Agreement
- ❖ Stock Certificate
- ❖ Terms of Use Agreement
- ❖ Trademark Assignment Agreement

Business Operations

Every business some or the other way involves into legal documentation. A paralegal should have information about the following business forms and agreements:

- ❖ Affidavit of Identity
- ❖ Affidavit of Service
- ❖ Affidavit of Title
- ❖ Arbitration Agreement
- ❖ Cease and Desist Letter
- ❖ End User License Agreement
- ❖ Hold Harmless (Indemnity) Agreement
- ❖ Invoice Form
- ❖ Letter of Intent
- ❖ Licensing Agreement
- ❖ Loan Agreement
- ❖ Manufacturing and Supply Agreement
- ❖ Photo Release Form

- Promissory Note
- Purchase Order
- Release of Liability Form
- Sales Agreement
- Toll Manufacturing Agreement
- Video Release Form

Business Property

Buying and selling property can be a real hassle which involves following legal documentation such as:

- Auto Bill of Sale
- Bill of Sale
- Boat Bill of Sale
- Buy-Sell Agreement
- Commercial Lease Agreement
- Construction Contract Agreement
- Deed of Trust
- Firearm Bill of Sale
- Horse Bill of Sale
- Land/Ground Lease Agreement
- Quitclaim Deed
- Warranty Deed

Employment

Whether you are hiring full-time employees or freelancers, legal document is required by the company or worker for safety which covers:

- Employment Agreement
- Independent Contractor Agreement
- Leave of Absence Agreement
- Leave of Absence Letter
- Non-Compete Agreement
- Non-Disclosure (Confidentiality) Agreement
- Resignation Letter

Financial

Legal documents are involved in business, purchases, sales, transactions and other finance related a legal affair which includes:

- Affidavit Templates
- Demand For Payment Letter
- Financial Affidavit
- Gift Affidavit
- IOU
- Loan Agreement
- Power of Attorney
- Promissory Note
- Revocation of Power of Attorney
- Stock Purchase Agreement
- Tolling Agreement

Personal & Family

There are certain legal forms related to personal and family needs which every paralegal should know which includes:

- Affidavit of Death
- Affidavit of Heirship
- Affidavit of Residence
- Affidavit Templates
- Child Medical Consent
- Child Support Modification
- Child Travel Consent Form
- Cohabitation Agreement
- Demand For Payment Letter
- Divorce Agreement
- Financial Affidavit
- Gift Affidavit
- IOU
- Last Will and Testament
- Leave of Absence Agreement
- Leave of Absence Letter

- Letter of Intent
- Living Will
- Medical Records Release Form
- Parenting Plan/Child Custody Agreement
- Pet Care Agreement
- Pet Custody Agreement
- Photo Release Form
- Postnuptial Agreement
- Power of Attorney
- Prenuptial Agreement
- Purchase Agreement
- Revocation of Power of Attorney
- Roommate Agreement
- Separation Agreement
- Tolling Agreement

Real Estate

On buying, selling or managing pieces of property, legal documents are required which needs to be signed from buyer, seller with a witness which covers:

- Affidavit of Heirship
- Affidavit Templates
- Commercial Lease Agreement
- Deed of Trust
- Eviction Notice
- Home Lease Agreement
- Land/Ground Lease Agreement
- Late Rent Notice
- Lease Agreement
- Lease Amendment
- Lease Application
- Lease Renewal
- Lease Termination
- Mortgage Deed
- Notice of Intent to Vacate

- Notice of Rent Increase
- Notice to Quit
- Pet Addendum to a Lease Agreement
- Property Management Agreement
- Quitclaim Deed
- Real Estate Purchase Agreement
- Rent-to-Own Agreement
- Rental/Lease Application
- Roommate Agreement
- Smoking Lease Addendum
- Sublease Agreement
- Tenant Removal Form
- Vacation Rental Short Term Lease Agreement
- Warranty Deed

Will & Estate Planning

Will and estate planning is the process of arranging the distribution of assets before and after the death.

- Advance Healthcare Directive
- Affidavit of Death
- Affidavit of Domicile
- Affidavit of Service
- Affidavit Templates
- Codicil to Will
- Cohabitation Agreement
- Last Will and Testament
- Living Will
- Medical Power of Attorney
- Power of Attorney

10.3 Formatting legal business letters and proofreading

10.3.1 Formatting

Business letters are backbone of a successful business house. If a businessman wants to establish contacts with the business world and government departments, wants to collect information, he has to make correspondence. Business letters are written to inquire about terms and conditions, to offer a new product, to complain for some problems, to calm down a furious customer, to place and cancel orders, to collect overdue amounts, to build goodwill, to widen the approach and so on.

Formatting of Business letter includes:

- Letterhead: Most companies have a specific letterhead that you will need to type letters on. This may make it necessary to adjust the margins so that words are not printed onto the letterhead area.
- Name and address: Always try to have the name of someone that the letter should go to, even if you have to call to find it out.
- Date: This is the date that the letter was written. It should be written out, such as January 15, 2017.
- Reference: This gives a short description of what the purpose of the letter is. For example, one might write "Lost Invoice" or "Account number 23654" or something like that.
- Salutation: If you do not know the person, use a more formal one, such as Dr. Brian Lowden.
- Subject matter/body: Single-space and left justify for modified block and block style letters. Have one blank line between paragraphs. The first paragraph should have a friendly opening and state the purpose of the letter. The subsequent paragraphs should support the purpose you stated in the first paragraph.
- Closing: This should be "Tthank you," "Sincerely," or something similar.
- Signature: This is the actual signature of the person the letter is from, which may be different from the person who wrote the letter.
- Typist Initials: These are the initials of the person who typed the letter. These are not the initials of the person who it is from. If they are both the same person, then this line is not necessary. Usually the first initials would be that of the writer, and the second initials are of the typist and are in lowercase. For example: JW/sc.
- Enclosures: List here anything else you may be sending, such as a brochure, samples, etc.

Business Letter Format

Heading

Your Street Address
Your City, State Zip
Date

Inside Address

First and Last Name of the Person to whom you are writing
Their Street Address
City, ST Zip

Salutation

Body

Dear Mr./Ms. Full Name:

You do not want to indent when you are using this format. This is the best format to use when you are writing a persuasive letter. You want to introduce yourself and the topic you are writing about to the reader. Remember that the first rule of writing is to know your audience. In a persuasive letter, you state your opinion or your feelings about something that is important to you after you have introduced yourself. You must sound as professional and passionate as possible. You do not want to belittle the reader or they will not finish reading your letter. Your letter needs to have the facts, reasons, and examples to support your position. Address issues that your reader may have in their argument.
In a second paragraph, you must have solutions. Without solutions, you are only complaining. Offer assistance in solving the problem. Remind the reader where they can contact you.

Sincerely yours,

Signature

Fig: Business Letter

To,
Mr. Michael Johnson,
46, Apple Valley,

Dear Mr. Michael,
Sub- Legal Notice for Non-payment of Loan Installment
Ref- Loan A/c No. 0000XXXX

Notice is being sent to you for the non-payment of previous three installments on your loan as mentioned in the reference. The loan was taken for the purchase of Car in the month of March 20XX and after paying two installments, you have not paid rest of the installments till today. However, we have already sent several reminders for the non-payment of installments on time, yet we have not got any response from your side. As a result we are supposed to take legal step of sending you legal notice.

If you do take appropriate action against your due with in 15 days from this notice we will be bound to take legal action against you. The legal action can result in confiscation of mortgaged property and penalty as per the law for defaulting.

Thank You,

Sincerely,
Legal Advisor,
City Bank,
California

Fig: Legal Business Letter

10.3.2 Proofreading

The format, or overall appearance of a document, determines a reader's first impression, favorable or not, about the author and the message. After you have created a business letter or document, you should start out by reading it over once. You want to first correct any errors in spelling, grammar, punctuation, and sentence logic. This is to see if it makes sense and if you have included the information you intended to include. Once you have finished that, you should set the letter or document aside for a while. You should not immediately begin to edit the work.

The process of proofreading should be the last step in the writing process. Once you have written a draft and edited it to your liking, you are then ready to do a quick spell-check on the computer. Once you have done that, you are ready to proofread the document.

In proofreading, you are looking for mistakes such as grammar, capitalization, typos, and misspelled words. While some people do this on computers today, making changes as they go along, others prefer to do it with a printed piece of paper in their hand. There is no right or wrong way to proofread. It does have to be done on the computer or on paper. Many offices today are becoming more environmentally friendly, which is one reason some would prefer to proofread right on the screen, thus saving all the extra sheets of paper.

To proofread, you will need to read the document very slowly. If it is possible for you to read the document aloud, that is even better. When you can read it aloud and hear what has been written, you are relying on more than just vision and may catch things that do not sound quite right. Some people also recommend reading the document backward, word for word, to catch things that are not correct. Another great option is to have someone else look the document over. You would be amazed at the spelling errors someone else can find even after you have gone over it several times. It never hurts to have a second pair of eyes go over the document if possible.

As you get started with your business writing, pay attention to whether there are errors you consistently make. Then you will know what to be more careful of and can try to avoid in the future.

Proofreader marks may be necessary for some academic or work purposes. While they were more commonly used years ago, before there were computers, some places still routinely use them today.

The task of learning the proofreader's marks and using them may seem daunting at first. However, after you have worked with them for a couple of weeks, they will be like second nature and you will know them well. The document is handy to have printed and readily available in the event someone asks you to proofread and be their second pair of eyes. You could easily use the marks, which are universal in the country, to proofread the document and then return it back to the first proofreader with your suggestions.

Common mistakes when proofreading:

- ❖ Words that have been spelled wrong.
- ❖ Homophones, or words that are pronounced alike but have different spellings and meanings, that have been used incorrectly; e.g., using "their" instead of "there" or the incorrect version of "to," "too," or "two."
- ❖ Punctuation to ensure that commas, periods, apostrophes, and question marks are in the appropriate place. Also, check to see that words that should be capitalized have been. While checking what is there, you should also check to see if something is not there. It is possible to leave out a word that belongs in the document.

There are other areas that you will need to be aware of and watch for when editing and proofreading, such as using active and passive voice, using numbers, word overload, and using clichés.

Numbers

In addition to using the numbers in a date or phone number, you inevitably will include some other numbers from time to time. There are some rules that should be followed when using numbers in your documents other than dates and phone numbers.

Active and Passive Voice

In most of the writing you will do, you will want to use the active voice. Documents that are written in passive voice tend to be scientific in nature. They can be unclear and cause confusion. Unless otherwise preferred for your type of position, you should aim for using active voice when writing your documents.

In passive voice, the subject is acted upon. In active voice, the subject clearly is performing an action. Active voice is considered direct, personal, and clear. Passive voice can often hide important details. In active voice, the subject is doing something (e.g., cleaning, cooking, writing, walking, etc.). You need your writing to be doing something, which means that the verb needs to be active. When writing the sentences, keep in mind that the subject (doer) comes first and is performing the action (verb).

Being Too Wordy

There is a tendency by some people to add fluff or flowery language or to be too wordy with their writing. Regardless of what term you use to refer to it, you should try to avoid it. Adding in words that are not necessary makes a document too wordy. When you are editing your work, you may notice that in removing some of these words the sentence still stands alone and may even become more concise. Here are some commonly used unnecessary words that can be trimmed out of your document to keep it from being too wordy:

- Just recently
- Basic fundamentals
- Very unique
- First and foremost

A common problem with the above examples is that two words are being written to say the same thing. If something is unique, then "very" is not necessary. Extra wording like this adds to a document and can make the message become lost or unclear. The reader has very limited time to spend on the document you have prepared. Aim to say the most with the least amount of words.

Avoid Clichés

When you are writing, it is a good idea to try to avoid clichés. They are phrases that have been overused and people have grown tired of or find annoying. Some common clichés include:

- Do not put off until tomorrow what you can do today.
- There is no place like home.
- A chain is only as strong as its weakest link.
- Don't throw the baby out with the bathwater.
- Kill two birds with one stone.
- All talk and no action.
- All's well that ends well.

10.4 Producing, formatting and editing multi-page legal documents

Writing Legal Document

The writing process includes these steps:

- Prewriting: This is done before you actually start writing. It is the point at which you start gathering information, details, notes, etc. that you will need to write the draft. It is wise to create an outline to follow along with as you write. You can jot down a brief outline that states topics to be discussed in each paragraph, pertinent information to include, etc. Doing an outline before beginning to write is like having a road map so you know where you are going as you write.

- Drafting: This is when you begin writing the draft. You will connect your ideas and write the letter or document you have set out to do. During this stage, it is best to keep writing and not worry about editing or stopping to mull over every paragraph. Just let the words flow and keep going until you finish.
- Edit: This is when you go back over the draft with a keen eye for detail. You will be looking for proper mechanics, spelling, grammar, etc.
- Proofread: This step should be the last step you do once all the others have been done. In this step, you will read over the document for any spelling, punctuation, or other such minor errors that you have overlooked.

When there are more pages than one in a letter it is normal practice to put nothing at the end of the first page. Since there is no closing line or signature it is obvious that there is another page. Subsequent pages do not contain the letterhead and are printed on plain paper. Instead they have a special identification of the letter, which is usually called "header" or "heading". It usually (but not always) contains the name of the addressee, the page number, and the date.

October 24, 2008

Mr. Colin Adams
134 Blossom St.
Chelsea, MA 02231

Dear Mr. Adams:

I would like to confirm your participation in our upcoming February 5-8 conference at the Hyatt Regency Hotel, Boston, Massachusetts. We expect 200 to 230 registrants to attend your session.

I will forward the complete agenda to you in late December. But in the meantime, let me give you a few preliminary details: you are scheduled to deliver your presentation on Asset Management on February 7. Topics that will be covered by different speakers during the conference include Financial Planning, Financial Software and Financial Services.

You will be responsible for preparing thoroughly for the session and presenting a well thought out presentation. It is our expectation that attendees should feel that they have gained valuable knowledge and insight after leaving your session. You will also prepare materials for the participant manuals. We will compile and multiply the manuals and will ship them to the conference site. Your materials should be forwarded to our office no later than January 5. Failure to provide the deliverables by the specified deadline and/or adjust them upon request of our staff may result in your session being cancelled.

Mr. Colin Adams — Page 2 — October 24, 2008

I will call you during this week to discuss your equipment needs for the presentation and the room setup, along with the promotional materials we need such as biographical data, your picture and a press kit. Please feel free to contact me if you have questions, suggestions or need additional information.

Our members are looking forward to having you as a speaker at our conference. You will also have an opportunity to benefit from the exposure to our member firms.

Sincerely,

A. Prescott

Anthony Prescott,
Public Relations Officer

Formatting Multiple Pages

- Use letterhead when necessary for the first page and plain stationery for any additional pages.
- Place a header containing the recipient's name, date and page number on all subsequent pages one inch from page top.
- Go down three spaces or so from the page header on page two (or any other continuation sheet) and then continue your letter from the previous page.
- Try to leave at least two lines on the first page if you must divide a paragraph between pages. It's good to have at least two lines from the divided paragraph on the subsequent page, as well.
- If the paragraph is short, it's better to move the whole thing to the second page.
- Have atleast two (better three) lines of text before the closing on the last page.
- Don't squeeze the letter onto one page if would look better on two pages. (Dixie just wanted to reiterate this point here)
- Follow the format used in first page except for the header instead of letterhead. All margins on the subsequent pages should match the first page (as well as the previous ones, Dixie is sure you realize that).

Glossary

Abate: To reduce, remove or minimize. To abate a nuisance is to remove or reduce it without violence or unnecessary damage. Abatement is an alternative to bringing a court action.

Abduction: Unlawful removal of a person, often a child, from their home environment.

Abrogate: To repeal or cancel. An act that repeals whole or part of an existing Act or a rule of common law is said to abrogate that Act or law.

Absolute privilege: The protection given to parliamentary and court proceedings that any information produced or revealed in them cannot give rise to an action for defamation.

Abuse of process: Misuse or unjust use of court procedure, e.g. long delay in bringing an action may disadvantage a defendant.

Acquit To discharge: To find an accused "not guilty" after trial.

Act of bankruptcy: An action of a debtor that shows an inability to pay their creditors.

Actus reus: Voluntary actions or omissions constituting a crime, the physical element of an offence. The actus reus may be a positive act or failure to act.

Adduce: To present as evidence in court.

Adjourn: To suspend a court hearing to a future specified day or sine die. Also, adjournment.

Adjournment without conviction: A sentencing order of a good behavior bond. A conviction is not recorded if the bond is observed. Can also known as a deferred sentence or suspended sentence.

Administrative act: A decision, or refusal to make a decision, by an officer of a government department and which is subject to review either internally or externally by the courts. see fiat.

Administrative law: Rules that govern the decision making process of public officials covering their powers, functions and procedures to follow.

Adversary system: The system used to decide court cases in Australia, where the opposing parties argue against each other, with a judge or magistrate as an independent decision maker or arbitrator.

Affidavit: A written document sworn on oath before a person with authority to administer it for the purpose of providing evidence for a court case. The person in whose name the document is sworn is called the deponent.

Affirmation: A pledge that statements made are true which may be made in place of an oath if an oath is contrary to a person's religious belief or if the person has no religious belief. It can be used where a person is giving evidence in a court or where a declaration or affidavit is being made.

Alibi: Defense to a criminal charge on the grounds that the accused was somewhere other than the scene of a crime when that crime was committed.

Alleged: Said to be the case, but not yet proved.

ADR (alternative dispute resolution): Process for resolving disputes outside the court system, e.g. through mediation, negotiation, arbitration or conciliation.

Amenity: Features, benefits or advantages of the local environment that people currently enjoy. A park, for instance, is a local amenity.

Amicus curiae Friend of court: Someone who advises the court on a particular matter but does not represent any of the parties in the action.

Annuity: A sum of money payable yearly, such as a payment made under a will.

Annul: To put an end to, cancel, render void in law.

Appeal: To have a case go a higher court in order that a decision from a lower court or tribunal be reviewed.

Appellant: A person who appeals a decision of a court or tribunal to a higher court

Arbitration: A procedure for resolving disputes that involves less formality than a court hearing. An arbitrator's decision is final and cannot be appealed.

Arrears: Payment that is overdue or made after the date when it fell due.

Arrest: To take into custody usually for the purpose of bringing the person to court

Assessable income: Income on which liability to pay income tax is calculated.

Assignment: Legal transfer of a right or an interest in property from the owner to another person.

Asylum: Refuge or protection from persecution, usually in another country. Alternatively, a place for the detention and treatment of the insane.

At large: not securely confined to the owner's property. A person who has committed an offence and is still to be captured or who has escaped from legal custody.

Attachment of earnings: A court order that a debtor's employer pays an amount of the debtor's wages regularly to the creditor until the debt is paid off.

Attestation Clause: A witnessing clause, e.g., a will contains an attestation clause stating the witnesses saw the testator sign and that they signed the will in the presence of the testator and each other.

Bail: The payment of money in order to be set free when one is in remand awaiting trial. This acts as a guarantee that the accused will appear in court to answer the charges otherwise the bail payment will be forfeited.

Bail bond: A form signed by a person released on bail setting out the conditions of release.

Bail justice: A person who is not a judge or magistrate but who has authority to grant or refuse bail, usually at a police station.

Balance of probabilities: The standard of proof required in civil law cases, i.e. it is more probable than not that what the person says happened is true. In criminal cases, the standard is proof beyond reasonable doubt.

Bankruptcy: A person or organization in a position of not being able to pay their debts in full to their creditors.

Beneficiary: A person who is left something in a will, or a person for whose benefit property is held by trustees or executors. Can also be known as a legatee or trust.

Bequeathed: The act of giving a person something by listing their name as the beneficiary (recipient) in a will.

Beyond reasonable doubt: The standard of proof required in criminal cases. If there is any doubt as to the guild of the accused, then a verdict of not guilty must be given. In civil cases, the standard is on the balance of probabilities.

Bias: A pre-existing attitude or opinion that favors one side over another in a dispute.

Bill of sale: A document that enables one person to possess and use goods, the possessor, while another has legal ownership, usually a person or company that has lent money for the purchase of the goods. See goods mortgage.

Bond: A deed in which a person undertakes to do or refrain from doing certain things, e.g. good behaviour bond. Also, money paid to a landlord by a tenant at the start of a tenancy as security in case of future damage to premises or non-payment of rent.

Breach of contract: Failure by one of the parties to a contract to satisfactorily perform the service or action agreed to in the contract.

Burden of proof: The obligation to prove what is alleged. In criminal cases, this obligation rests on the prosecution, which must prove its case beyond reasonable doubt. In civil cases, it rests on the plaintiff, who must prove their case on the balance of probabilities. Sometimes, however, this burden shifts, for example, where the defendant raises particular defenses.

Business purpose declaration: A statement signed by a debtor before entering a credit contract that the credit is for business, not domestic, purposes.

Capacity: The ability to understand and give legal consent to an action or arrangement. Full legal capacity is reached at 18 years of age when a child becomes an adult.

Case law: The law based on decisions made by judges in previous case. see common law.

Caveat: Translated from Latin it means to 'beware'. A notice given to an appropriate officer ordering them not to take a certain step until the person giving the notice (the caveator) has had an opportunity to object e.g. to a transfer of land.

Certificate of title: A document prepared by the Titles Office that shows details of land registered under the Torrens system, particulars of the location, encumbrances and owners.

Certiorari: A form of writ by which actions for review of administrative decisions are commenced in the Supreme Court. Now termed "an order in the nature of certiorari".

Character witness: A person who appears in court to give a reference for an accused person. see witness.

Charge: An accusation made against a person or organization that they have committed a criminal offence. Also, a judge's directions to a jury at the end of a case.

Chattel: Any property that is not freehold land. It may be leasehold, called a chattel real, or a movable article of property, a chattel personal.

Child maintenance order: A parenting order setting out arrangements for the financial support of a child after marriage breakdown.

Citizen's arrest: An arrest by any person who is not a police officer or who does not have a warrant to arrest.

Civil action: Legal proceedings between two or more private persons. Sometimes a private person may bring a civil action against the state.

Civil law: Law that is not criminal or church law, usually the former, it may mean law based on the Roman system. The body of law relating to civil matters between private individuals and/or organizations as opposed to the criminal law. Throughout this book, civil law means non-criminal law.

Civil matters: Disputes between private individuals and/or organizations in contrast to criminal law matters that are between the state and an individual and/or an organization.

Clear title: Outright ownership, without any debts or charges on the property.

Code of practice: A set of guidelines for fair practice developed for a specific industry, occupation, trade or profession. May be voluntary or statutory.

Codicil: A document signed by a will maker that alters or adds to an existing will.

Cohabitation: Living together as a couple sharing an emotional and sexual relationship. Also, where any number of people lives together on a long-term basis as do members of a family.

Collateral contract: A separate contract that precedes or exists alongside the main one.

Combined custody and treatment order: A sentence that is served partly in prison and partly in the community undergoing supervised alcohol and/or drug treatment.

Committal proceedings: Where a Magistrates' Court hears evidence on an indictable charge and decides whether the accused should be sent for trial.

Common law: The part of English law traditionally based on common custom and being unwritten. Law that is not equity, statute, ecclesiastical, or civil.

Common law defense: A defense based on decisions in previous cases.

CTO (community treatment order): Treatment of an involuntary patient by a medical practitioner in the community, not in a mental hospital.

Community Visitor: A voluntary, independent person with authority to monitor and report on the performance of mental health services and the welfare of their patients.

CBO (Community-Based Order): A sentencing order, as an alternative to imprisonment, requiring a person to undertake unpaid or educational work in the community for a set number of hours under the supervision of the Office of Corrections.

Compensation order: A court order that a person found guilty of a criminal offence must pay for loss or damage of property caused by the offence. The payment would be paid to the affected individual or business.

Compensatory damages: Damages paid to the winning party in a civil action to compensate them for damage they have suffered as a result of the actions of the losing party.

Complainant: A person who begins a criminal prosecution against another in the Magistrates' Court. In a civil action they could also be referred to as a plaintiff.

Comprehensive insurance: Insurance that covers claims against the insured by other persons for damage to their property as well as covering the insured for damage to their own property.

Conciliation: Process of resolving disputes that involves negotiations between parties, assisted by a conciliator. Conciliation aims for mutual agreement rather than a decision in favor of one side.

Condition precedent: A condition that delays the coming into effect of a right, usually under a contract, until that condition is fulfilled.

Conduct money: Money that must be provided to a witness subpoenaed to court to cover the cost of travel, and other associated costs, to and from court.

Confidential relationship: A relationship where one party depends on or trusts the authority or professional independence of the other party.

Confidentiality: Protection against disclosure to an outside person of information revealed in a professional relationship, e.g. doctor–patient.

Conflict of interest: A situation where a person's own interests, or a duty towards someone else, may corruptly affect the way they carry out a duty towards others.

Consent: Agreement to an action or arrangement. see informed consent.

Consumer lease: A contract for hire of goods by a person for a specified period and rental payment/s.

Contact order: A parenting order that states the kind and frequency of contact between a child and another person – usually the parent with whom the child is not living.

Contempt of court: The failure to obey a court order or an act that shows a disregard for the authority of the court or judge. A person in contempt may face imprisonment.

Contests mention hearing: A preliminary hearing/examination in criminal cases where parties can try to reach agreement on some matters before the full hearing.

Contract: A legally enforceable agreement between two or more people or organizations with enforceable obligations and promises.

Contravene: To breach, neglect or refuse to comply with a particular requirement, condition or court order.

Contributory negligence: A defense in an action for damages for injuries arising from the defendant's negligence. The defendant attempts to prove that the plaintiff's own negligence caused or contributed to the injuries suffered.

Conveyance: A transfer of real property.

Convict: At the end of a criminal trial to find the accused guilty of a crime.

Cooling-off period: The time during which a purchaser can withdraw from a contract after signing.

Copyright: The rights belonging to the owner or licensee of literary, artistic and dramatic works, films and sound recordings, to reproduce, perform or otherwise deal with these works.

Corporal punishment: Any physical punishment, usually one causing pain.

Corroboration: Independent evidence that supports the main evidence.

Cost indemnity rule: The rule, applying in many court proceedings, that the losing side must pay the legal costs incurred by the other side in the action. see costs.

Costs: The legal fees and expenses incurred by each party in legal proceedings. The losing party usually must pay the costs of the winning party. See cost indemnity rule.

Counterclaim: Where the defendant has a claim against the plaintiff that might have been brought by bringing a separate action, the defendant may raise it in the existing action by adding a statement of the facts on which the claim is made to the statement of defense.

Covenant: An agreement creating an obligation contained in a deed or land title. A covenant may serve the same purpose as a.

Cover note: A document provided by an insurer as evidence of temporary insurance cover before a formal policy is issued.

Credit charges: Charges for which a consumer who enters into a credit contract will be liable in addition to the sum borrowed and any interest payable.

Credit Contract: A contract for deferred payment of a debt owed by one person or organization to another.

Creditor: A person or company to whom a debt is owed.

Cross-vesting: Process by which a superior court can exercise the jurisdiction of another, e.g. between state supreme courts and federal courts.

Cumulative sentence: An order by a court for two or more periods of imprisonment is served one after the other. See concurrent sentence.

Custodial sentence: A sentence of imprisonment.

Custody: Control over a person by keeping them in custody; e.g. when arrested and not free to leave; formerly, care and control of a child.

Damages: A court order for money to be paid as compensation for a loss suffered as a result of a civil wrong or breach of contract. see compensatory damages; general damages; nominal damages; special damages.

Debt: Money that is owed by one person or business to another.

Debt agreement: An arrangement between the creditor and debtor for dealing with unpaid debts that is less formal and intrusive than bankruptcy.

Debtor: A person who owes a debt.

Decree absolute: A final order from the Family Court that a marriage has been terminated. Both parties are now free to remarry. see decree nisi; divorce; marriage.

Decree nisi: An order that a marriage is terminated until a decree absolute is issued. During a decree nisi neither party may remarry. see decree absolute; divorce; marriage.

Decree of nullity: An order that a marriage is not legally valid.

Deed: A written document that is signed sealed and delivered. "Sealing", attaching a seal with wax, is no longer necessary. "Delivering" is traditionally completed when the person signing the document says, "I deliver this as my act and deed".

Deemed: To be treated as.

Defamation: Publication, in the press, electronic media or by word of mouth, of false and derogatory statements about another person, without any justification recognized by law.

Default: To fail in some duty, i.e. to fail to do something you were meant to do. So, default rate – rate of interest charged on overdue payments; default summons – summons that alleges the debtor/defendant has failed to pay money due and owing. The summons may be ordinary or special.

Defendant: A person who has been charged with a criminal offence, or against whom a civil action has been brought.

Delegated legislation: Laws made by bodies subordinate to parliament. These laws may be regulations/rules, local laws or Orders-in-Council.

Delegation: Allowing lower ranking officials to make decisions on behalf of the person responsible by law for making the decision.

Deportation: Expulsion from a country of a resident non-citizen who has committed a serious crime or is considered a threat to national security.

Determination: A judicial decision or termination, ending or cessation of an estate.

Dictation: Situation where a decision making body improperly allows itself to be directed by another person or body when making a decision.

Directions hearing: A hearing held before the full hearing so that the court or tribunal can give directions to the parties about the law, admissibility of evidence or questions of face and how the action should proceed.

Disbursement: Money paid out on behalf of another. In a solicitor's bill, a disbursement may include payments made on lodging documents, and stamp duty, for example.

Discharge: To fulfill or be released from an obligation. A debt is discharged when it is paid.

Disclosure: Giving particular information to another party as required by a contract or legal process.

Discoverable date: The first day it is, or should have been, known that death or personal injury has occurred, that it was caused by the fault of the defendant, and that the injury was serious enough to justify bringing an action for damages.

Discovery: A procedure by which documents relevant to a civil action are exchanged between the parties before the case comes on for hearing.

Discretion: Power to choose whether to do or not to do a certain thing, e.g. investigate a complaint.

Distrain: To seize property or goods belonging to a debtor to enforce payment of the debt. A court order must be given before distrait can be undertaken by the Sheriff.

Divisible property: Property that can be taken by the trustee of a bankrupt to pay off debts. It would include a house or a car but not furniture or household items. see protected property.

Divorce: The bringing of a marriage to an end. A marriage is legally divorced when a court issues a decree absolute where there has been an irretrievable breakdown of the marriage.

Doctrine: A framework set of rules, procedural steps, or test, often established through precedent in the common law, through which judgments can be determined in a given legal case.

Domestic relationship: A relationship where two people, of the same or opposite sex, are not married but are living or have lived together as a couple.

Domicile: The place where a person has their legal home – therefore, the place that determines the legal system relevant to that person.

Double jeopardy: A situation in which a person may be tried twice for the same offence. There must be fresh and compelling evidence to warrant a retrial of a previously convicted or acquitted person. See convict; acquit.

Duress: Undue pressure placed on a person to force them to do something or refrain from doing something.

Duty lawyer: A lawyer at the court who provides free legal assistance to people appearing in court on criminal charges who have not yet had legal advice.

Duty of care: The obligation of a person to exercise reasonable care in the conduct of an activity. Breach of a duty of care that causes damage or loss to another may give rise to an action in tort.

Encumbrance: A charge or liability, e.g. a mortgage. An encumbrance operates to limit the right of a person to deal with an item as they wish without also paying attention to the terms of the encumbrance.

Endorse: To write on the back of a document to indicate its authenticity or ownership

Enduring power: A power of attorney or guardianship that continues to have effect even if the donor ceases to be mentally competent. see guardian; power of attorney.

Enforce: To make people obey a law or the terms of an agreement, etc.

Entrapment: Action of a law enforcement officer that induces someone to commit an offence that they would not otherwise have committed.

Equitable estoppel: A type of estoppel that bars a person from adopting a position in court that contradicts their past statements or actions when that contradictory stance would be unfair to another person who relied on the original position.

Equity Fairness: A system of legal rules developed by the Lord Chancellor and special courts in England to make the common law fairer.

Estoppel: A legal rule of evidence that prevents or stops a person from denying what they have previously said or done.

Eviction: The action of recovering land or property from an occupier or tenant by legal proceedings. The court would be asked to issue an ejectment order to remove the person.

Evidence: Anything the supports or disproves the truth or existence of a fact. Evidence can be oral, documentary or real.

Exclusion clause: A clause in a contract that attempts to exclude, vary or avoid liability.

Executor: The person whose duty it is to carry the provisions of a will into effect. Where that person is female, she may be called an executrix.

Exhibit: A document or thing shown to a witness when giving evidence, produced for inspection to the court or referred to in an affidavit.

Express: Warranty an undertaking or statement made when offering goods for sale that would naturally encourage people to buy the goods. Breach of an express warranty can give rise to a right to sue for damages only.

Expulsion: Permanent exclusion of a student from a school; compare: suspension.

Extradition: The process used when a person in one state or country has committed a crime in another state or country, and is to be taken into custody and sent for trial to the place where the offence allegedly occurred.

Fair dealing: Legitimate use or reproduction of part or all of copyright material by someone other than the copyright owner, for defined purposes.

False imprisonment: Confinement of a person without legal permission.

Fiat: Consent by the Attorney-General to start proceedings on behalf of someone else for review of an administrative act.

Forensic procedure: Examination of a crime scene or the body of a person suspected of having committed an offence, with the taking of certain body samples. Samples may also be taken in a civil action for paternity reasons.

Fraud: Intentionally dishonest act, or lack of action, done to deceive someone and intended to bring some advantage over those who have been defrauded.

Freedom of association: The right to belong, or not belong, to an industrial association, such as a trade union, or other group, such as a religion.

Freedom of information: The right of any person to have access to documents held by government agencies, except those exempted by legislation.

Gazumped: Accepting a higher offer on a property after having agreed on a purchase price with another buyer.

General damages: Damages paid for expenses that are difficult to accurately assess. They include payments for pain and suffering, loss of enjoyment of life, loss of future income, embarrassment and discomfort. See damages; special damages.

Grievance procedure: A defined process for attempting to settle employment disputes within an organization.

Guardian: A person who has the right and duty to protect another person, their property and rights. A plenary guardian has all the powers of a parent.

Habeas corpus: To have the body. A prerogative writ directed to a person who holds someone in custody commanding them to produce that person before a court.

Hand-up brief: Documents tendered by the prosecution in a committal hearing containing the charges and a summary of evidence on which the prosecution proposes to rely.

Hospital order: A court order, known as a hospital security order, by way of sentence, that a person be admitted to a mental hospital as an involuntary patient.

Identification material: Material such as fingerprints, voice recordings, handwriting samples or photographs collected by police to help identify a person suspected of committing an offence.

Identification parade: A police "line up" held so a witness to an offence can try to identify a suspect among other people of similar appearance.

Implied terms: Terms set out in legislation that are automatically part of a contract, without having to be stated in the contract document.

Inadmissible: Not allowed, i.e. not able to be used as evidence in a court action.

Incorporated Associations: A not-for-profit community organization with a separate legal identity and a structure regulated by legislation.

Incorporated documents: Documents added to and considered part of planning schemes that regulate land use and development in a local area or municipality.

Indemnity: Compensation for a wrong done, or an expense or loss suffered as a result of the act or default of another. Verb: indemnify.

ITP (Independent Third Person): An impartial person required to support and assist a person with an intellectual disability, mental illness, brain injury or dementia during questioning by police.

Indictable charge: An accusation against a party who is suspected of having committed a serious crime that is generally tried before a judge and jury. Examples include burglary or theft.

Indictable offence: A serious crime that is generally triable before a judge and jury.

Indictment: The document that lists the accused's name, the charges against the accused and the particulars of the offence relating to each in County or Supreme Court proceedings. Criminal proceedings commence upon its filing with the court.

Industrial disease: A disease linked to a particular industry or to doing a particular type of work.

Infant: The legal term for a person under 18, used particularly in family law, criminal law and civil actions.

Informant: Generally someone who tells. A person who lays information, i.e. a criminal charge. Usually a police officer.

Informed consent: Agreement given for something to be done, after the procedure has been fully explained so that the person understands the procedure and their right to agree or refuse.

Infringement notice: Notice showing that an offence, usually a driving offence, has been committed and the penalty to be paid.

Injunction: A court order that directs someone either to do, or to refrain from doing, a particular thing. An injunction may be interim or perpetual.

Insolvent: Unable to pay debts in full.

Installment order: A court order allowing or requiring a debtor to pay a judgment debt by regular specified payments.

ICO (intensive correction order): A non-custodial sentence with very strict conditions attached.

Interested witness: A witnesses to a will who, or whose spouse is given property or power under the terms of the will.

Interim order: A temporary court order allowing or preventing certain action, until a full hearing can make a decision on the matter and a final order is given.

Interpleader: summons An action by which a person who claims a right to property can bring the question before a court to determine ownership.

Interrogation: The asking of questions. In criminal cases, the questioning of suspects by police. In civil proceedings, the pre-hearing process, by which a party asks the other party a series of written questions, interrogatories, that are then required to be answered on oath.

Intervention order: Court order restraining a person from harmful or annoying conduct.

Intestate: One who dies without leaving a valid will. The deceased's property is distributed to the nearest relatives in an order set by law.

Invalid Not valid; without legal effect.

Involuntary patient: A patient admitted to a mental hospital on a doctor's recommendation and without the patient's consent.

Irreconcilable difference: Serious long-term disagreement between parties that cannot be overcome.

Joint tenants: Persons who own land in an undivided share in common; on the death of one owner their interest passes to the surviving owner(s), and cannot be disposed of by will or deed, unlike tenants in common.

Judgment debt: The amount awarded to be paid under a court order.

Judicial review: Review by a court of an administrative act on the basis of fault in the decision-making process. Compare: review on the merits.

Jurisdiction: The authority of a court to decide matters brought before it; the geographical limit within which a court order can be enforced.

Juror: A member of a jury.

Jury: A panel of people selected from the general public to decide the guilt or innocence of people tried in criminal cases, or questions of fact and the amount to be awarded as damages in civil cases.

Knowingly concerned: Consciously and deliberately involved in committing an offence.

Lawyer-client costs: Those costs that a lawyer can rightly charge their client. These would include fees, disbursements, postage and stamp duty.

Lease: A document of agreement between a landlord and a tenant, for rental of premises.

Legally binding: Able to be enforced by law.

Legatee: A person to whom property is bequeathed in a will.

Legislation: Statutory rules made either by parliaments or delegated bodies. see delegated legislation; statute.

Lessee: A person to whom property is leased.

Lessor: A person who leases property to another.

Letter of demand: A notice from a creditor that legal action will be taken if a debt is not paid.

Letters of administration: The document by which a person is empowered to manage the estate of a deceased who left no valid will.

Liability: To be responsible for something or to owe something to another under a legal responsibility, e.g. for breaking a contract, committing a crime. It may be civil or criminal, and is enforced by civil or criminal courts.

Libel: Any defamatory written, drawn, painted or other permanent form of communication that has been published.

Lien: The right to hold a person's property as security for the performance of an obligation e.g. the payment of money owing.

Linked credit provider: A credit provider that has an arrangement with a supplier of goods that people wanting to borrow money to buy those goods will be directed to that credit provider.

Litigation: Court proceedings in civil matters. A litigant is one of the opposing parties in a civil proceeding.

Litigation guardian: An adult through whom a person under 18 or a person with an intellectual disability can act in court, and who is liable for the costs of such action if unsuccessful. See McKenzie Friend; Next friend.

Local laws: Laws made and enforced by municipal councils within their boundaries. Previously called by-laws. see delegated legislation.

Long stop limitation period: In personal injury cases, a period of 12 years, from the date of the act or omission that caused death or injury, within which court proceedings for damages must be issued.

Malice: A desire to cause harm to someone intentionally, particularly in relation to an action for defamation.

Mandamus: A form of writ to commence an action for review of an administrative decision, such as a failure to perform a duty, in the Supreme Court.

Mandatory: Having to be strictly complied with. Mandatory reporting: obligation to report, e.g. cases of abuse of children, to authorities. Mandatory sentencing: automatic goal term for certain offences.

Marriage: The union of a man and a woman to the exclusion of all others voluntarily entered into for life.

Material: Relevant or important; information that may influence a decision.

Material form: Any form of storage from which a copyright work can be reproduced.

McKenzie Friend: The general term used to describe a person who sits with and assists a party in court proceedings if they do not have any legal representation and the court agrees. They assist by taking notes and offering quiet advice. See litigation guardian; next friend.

Means test: Assessment of income and assets to see if a person qualifies for financial assistance.

Mediation: Form of dispute resolution where an impartial third party helps communication and negotiations between the parties, but does not decide the dispute.

Men's rea: The state of mind required to constitute a particular crime; the mental element of an offence. Generally, every crime requires a mental element, which varies depending upon the nature of the crime. There may be more than one mental element of an offence and it may include intentions, recklessness, negligence, dishonesty, or malice.

Mention date: In Magistrates' Court criminal matters, the first day on which a matter is listed at court. A case can only be heard on the mention day if it is a plea of guilty.

Merchantable quality: Reasonable quality, being in a good enough condition to be sold.

Misleading and deceptive: conduct generally, an action or behavior that leads another person into error, or that is unfair.

Misrepresentation: Making a false statement, either deliberately or unintentionally, to induce someone to do something they would otherwise not have done, e.g. buys something.

Mitigation: Circumstances that go towards reducing the damages or punishment that the court may order against a defendant or prisoner.

Moral rights: The rights of the creator, not the owner, of an artistic, dramatic or literary work or film to have their authorship acknowledged and to protect the integrity of the work or film.

Mortgage: A transfer of real property (land) or personal property as security for the repayment of money borrowed. The creditor to whom the mortgage is made is the mortgagee; the debtor who makes it is the mortgagor.

Native title: A form of communal title whereby land is not owned but is used by those who have rights over it.

Natural justice: The rules and procedures against bias to be followed by a person or body with the power to settle disputes. Some rules of natural justice are to act fairly, without bias, and the right of all parties to be heard. see administrative law.

Necessaries: The basic requirements for a reasonable lifestyle given a person's station in life and specific requirements at the time of purchase, e.g. food, clothes, housing, etc.

Negligence: A tort involving the breach of a duty of care resulting in loss or damage to another person.

Negotiation: A dispute resolution procedure where both parties discuss the matter in dispute with one another with the aim of reaching a settlement through a consensus, compromise or agreement. See ADR (alternative dispute resolution); arbitration; conciliation; mediation.

Next friend: Any person who sues for, and on behalf of, another person. Typically this would be a parent acting for their child.

Nominal damages: Damages of a small amount ordered where a right has been affected but no damage done.

Nominee: A person acting as a buyer on behalf of someone else.

Non-custodial sentence: A sentence for a criminal offence that does not involve imprisonment. The person would normally be sentenced to a form of rehabilitation. See custodial sentence/non-parole period. The minimum term a prisoner must serve before being eligible for parole.

Notice of defense: In civil proceedings, written notice that a defendant is required to give within a certain time stating that they intend to defend the action or cross-examine witnesses.

Nuisance: Any inconvenience that interferes with normal physical human comfort. A nuisance may be either a private nuisance or public nuisance.

Oath: A pledge that statements made are true, which is made with one's hand on the bible, the New Testament, the Old Testament or another relevant religious text, such as the Koran. Witnesses in court are required to take an oath or make an affirmation, if they do not want to swear on a religious text, before giving evidence.

Obiter dictum: An opinion voiced by a Judge that has only incidental bearing on the case in question and is therefore not binding. Latin definition: said in passing.

Offence: A summary (minor) or indictable (serious) crime prohibited by state or commonwealth criminal law.

Offender: A person who commits an offence.

Ombudsman: A public official appointed to investigate citizens' complaints against the administrative agencies of government, or against members of a particular profession.

Onus of proof: The responsibility for proving allegations are true. Usually it is the Crown in criminal cases and the plaintiff in civil cases who hears the responsibility of proving their version of the law and facts to the required standard of proof before they can win the case.

Order to review: An appeal to a higher court if it is believed an error in law has been made.

Orders-in-Council: Laws made by the Governor-in-Council, or at the federal level, by the Governor-General-in-Council. They are made under the authority of relevant Acts of Parliament and may also be known as regulations. See delegated legislation.

Own motion: Decision by a body to take action, e.g. to start an investigation, without a complaint having been made.

Paramount: Most important. An act of paramount force is one that cannot be made subject to another for its operation. See paramount principle.

Paramount principle: A shorthand expression for the rule in the Family Law Act 1975 (Cth) that when the court makes certain decisions relating to a child, the best interests of the child must be regarded as the paramount consideration.

Parenting orders: Court orders made in relation to care of children, where agreement cannot be reached on a Parenting Plan, and covering aspects such as residence, contact, maintenance and other issues.

Parenting Plan: After a divorce where children of the couple are involved, a written agreement between the parties detailing the parenting arrangements for the children.

Parole: To free a prisoner on their own recognizance after serving a minimum term.

Party/parties: A person or organization that participate in civil or criminal proceedings.

Party-party costs: The costs of a court action that a court can order to be paid by one party to the other party. See lawyer–client costs.

Pecuniary loss: loss of an amount of money; pecuniary penalty - fine; pecuniary interest - financial interest in property.

Perjury: Lying under oath when questioned in a court proceeding or when making a sworn statement. A person found guilty of perjury may face imprisonment.

Permanent care order: A court order that a person who is not a child's parent have long-term care and responsibility for the child.

Perpetrator: Person who committed the offence.

Perpetual succession: Ownership of property remains with a group or organization as a whole, not individual members of the group.

Person responsible: The person highest on a designated list who is available and able to make decisions on medical treatment for a patient who is unable to give informed consent.

Petition for bankruptcy: Formal action by either a debtor or a creditor to file for bankruptcy.

Plaintiff: Person who initiates legal proceedings against another in a civil dispute. See complainant.

Police brief: The evidence the police prosecutor relies on to prove the guilt of a person charged with a criminal offence.

Portability: Right to carry the benefits of e.g. a pension, entitlement or protection order from one state, country or workplace to another.

Power of attorney: A formal written legal document by which one person gives another power to represent them or act in their place for certain purposes. See enduring power.

Pre-hearing conference: An informal, compulsory and confidential conference between the parties in a court action to try to reach a settlement or clarify any matters in dispute before the full hearing.

Pre-sentence report: A report, usually prepared by the Department of Human Services, for the court to consider before sentencing a young person.

Precedent: The doctrine by which courts are obliged to follow past decisions when hearing similar later cases. The precedent comes from the reasoning given by judges when delivering the decision in a case.

Prerogative writ: A writ issued by a higher court, such as the Supreme Court, to prevent lower courts and officials from exceeding their powers or to compel them to exercise their functions. E.g. habeas corpus, mandamus, certiorari.

Prescribed Owners Corporation: A prescribed owner's corporation is an owner's corporation that levies annual fees in excess of $200,000 in a financial year; or an owner's corporation that comprises more than 100 lots including any accessory lots such as a car park or storage area.

Prima facie: At first sight or on the face of it.

Prima facie case: A serious, opposed to a speculative, case which has a real possibility of ultimate success.

Prima facie evidence: The sufficiency of evidence upon which a person could be convicted of an offence or taking the evidence of the prosecution at its highest; evidence which is capable of proving the elements of the offence beyond reasonable doubt.

Primary victim: A person who is injured or dies as a direct result of an act of violence.

Private nuisance: A nuisance that you cause that interferes with a right of your neighbors.

Private ruling: An opinion given by the Australian Taxation Office to an individual taxpayer that is binding on the ATO with regard to that taxpayer.

Privative clause: A provision in a statute that seeks to prevent judicial review of decisions made under that statute.

Probate: The proving of a will. The acceptance by the Probate Division of the Supreme Court of Victoria that the deceased's will is valid and the last will in existence.

Probation: A non-custodial sentencing order that involves good behavior and supervision by a probation officer under defined reporting conditions for a specified period.

Procure: To encourage or persuade someone to commit an offence.

Professional indemnity insurance: Insurance that provides cover for a person against claims for negligence arising out of the performance of their professional duties.

Prohibited name: A name that cannot be registered because it is obscene or offensive, impracticable or against the public interest.

Prohibition: An order to stop decision-making proceedings in a lower court or tribunal.

Prohibition notice: a notice banning a workplace activity that may risk safety or health of any person.

Prosecution: The party presenting evidence against the person accused of committing a crime.

Protected property: Property that cannot be seized for later sale in order to pay a debt that owes. It would include furniture, tools of trade and household appliances.

Protection application: An application to a court by the Department of Human Services for intervention to protect the welfare of a child; may involve removal of the child from the family.

Protection order: A court order resulting from a protection application with various options for supervised care of a child.

Provable debt: A debt that must be accepted for proportional payment from available funds by the trustee of a bankrupt, and from which the bankrupt is released on discharge from bankruptcy.

Proxy: A person authorized to represent or act for another or the use of such a person, e.g. voted by proxy.

Public nuisance: A nuisance that interferes with a public right to do something.

Public officer: Person appointed to act on behalf of an incorporated association in any public dealings.

Pursuant to: According to, as directed by an Act or Regulation.

Qualified privilege: Limited protection against an action for defamation except where the person revealing the information did so out of malice.

Quantum: The amount of money or compensation awarded as damages.

Quo warrant: By what authority; a prerogative writ to remedy improper use of public office. Today the Administrative Appeals Tribunal, or an appeal to the Ombudsman, would be the most likely avenue to use to have the authority of the decision-making body reviewed.

Quorum: The number of members of a body required to be present to transact business legally.

Real property: Land or other real estate.

Rebuttable: Capable of being proved wrong in court.

Recognizance: A bond the object of which is to secure the performance of an act by the person bound by it, e.g. to be of good behavior.

Referral authority: An authority or government department to which a planning permit must be referred for advice before it is granted.

Regulations/rules: Laws made by government departments and statutory bodies under authority granted by a relevant Act of parliament. See delegated legislation.

Related victim: A person with a close family or personal relationship to a primary victim who has died as a result of an act of violence.

Remand in custody: Order that a person who is charged with an offence be detained or imprisoned until the charge is heard by a court.

Renewable insurance policy: Insurance provided for a particular period of time, of a kind that is usual to renew at the end of that period of time.

Repairer's lien: The right of a repairer to hold repaired goods, e.g. a car, as security for payment.

Repeal: To abrogate or cancel legislation or a regulation.

Repossession: The taking possession of goods by a creditor from a debtor who has breached a term of a credit contract.

Represented person: A person whose financial affairs are controlled by an administrator as a "publicly represented person", the state trustees.

Rescission: A revocation or stopping action, particularly of a contract. Rescission is only allowed where restitution is possible.

Residence order: A parenting order stating with whom a child is to live following separation or divorce.

Respondent: A person against whom a summons has been issued or an appeal brought.

Responsible authority: The body that has the power to grant or refuse permits, often a local council.

Restitution: Giving back what has been provided under a contract, stolen, or seized to pay a debt.

Restraining order: In family law, an order preventing a specified person from harassing or molesting the person applying for the order.

Restraint of trade: A commercial arrangement that prevents a business from freely buying or selling goods or services.

RCTO (Restricted Community Treatment Order): If treatment can be safely obtained in the community, patients on hospital orders can be put on a RCTO under section 15A of the MHA, which provides for release into the community on certain conditions.

Retrospective: Applying to circumstances existing before the date on which a law came into effect.

Review on the merits: A review, or rehearing, of a case in order to determine whether it was the correct decision to have been made on the basis of the facts presented.

Revocation: Cancelling the effect of a previous act, e.g. an earlier will.

Sanction: A penalty or punishment imposed on someone found guilty of an offence.

Secondary victim: A person who is injured, physically or psychologically, as a direct result of witnessing an act of violence, or through being the parent or guardian of a primary victim aged under 18.

Secured creditor: A creditor who holds a mortgage, charge or lien on the property of the debtor.

Security interest: An interest in or power over goods to secure payment of a debt or obligation.

Self-incrimination: The privilege against self-incrimination means the right, with certain limitations, not to do or say any-thing that might later be used as evidence against you.

Self-representation: Presenting your own case in court without a lawyer being there to assist you.

Sentencing order: A court order imposing a sentence of imprisonment on a guilty accused in a criminal case. See non-custodial sentence.

Sequestration order: An order that property be seized to satisfy a debt.

Serious indictable offence: An indictable offence for which the penalty is imprisonment for five years or more, or life imprisonment.

Serious injury: In relation to transport injuries, a serious long-term impairment, disfigurement or loss of a body function, or severe long-term mental or behavioral disturbance, or loss of a fetus.

Servitude: Being completely under the control of another, such as sexual servitude (slavery).

Sheriff: An officer of the court responsible primarily for enforcement of court orders.

Sine die: To adjourn, put off, postpone or suspend a court hearing to a later specified date. This Can also be referred to as "stand down", "stand over" or "postpone".

Show cause: A reversed onus of proof that applies to applications for bail for some drug offences.

Slander: Defamation that consists of spoken words or actions. See defamation; libel.

Solvent: Ability to pay all debts when they are due.

Special damages: Damages paid for expenses that are easy to determine and assess precisely. These damages would include payments for out-of-pocket expenses, e.g. medical costs, lost wages, rehabilitation costs. See damages; general damages.

Specific performance: Doing exactly what is stated in the terms of a contract.

Spent conviction: A conviction for a minor criminal offence, that after a certain time without re-offending, is considered to no longer exist.

Stale: A complaint that cannot be pursued because the complainant has delayed too long in taking action on a grievance.

Stamp duty: A state tax on transfers of ownership of assets or property, or on leases.

Standard of proof: The required level to which something must be proved in court. In criminal matters, the standard is "beyond reasonable doubt"; in civil matters, on the "balance of probabilities"

Standing: The right to take action in court or to be heard or represented in a case.

Status quo: The existing situation.

Statute: A law made by parliament, either state or Commonwealth. This also be known as an Act.

Statute barred debts: Debts for which the right to take action to recover payment is limited to a specified period, after which such action will not succeed in court.

Statutory: A law developed by parliament or delegated bodies in the form of an act, regulations or local laws. It must be followed otherwise the relevant penalty may apply for any breach of the law.

Statutory declaration: A written statement of facts that the person making it signs and solemnly declares to be true before a person authorized to take declarations.

Statutory defense: A ground for defense included in a particular law that, if argued successfully, would prevent a person from being found guilty of an offence under the law.

Subpoena: A writ that commands the appearance of a person or the production of specified documents in a court.

Substantiation: Providing evidence to prove that an event took place, e.g. an expense was incurred.

Sue: To take legal action in a civil case.

Sufficiently interested party: A person or company, not a party to a contract, that has been involved in a transaction giving rise to a claim under the contract and can be named as a party to the claim.

Summary offence: A minor offence heard and decided in a Magistrates' Court and not sent for trial before a judge and jury.

Summons: A document that is issued by the court requiring the attendance of the person named in the summons at court on a specified date.

Supervision order: An order that the Children's Court may impose where a young person is found to be in need of care and attention. A probation officer is appointed to supervise the young person. In addition, the court can impose conditions to be observed by the young person's parents or persons with whom the young person is living. Also, a supervision order requires a person arguing substantial mental impairment in a serious criminal case to be admitted to a mental institution.

Surety: A person who binds themself to be answerable for another by paying an amount of money to the court. If there is a default, the surety will be liable and any money paid will be forfeited. The person who pays the money is also referred to as the surety or guarantor.

Suspended sentence: A sentence of imprisonment that is only served if the convicted person commits further offences. May be partially or wholly suspended, or a combined custody and treatment order.

Suspension: Exclusion of a student from school for a specified period as a disciplinary measure; less severe punishment than expulsion.

Sworn evidence: Evidence given under oath or affirmation.

Taxable form: Refers to a lawyer's bill of costs that shows details of all the lawyer's charges.

Tenancy: The relation between a landlord and a tenant for rented premises See lease.

Tender: An offer by someone who owes money to pay the debt, or part of it, to the person it is owed to. Also, a tender can be a quote submitted offering to construct a building or undertake renovations for a given price.

Terms of reference: The preset terms under which an inquiry is conducted or a decision is made.

Testamentary capacity: The legal and mental ability to draw up a valid will. The mental capacity to understand about property rights and family responsibilities is an important aspect of capacity in this regard.

Testator: A person who makes a will. A female testator is sometimes called a testatrix.

Therapeutic privilege: Right of doctors and other health professionals, in some circumstances, not to give patient information that they believe might cause harm to the patient.

Third party objector: A person appealing against a decision to grant approval for developments that may produce discharge harmful to the environment.

Trafficking: In common law, movement from source to end user in the course of trade. In criminal law the act of dealing with something illegal, such as humans. Also, drug trafficking has a much wider definition. See servitude.

Treatment order: A court order that a person suffering from mental illness be sent to a psychiatric hospital for treatment instead to prison after conviction for an offence.

Trespass: Wrongful entry onto or interference with property or with a person's goods or property without the permission of the lawful owner or occupier.

Tribunal: A body set up to hear and decide disputes, usually with less formality and less strict rules of evidence than in a court proceeding.

Trust: Items held by one party known as the trustee for the benefit of another party referred to as the beneficiary. See trust account; trust deed.

Trust account: A special bank account where a lawyer deposits money held on behalf of other people, subject to strict accounting rules.

Trust deed: A document that sets out the rights and obligations of the trustee and beneficiaries of a trust.

Unconscionable conduct: Action that takes unfair advantage of another party that is under a special disability in a contract or transaction. See special disability or disadvantage.

Undertake: To promise, in the course of legal proceedings, to do or refrain from doing an act. An undertaking is enforceable by attachment or like an injunction.

Undue influence: Taking unfair or improper advantage of the weakness of another party to make them agree to do or refrain from doing something without the benefit of their free will.

Unliquidated: Undetermined, unascertained, e.g. when damages are left to a judge or jury to determine. Also, any debt that has not been paid or cleared by agreement. Valid Legally binding or effective.

Vendor terms: Contract of sale of property where the seller allows the buyer to pay over a set period. Ownership remains with the seller until the final payment is made.

Vendor's statement: A document that must be provided to the buyer of a property by the seller that gives certain information about the property and matters affecting it. This Can also be referred to as a Section 32 statement.

Vexatious: Legal action that is unnecessary or undertaken only to cause trouble or inconvenience for the other party.

Victim impact statement: A statement to the court by the victim of a crime setting out details of injury, loss or damage caused by the crime.

Visa: Permit that allows either temporary or permanent stay in a country.

VoIP (Voice over Internet Protocols): A general term for a family of transmission technologies for delivery of voice communication over the Internet or other networks. Void Of no legal effect.

Voidable: An agreement, or other act, that either of the parties is entitled to rescind and until that happens has full legal effect. There are certain restrictions on the view of what is, and is not, Voidable that require advice from a lawyer. See rescission.

Voluntary: That which is done by one's own free will.

Voluntary patient: A patient admitted to a mental with the patient's consent.

Waive: To give up a legal right or claim usually for another benefit or the benefit of another.

Warrant: A document issued by a court directing an officer to take certain action. May be a warrant of apprehension, directing that a person be arrested and brought before a court; a warrant of commitment, directing that a person be arrested and imprisoned; a warrant of distress, directing that a person's goods be seized to satisfy a debt; or a warrant of seizure and sale of real estate.

Warranty: A minor clause in a contract, the remedy for breach of which is damages for any loss. Also, a promise to repair or replace defective goods.

Waste: Something that does lasting damage to land or alters the nature of the property.

Witness: A person who can provide direct information based on their own knowledge about a relevant fact in issue, and appears in court to do this or who provides a deposition setting out their evidence if they are not able to attend court.

Writ: A document in the monarch's name and under the seal of the Crown that commands the person to whom it is addressed to do or refrain from doing some act

Further readings

Boyer, Paul S. 2001. Oxford Companion to United States History. New York: Oxford Univ. Press.

Jolls, Christine. 1997. "Contracts as Bilateral Commitments: A New Perspective on Contract Modification." Journal of Legal Studies 26 (January): 203-237.

Hylton, J. Gordon, et al. 2003. Property Law and the Public Interest: Cases and Materials. 2d ed. Newark, N.J.: Lexis-Nexis.

Singer, Joseph William. 2002. Property Law: Rules, Policies and Practices. 3d ed. New York: Aspen Law & Business.

Sprankling, John G. 2000. Understanding Property Law. New York: Lexis.

Index

D

E

F

G

H

I

J

L

M

www.ingramcontent.com/pod-product-compliance
Lightning Source LLC
Chambersburg PA
CBHW071330230926
51849CB00002B/362
* 9 7 8 9 3 6 0 8 4 5 6 6 7 *